Darren Aronofsky's Films
and the Fragility of Hope

Darren Aronofsky's Films and the Fragility of Hope

Jadranka Skorin-Kapov

Bloomsbury Academic
An imprint of Bloomsbury Publishing Inc.

B L O O M S B U R Y
NEW YORK · LONDON · OXFORD · NEW DELHI · SYDNEY

Bloomsbury Academic

An imprint of Bloomsbury Publishing Inc.

1385 Broadway	50 Bedford Square
New York	London
NY 10018	WC1B 3DP
USA	UK

www.bloomsbury.com

BLOOMSBURY and the Diana logo are trademarks of Bloomsbury Publishing Plc.

First published 2016
Paperback edition first published 2017

Library of Congress Cataloging-in-Publication Data

Skorin-Kapov, Jadranka, 1955–
Darren Aronofsky's films and the fragility of hope / Jadranka Skorin-Kapov.
pages cm
Summary: The first sustained analysis of the current oeuvre of film director
Darren Aronofsky, examining the many intersections between his filmic work
and his philosophical positions—Provided by publisher.
Includes bibliographical references and index.
ISBN 978–1–5013–0697-6 (hardback)
1. Aronofsky, Darren—Criticism and interpretation. I. Title.
PN1998.3.A7615S58 2015
791.4302′33092—dc23
2015018668

ISBN:	HB:	978-1-5013-0697-6
	PB:	978-1-5013-2015-6
	ePub:	978-1-5013-0698-3
	ePDF:	978-1-5013-0699-0

Typeset by RefineCatch Limited, Bungay, Suffolk

For Nela and Marin

Contents

Preface

This book appears as a natural consequence of a lifelong fascination with movies. There are many films and many directors that I could write about, so why Aronofsky? In this Preface, I offer some personal information in order to describe the path that led me to write about Aronofsky's filmography, and to engage in a conversation with him as presented in the Appendix. Aronofsky's work combines elements of the auteur voices of the 1970s New Hollywood and of the European film scene, employing an authentic directorial style. In exploration of the human condition, his films appear quite analytical in dissecting a character's extreme states, and quite philosophical in providing a broader picture of human weaknesses and strengths, tying up with a number of philosophical writings. Moreover, his films present interesting narratives, leaning toward commercially successful films. Aronofsky's filmic sensibility attracted me as a way to interrogate my dual upbringing and inclinations, including European auteur films versus American blockbusters, and mathematics versus philosophy and art.

Growing up in Pula, a small town on the tip of the Istrian peninsula in the northern Adriatic in Croatia on the border of the Gulf of Venice, I was exposed to movies at an early age. Pula is indebted to the Roman emperor Vespasian, who in addition to building the Colosseum in Rome, enlarged an amphitheater in Pula that we call the Arena. After many centuries, in 1954, the Arena became the site for the yearly film festival, and my childhood was filled with memories of nights in the Arena watching movies in a spectacular historic place. In 1973, I left Pula and enrolled at the University of Zagreb to study mathematics, my favorite subject. As it happened, I rented a room close to Kinoteka, at that time a trendy cinematheque of Zagreb, and had a chance to see various movies from the first silent movies to retrospectives of Ingmar Bergman and other auteurs. The 1970s was a very exciting decade for the movies, and we would contemplate and have long discussions after seeing movies such as *Straw Dogs* (Sam Peckinpah, 1971), *The Devils* (Ken Russell, 1971), *Amarcord* (Federico Fellini, 1973), and *One Flew Over the Cuckoo's Nest* (Miloš Forman, 1975), to name but a few. On the other spectrum were adorable French comedies with Louis de Funès and movies such as *Saturday Night Fever* (John Badham, 1977) and *Grease* (Randal Kleiser, 1978).

When I saw *2001: A Space Odyssey* (Stanley Kubrick, 1968) for the first time in the 1970s, a film that exceeded all my expectations, it triggered a defining moment in my future career. After undergraduate studies, fascinated by the promise of computers, I took a job in the University Computing Center at the University of Zagreb, as a software engineer for mathematical applications. We had a big UNIVAC computer occupying the whole room, which I affectionately called my HAL. HAL stands for **H**euristically programmed **AL**gorithmic computer, which indirectly motivated my future research in metaheuristic algorithms. In 1984, I moved to Canada with my husband and two daughters to pursue graduate studies at the University of British Columbia in Vancouver. We subsequently moved to the Unites States, where I accepted a tenure-track position at Stony Brook University in the College of Business and began my academic career. Going to see a new type of movie, the blockbuster of the 1980s and early 1990s, was a regular pastime for my family. We also revisited some earlier movies, for example, *Grease*: we watched it for the nth time and had a competition with our daughters as to who would know more dialogue, talking before the actors could say their lines. When we (again) watched the *Back to the Future* trilogy (Robert Zemeckis, 1985, 1989, 1990) in one night, we let our daughters sleep in the next morning and skip school while inventing an excuse for their absence. But while we were never tiger parents, Lea and Nina turned out quite well, both pursuing academic careers in engineering.

After many years of algorithmic research, I decided to follow my wish to study philosophy, a wish certainly stimulated by challenging movies and their provocative questions regarding the human condition, especially the nature of aesthetic experience. In the work entitled *The Aesthetics of Desire and Surprise: Phenomenology and Speculation,* I consider the properly aesthetic experience and propose the term *desire∥surprise*, indicating a break separating desire stemming from our past experience, and the surprise of acknowledging the rebirth of our sensibility followed by reflection.[1] The representational break between desire and surprise is a consequence of the impossibility of presenting immediacy. Every presentation is mediated, but immediacy leaves a trace as a presence that cannot be presented, and it lingers in the surprise that follows the encounter. Such immediate presence characterizes excess and unexpectedness, bringing to my flow of experience something that was not there before, a new

[1] Jadranka Skorin-Kapov, *The Aesthetics of Desire and Surprise: Phenomenology and Speculation* (Lanham, Maryland: Lexington Books, 2015).

beginning. Hence, by assigning such importance to surprise, I basically argue that perfection is characterized by surprise, as the attainment of something new, resulting with experiential augmentation. With respect to art, I most strongly experienced such surprises in relation to film.

In addition to provoking my philosophical interests, film opened another direction of interest for me: Jungian analytic psychology. This happened while watching *Full Metal Jacket* (Stanley Kubrick, 1987). Namely, when Sergeant Joker explains contradictory signs (a peace sign on his button and the phrase "Born to Kill" on his helmet) as representing "the duality of man, the Jungian thing," I had to explore Jung further. I did not know much about Jung and was intrigued that one of my favorite directors would invoke Jungian psychology. As it turned out, I found Jungian analytic psychology, the process of individuation, his archetypes, and subsequent work by Joseph Campbell on mythology, extremely relevant to interpreting movies.

Darren Aronofsky's films intrigued me in different ways. His portrayal of a mathematician in π resonated strongly with an experience I had in the late 1980s when trying to heuristically solve a notoriously hard combinatorial problem (Steinberg's 36-dimensional quadratic assignment problem with rectangular distances, published in 1961). I programmed the algorithm so that, whenever an improved solution is discovered, a line indicating the solution and the iteration number appears on the computer screen. One morning, the computer screen displayed the new and improved solution for this problem, and I can still remember the excitement of getting the number on the screen. This project helped me in getting tenure and a promotion. But, while I somehow could identify with Max from π, I was not nearly as obsessive.

Aronofsky's casting of Mickey Rourke in the lead role of an aging wrestler was poignant in various ways: looking at Rourke, so different from the sex symbol from *9 ½ Weeks* (Adrian Lyne, 1986) and in a role so close to his real life, invited contemplation about imitations between art and life. It reminded me of my favorite director of the silent era, Erich von Stroheim, and his art-imitating-life role in *Sunset Boulevard* (Billy Wilder, 1950).

When seeing Aronofsky's *Black Swan* for the first time and hearing the choreographer Thomas Leroy instructing his ballerina, Nina Sayers, with the statement that perfection relates to surprise, I knew instantly I would have to look more closely into Aronofsky's filmography and write about it.

So, I embarked on the challenging task to write about Aronofsky's filmography from 1998, beginning with π, to 2014, with the just-released *Noah*. Indeed, the interpretation and evaluation of his movies were challenging and rewarding experiences, and a number of people deserve acknowledgment.

First, I would like to express my sincere gratitude to the faculty and students from the Department of Art, the Department of Cultural Analysis and Theory, and the Department of Philosophy at Stony Brook University. They all added to a lively academic atmosphere and enforced my wish to pursue the study of film art. In producing this work, I am indebted to Andrew V. Uroskie for insightful comments. In addition, I would like to thank John Lutterbie, Zabet Patterson, and Krin Gabbard, for their support and useful comments. Ed Casey provided proper guidance for my philosophical directions or research. I also wish to acknowledge the support of my colleagues at the College of Business at Stony Brook University.

María Elena de las Carreras and an anonymous reviewer gave valuable comments resulting in an improved manuscript. I am grateful to Dan Pal for his many constructive comments that helped in producing the final stage of the manuscript, while Ashar Foley was very helpful in the editing.

The editorial and design team at Bloomsbury Academic was instrumental in producing this book. In particular, Katie Gallof, my editor at Bloomsbury Academic, was highly supportive, and I greatly appreciate it. Mary Al-Sayed's assistance was very effective in preparation of the book. It was a pleasure to work with the Bloomsbury team.

I am truly indebted to Darren Aronofsky for his artistic force and his films that motivated this work. Also, I am thankful for the time he spent on our conversation, in the midst of the postproduction of *Noah*, certainly a very busy time. His assistant, Dylan Golden, was indispensable for our communication, and I thank him for his efforts.

Finally, I wish to thank my husband Darko and our younger generations for their support in all my various endeavors and for their companionship in the adventure of film spectatorship. This book is dedicated to the youngest movie buffs in my family, my grandchildren Nela and Marin. We have already watched some movies together. Even some older movies were fun to view. It was memorable to watch with them *Animals Are Beautiful People* (Jamie Uys, 1974), a humoristic documentary about South African animals. Their laughter when seeing drunk elephants (which might be staged or not) was so delightful, and their repeated desire to see something again and again ... and again points to a continuing generation of movie aficionados, enthralled by good stories. Regardless of the change in medium, celluloid or digital, it seems that desire for movies continues.

Introduction

The subject of the proposed work is the filmography of the film director, screenwriter, and producer Darren Aronofsky (b. 1969) in the period 1998–2014. In that period, he directed six feature-length films: π (1998), *Requiem for a Dream* (2000), *The Fountain* (2006), *The Wrestler* (2008), *Black Swan* (2010), and *Noah* (2014). Aronofsky's style evolved, varying with different themes, but one constant seems to emerge: the sensitivity of an artistic eye observing the human condition, its weaknesses and strengths, with compassion and concern. A film is a joint product of various talents—from actors to artists producing screenplays, music, cinematography, editing—but the glue that holds it together is the director, the conductor of the audio/visual symphony.

While this book is restricted to consideration of the work of a specific filmmaker and does not take up cinema in general, it is necessary to frame the expository arguments. I wish to offer an analysis of my aesthetic experience with Aronofsky's filmography and reiterate Deleuze's statement that writing about an author implies a liking of that author's work. The starting point for the inquiry is a film itself, viewed as an artwork capable of inducing an aesthetic experience. In order to experience an artwork, we need to approach it directly, to let it speak for itself, which leads to subsequent reflection, criticism, and evaluation. This sounds like Adorno, who argued that because artworks are inherently particular, they should be examined as such. However, because "... in its particularization, art is more than simply its particularity,"[1] evaluation of individual artworks, while necessary, is not sufficient, and we need a "second reflection" to situate an artwork in its cultural and historical environment. Without going into Adorno's analysis of the subjective content of art versus its socially significant form, let me argue for the proposed approach in presenting Aronofsky's films to date. Aronofsky's films work in different ways: as interesting narratives dealing with intriguing and extreme aspects of human nature, and as captivating audio/visual representations inducing preconscious bodily response, followed by different levels of philosophical (aesthetical and ethical) reflection. It is not the case of starting

---

[1] Theodor W. Adorno, *Aesthetic Theory*, trans. R. Hullot-Kentor (Minneapolis: University of Minnesota Press, 1997), 358.

with a philosophical position and then reading a film through glasses adjusted to that position. On the contrary, I wish to approach a film with the same openness required when approaching an artwork—for example, a novel, a painting, a play—and let it speak to me. While the analysis and interpretation is subjective, its relevance could attain objective validity due to consideration of various writings supporting the claims.

One of the most prominent questions in film studies is the issue of spectatorship: what is the relation between a spectator and a film? The interest in spectatorship is analogous to the interest in the reader in literary studies or in the subject in philosophy. Judith Mayne provides one of the first systematic treatments of the history and role of the cinema spectator.[2] She distinguishes between the "subject" as the viewer assumed by the cinema industry, and the "viewer" as the real person going into movies. In *Film Theory: An Introduction through the Senses* (2010), Thomas Elsaesser and Malte Hagener summarize major spectatorship theories (psychoanalytic, apparatus, phenomenological, cognitivist).[3] Instead of distinguishing between formalist and realist film theories, they group different approaches according to their relationships among cinema, perception, and the human body, arguing for cinema as: window and frame (preference for the visual sense, i.e., ocular-centric perception), door and screen (identification via narrative), mirror and face (character identification), eye and look (psychoanalytic approach), skin and touch (phenomenological approach), ear and sound (importance of acoustics and sound), mind and body (relating cognitivism, phenomenology, and empathy). The last chapter questions the role of digital cinema and its impact on the spectator's senses. Elsaesser and Hagener write:

> The idea of the body as a sensory envelope, as perceptual membrane and material-mental interface, in relation to the cinematic image and to audio-visual perception, is thus more than a heuristic device and an aesthetic metaphor: it is the ontological, epistemological and phenomenological "ground" for the respective theories of film and cinema today.[4]

The role of body—not only visual, but in its full sensual capacity—provides a starting point for the spectator-film encounter.

Contemporary film studies usually start with a theory (e.g., Lacanian psychoanalysis or neo-Marxism) or with a strand characterizing an aspect of

---

[2]   Judith Mayne, *Cinema and Spectatorship (Sightlines)* (London: Routledge, 1993).
[3]   Thomas Elsaesser and Malte Hagener, *Film Theory: An Introduction through the Senses* (New York: Routledge, 2010).
[4]   Ibid., 11.

reception (e.g., feminism or postcolonialism), and read the film through the lenses of a stated theory or ideology. While such studies are often revelatory and insightful, and were a predominant trajectory in criticism during the second part of the twentieth century, nowadays there is significant research that signals a return to humanistic concerns, almost having a retro feel. Humanism of the previous era was critiqued by modernism of the early twentieth century as serving the bourgeois philosophy of the unique, centered individual, and as scientifically ungrounded, unlike positivism relying on science and formal structure. After World War II, and especially during the turbulence of the 1960s, poststructuralism provided a way for considering a fragmented and neurotic individual, with emphasis on disintegration of individuality, in line with Derridian deconstruction for interpretation of a work, and Barthes's "death of the author" for characterizing a work. Lacanian psychoanalysis continued the structuralist strand and was adapted to read films through specific structures, for example, feminism. However, in light of technological advances and environmental threats facing us in the twenty-first century (*us* meaning humans as such—regardless of gender, race, sexual orientation, or nationality), postmodernism gave way to a new paradigm of approaching the human condition. Some call it postpostmodernism, some call it meta-modernism. Regardless of the title, the fact is that the humanities and the sciences are very much intertwined in aspects previously solely in the domain of humanities. For example, today we have biogenetics dovetailing with bioethics, and we have social environmentalism looking into the profound ways technology is changing our way of life. The (old-fashioned) question of what characterizes humanity, that is, what it means to be human, enters the first row of investigation, in the sciences as in humanities. The cognitive—with its emphasis on scientific, experimental confirmation of hypotheses—becomes a valuable tool in investigations reshaping contemporary film theories.

In general, the concept of theoretical research should apply differently to science and humanities, acknowledging differences between quantitative and qualitative research. In science, when faced with data, it is appropriate to create models (as simplified descriptions of reality) and work on solving those models. Strict positivism is inappropriate for humanities since the analysis becomes too restricted, unable to capture the qualitative character of human behavior. While we know that art in general defies conceptual characterization, narrative cinema presents an interesting case as a complex and expensive product involving many people and creating visual depictions of characters that can be analyzed in various ways (e.g., psychological or ideological). It is not surprising that narrative cinema triggered film studies based on scientific approaches applied to psychology, ideology, linguistics, semiology. In fact, we can think of a narrative film as a model for analyzing human behavior, in analogy of creating models in engineering (e.g., a prototype model for a car) or models in architectural design. But an overly theoretical approach to cinema misses the artistry of the work, the aesthetic import. In *Elegy for Theory* (2014), D.N. Rodowick discusses various approaches to film theory and argues eloquently for a need to free cinema, and arts and humanities in general, from the constraining submission to theoretical-scientific examination and explanation, and to provide more space for aesthetic and ethical experience of humanistic subjects.[5]

The wish to consider an individual movie in its own right as an artwork, capable of inducing senses and reflection, is the main motivation behind the present work. Diverging from an explication of film either via the formalist film theory regarding film as an object to be formally analyzed, or via a contemporary film theory regarding film as a polygon for illustrating a given ideology, I consider the *experience of watching a film*, treating film as an artwork that stimulates the senses and subsequent reflection. This approach could be labeled as the composite of *existential, semiotic, and hermeneutic phenomenological* approaches, starting with the existential philosophy of preconscious perception and continuing with reflections toward interpreting film's meaning and significance.

I propose a composite experience consisting of two intertwined phases: (1) the implicit prereflective bodily phase, and (2) the explicit conscious phase engendering reflection in various directions. This framework needs some clarification. To provide a comprehensive analysis of an aesthetic experience in general is beyond the scope of this work, so let us understand it as Dewey would argue in his elaboration of "art as experience."[6] For Dewey, aesthetic quality in experiencing contributes to the unity of experience, resulting with "*an* experience," a distinctive unit in the flow of experience. In describing the beginning of an aesthetic experience, Dewey distinguishes the first overwhelming impression followed by reflection. He writes, "While both original seizure and subsequent critical discrimination have equal claims, each to its own complete development, it must not be forgotten that direct and unreasoned impression comes first."[7] The difference between philosophy and art, argues Dewey, is that

---

[5]   D.N. Rodowick, *Elegy for Theory* (Cambridge, MA: Harvard University Press, 2014), 265.
[6]   John Dewey, *Art as Experience* (New York: A Wideview/Perigee Book, 1980).
[7]   Ibid., 145.

philosophy begins in wonder and ends in understanding, while art starts beyond understanding and ends in wonder.[8] His suggestion for understanding the philosophical concept of experience is via aesthetic experience: "To esthetic experience, then, the philosopher must go to understand what experience is."[9] Hence, art starts unexpectedly, beyond understanding, preconsciously, and leads to wonderment when philosophy and reflection take over. Wonder leads to complex reflections in different directions (admiration of art, assessment of cultural significance, sense of responsibility related to ethics and morality, sparks of creativity leading to scientific discoveries).

Of all the art forms, a narrative film can best illustrate the metamorphosis of an aesthetic experience, from its purely aesthetic (i.e., sensual) trigger, to a further development of reflection. First, a narrative film is a *composite* of elements from literature, visual, and audio arts (this also applies to performing arts). Second, film has a *duration*, measured in everyday time, allowing for reflection to unfold, and allowing for interplay between elements of pure surprise affecting bodily response and for directions of subsequent reflection (this also applies to the performing arts and to literature). Third, film can be *shown repeatedly*, allowing for multiple viewings and facilitating further reflection (this also applies to literature, which allows for multiple readings). Fourth, film employs *editing and special effects* as cinematic language, best suited for triggering initial bodily response from a spectator due to surprise when faced with convoluted senses of space and time. This last point, that is, editing, pertains only to film, and "is the only unique aspect of filmmaking that does not resemble any other art form," to quote Kubrick.[10]

While an aesthetic experience can happen in any encounter with the environment, film experience can most forcefully delineate its two aspects (initial surprise and subsequent reflection) as if putting it under the microscope. Hence, to paraphrase Dewey, let me state that *to film experience, then, the philosopher must go to understand what aesthetic experience is*. This statement is compatible with that of Cavell: "the creation of film was as if meant for philosophy."[11] Cavell's approach to philosophy through film (and literature) was

8   Ibid., 270.
9   Ibid., 274.
10   Alexander Walker, *Stanley Kubrick, Director: A Visual Analysis* (New York: W.W. Norton & Company, 1999), 22.
11   Stanley Cavell, *Contesting Tears: The Hollywood Melodrama of the Unknown Woman* (Chicago: University of Chicago Press, 1996), xii.

to start from the work itself (film or literature), and find a philosophical meaning beneath the face value of the narrative, illustrating his view most forcefully through classic Hollywood comedies of remarriage. In *Cities of Words* (2004), Cavell further explicates his notion of *moral perfectionism* through the reconstruction of the everyday, as repetitions of leaving and returning, but with a changed state of mind, more ethically attuned. Film can help in this aspect because, writes Cavell, "The implied claim is that film, the latest of the great arts, shows philosophy to be the often invisible accompaniment of the ordinary lives that film is so apt to capture (even, perhaps particularly, when the lives depicted are historical or elevated or comic or hunted or haunted)."[12] At times, it might seem that Cavell overread the narrative of a Hollywood movie, and he indeed acknowledges it in saying that his consideration of film is not on the level of Plato's consideration of the role of tragedy, but due to vast audience and the power to induce affection, films surpass all arts in contributing to "moral education for the culture contemporary with them."[13] This brings to mind a book by C. Davis entitled *Critical Excess: Overreading in Derrida, Deleuze, Levinas, Žižek and Cavell* (2010), in which he singles out exceptional contemporary readings of films and texts selected for their symbiosis with philosophy or psychoanalysis.[14] For example, Davis asks, "Does the blanket hung up in a motel room in Frank Capra's romantic comedy *It Happened One Night* (1934) invoke the Kantian divide between the knowable phenomenal world and unknowable things in themselves, as Cavell argues?"[15] Davis concludes that overreading is important to augment the perceived world of a film or a novel, thereby augmenting our experiential space. We might not agree with all the assertions of an overread film or text, but such an approach provokes critical thinking, possibly opening new avenues of thought and emotion. I will take this point as a disclaimer if my (philosophical) readings of Aronofsky's films may seem excessive.

Let me elaborate on the proposed film experience consisting of two-phase sequences: (1) the initial preconscious reception and bodily response, and (2) the subsequent reflection.

---

[12] *Cities of Words: Pedagogical Letters on a Register of the Moral Life* (Cambridge, MA: Harvard University Press, 2004), 6.
[13] Ibid., 318.
[14] Colin Davis, *Critical Excess: Overreading in Derrida, Deleuze, Levinas, Žižek and Cavell* (Redwood City, CA: Stanford University Press, 2010).
[15] Ibid., xii.

prvj gcie
Preconscious reception and bodily response

A prereflective bodily identification is usually described as an individual's being drawn into the story presented on screen, experiencing bodily reactions as if participating in the story before reflecting on the story. Since such identification strongly depends on the use of cinematic elements in a film, the elements specific to Aronofsky's films will be discussed while writing on separate films and in the concluding chapter. This introduction will offer insight into relevant theoretical work, in support of the approach used in the book. The prereflective bodily identification is *the prerequisite silent phase.* It is a prerequisite for triggering reflection, a provocation of the senses—because without this initial bodily reception a film would stay on the level of "what you see is what you get," that is, on the surface level of distanced observation, unworthy of further reflection to grasp the deeper meaning. It is silent because the reflection is not present, hence it belongs to the anonymous beginning of an aesthetic encounter, in commonality annulling the subject–object dichotomy. A spectator is not a subject reflecting on an object, and the interiority of the spectator and the exteriority of the screen are intertwined, my body feeling what (presumably) the character feels as presented on the screen.

In general, phenomenology is the study of the structure of experience as it relates to consciousness. Husserl proposed transcendental phenomenology, arguing that consciousness is intentional, as "consciousness of." Merleau-Ponty extended and modified Husserl's approach by describing perception and the prereflective phase when an individual's sensibility is provoked by the environment, creating a commonality between the observer and the observed. Merleau-Ponty's prereflective phase of perception seems to be the proper starting point for developing a phenomenology of cinema, the experience of a prereflective allure of cinema, and the subsequent reflection triggering aesthetic admiration and ethical respect and responsibility. Hence, some film theorists raised objections to considering a unidirectional relation between a spectator and a film as between a subject and an object, arguing for a two-way relationship, that is, a mutual intertwining of a spectator and a film: as I read a film, it reads me back. The phenomenology of film based on Merleau-Ponty's phenomenology of perception was proposed by Vivian Sobchack in *The Address of the Eye* (1992).[16]

---

[16] Vivian Sobchack, *The Address of the Eye: A Phenomenology of Film Experience* (Princeton, NJ: Princeton University Press, 1992).

That approach, termed *existential semiotic phenomenology*, argues for an embodied symbiosis between a viewer and a film, based on the act of vision proposed by Merleau-Ponty. Sobchack's commitment to perceptive readings of films stays clear of approaching a film as a conscious subject with established ideological views, searching for filmic elements to reinforce and illustrate his or her theoretical position. Starting from a theory and interpreting every film through the lenses crafted by that theory (a Grand Theory capable of explaining everything) seems too restricted when approaching film as an art form with its own voice. Culture and ideology certainly influence our perception, but some level of freedom and openness (for Sobchack, "not merely naïve conception of liberal humanism") should accompany our experience of film. While Sobchack's book applies Merleau-Ponty's phenomenology of perception and his concept of "flesh" to an embodied experience of film, it stays on the general theoretical level without considering specific films (with a few exceptions). However, a general question regarding the cinematic experience as an aesthetic experience would benefit from subjective readings of specific films considered as artworks. From a question regarding the phenomenology of aesthetic experience, in general, to a question regarding a specific film, there are different levels of diminishing generality: art in general → film as an artwork → a specific genre, or a specific filmmaker → a specific film.

The existential phenomenology of Merleau-Ponty and its adaptation by Sobchack received a cognitive nod via neurobiology. Namely, the problem of spectator identification with the fictional world presented on the screen embarked upon a new direction when neuroscientists discovered the activity of mirror neurons in the brain. This occurred in the early 1990s in laboratory work by a group of neuroscientists from the University of Parma that detected neuronal activity in macaque monkeys' brains that was identical whether the action was performed or merely observed by the monkeys. Vittorio Gallese, one of the scientists from that group, coined the term *embodied simulation* to describe this effect. In a subsequent work, Gallese and Guerra relate embodied simulation to film studies arguing for its power to generate social cognition: people share bodily representations and can map other's emotions and sensations onto their own body.[17] According to the authors, this presents a way to explain the feeling of empathy triggered in movies: I can put myself in the position of the other, and this positioning does not need a

---

[17]   Vittorio Gallese and Michele Guerra, "Embodying Movies: Embodied Simulation and Film Studies," *Cinema: Journal of Philosophy and the Moving Image*, no. 3 (2012).

conscious effort; it follows from the fact that we are similarly wired by neuronal activity. Gallese and Guerra write: "We believe ES can enrich the philosophical debate within film studies both at the receptive level and the creative one, by shedding new light on at least three types of embodiment related to cinema: i) film style as embodiment; ii) acting style as embodiment; iii) viewer's responses to filmed bodies and objects as embodiment."[18] With respect to viewers, this statement concurs with an earlier statement by Deleuze that "cinema not only puts movement in the image, it also puts movement in the mind."[19] Deleuze states that the biology of the brain is relevant for cinema. With respect to film style, the award-winning film editor Walter Murch offers insights into film cutting and editing, analyzing how these processes create a response in the viewer.[20] I will refer to the impact of cutting and editing in more detail in the concluding chapter when discussing Aronofsky's cinematic style.

Subsequent reflection

Following the initial sensual encounter with the presentation on the screen, the spectator's reflection starts in two directions: aesthetical and ethical. The aesthetical direction leads to reflection on the cinematic style and to comparison with relevant films in order to position the film among other comparable works. Reflection in the ethical direction invokes the meaning and significance of the narrative, relating it to the current social (cultural, political) environment and to philosophical questions regarding human existence. Various directions of analysis as triggered by the film, for example, psychoanalysis and anthropology, could be used to understand the fictional character and the spectator's response to the character.

Let me go back to Aronofsky's films considered in this book. This introduction provides a framework for considering his themes and characters, for positioning his films inside genre classification, for comparing his films with other films and directors, and for referencing relevant philosophical positions. A chapter is dedicated to each of the six Aronofsky's films from 1998 to 2014. The final

---

[18]   Ibid., 206.
[19]   Gilles Deleuze, "The Brain Is the Screen: An Interview with Gilles Deleuze," in *The Brain Is the Screen*, ed. Gregory Flaxman (Minneapolis: Minnesota University Press, 2000).
[20]   Walter Murch, *In the Blink of an Eye: A Perspective on Film Editing* (Los Angeles: Silman-James Press, 2001).

chapter summarizes themes occurring in multiple films and some stylistic elements characteristic of Aronofsky's work. The Appendix to this book includes a transcript of my conversation with Aronofsky on December 2, 2013.

Aronofsky's themes and characters

From the beginning of the early twentieth century, with the creative force subsequently unleashed in silent movies of the 1920s, to the golden years of Hollywood in the 1940s and the 1950s, continuing with foreign (predominantly European) art movies and New Hollywood of the 1970s, the blockbusters of the 1980s, and the proliferation of technology and video of the 1990s, we arrived at the beginning of the twenty-first century with a varied set of productions, directors with differing styles, a spectatorship that has seen it all, technology that allows massive dissemination and incredible manipulation by means of computer-generated imagery (CGI), ratings that reflect populist codes of decency, and budgets that have to cover it all. For a talented film director, the situation presents a challenge: either go with the flow, embark on a populist bandwagon, create a superhero trilogy and enjoy financial success allowing future projects, or remain an independent filmmaker à la Jim Jarmusch, attaining a respectable following and praises, but not blockbuster success. Some filmmakers, not many, seem to attain both ends: to stay sincere to their artistic credo and to obtain commercial success. An interview Martin Scorsese gave to Siskel and Ebert in 1991 comes to mind. Scorsese said that in reference to the ending in his *New York, New York* (1977), George Lucas told him, "Well, if they go away together at the end you can add $10 million more to your box office."[21] Liza Minnelli and Robert De Niro did not go away together, and *New York, New York* did not do well at the box office, but Scorsese managed to make subsequent commercially successful movies. Of course, it would be silly to equate commercial success with questionable artistic success—testified by a number of commercially successful and critically highly-acclaimed movies that audiences love, with the director's sensibility reverberating alongside spectators' sensibility, without the need to court the prevalent and fashionable public taste in an artificial way. Sometimes there is a temporal gap between the movie release and the acceptance by the audience, which is a price paid for artistic creativity surpassing established

---

[21] Robert Ebert and Gene Siskel, *The Future of the Movies: Interviews with Martin Scorsese, Steven Spielberg, and George Lucas* (Andrews and McMeel: A Universal Press Syndicate Company, 1991), 6.

rules and the contemporary public taste, for example the case of *2001: A Space Odyssey* (Stanley Kubrick, 1968). Aronofsky is a director with stylistic and thematic elements connecting his films into a recognizable body of work at the intersection of art film and the commercial blockbuster, contributing to his awards and financial success in most cases, but also to the criticism and controversy surrounding some of his films. However, such varied reception seems to be the case when an artist takes his or her own direction incongruent with the well-established path.

The themes in the six Aronofsky's films from 1998 to 2014 include the search for perfection, the search for happiness, longing for love, intoxication with publicity, the pain of alienation, and the burden of responsibility. Although such themes characterize humanity in general, they seem particularly pronounced in our times. The wish to achieve something extraordinary is present in all his main characters, from the past, the present, and the future. The characters from the past and the future are determined to accomplish *impossible* tasks: to relieve humanity from mortality (Tomas the Conquistador and Tom the Space Traveler in *The Fountain*), and to relieve humanity from the duality of innocence and guilt by starting anew (Noah in *Noah*). The rest of Aronofsky's characters, the contemporary ones—scientists, artists, performers, common people—are all prone to obsession as a way out when confronted with the challenges of biological constraints and pressures from the social environment. The fixation with numbers and markets addressed in π, the allure of appearing in a TV game show in *Requiem for a Dream*, the stubbornness of a scientific mind to find a cure for cancer in *The Fountain*, the longing for public exhibition and admiration in *The Wrestler*, and the drive to achieve artistic perfection in *Black Swan*—these themes point to a contemporary relation of an individual to the public, the crowd. A need for distinguishing ourselves from the rest of the crowd seems timeless, but today's technology, starting with TV and now the Internet, allows instant fame and increases the competition, raising the bar for achieving perfection, whatever is meant by that term. The contemporary public machinery is merciless, and Aronofsky's characters struggle for survival and recognition in a society characterized with high expectations, public entertainment, and instant gratification, ending in a fictitious world, creating a fabricated reality, and finally, succumbing to it. Usually, a film director gets the attribute *auteur* when his or her work conveys a recognized personal style and recurring elements serve as a signature. Despite a changing style and changing themes, from the black-and-white π with hip-hop montage to the spectacle of *Noah*, Aronofsky's sensibility in depicting characters in their internal turmoil remains his signature move. This will be further discussed in the concluding chapter after analyzing separate films.

Aronofsky's extension of the melodrama genre

The development of cinema genres is related to tradition, established via the audience's expectations, and to the prospect of curbing such expectations in propagating a certain ideology and increasing possible revenue.[22] Hence, right from the start, the concept of the film genre contains the duality of conforming to the established order and of creating a frame for innovations. When films started to be labeled as belonging to a certain genre, for example western, the audience started to have expectations of how events and characters should be treated. Hence, *genre* became a concept worthy of critical analysis, in order to evaluate films as belonging to them. Hollywood's film machinery, with large studios and profit-making outlook, was instrumental in the development of genres as repeating formulae shown to be successful in previous releases. As genres developed and matured, spectators and critics found it interesting to evaluate their tradition and the place of an individual artist in it; the genres brought together the work and the audience in constant mutual influence. It is not surprising to have opposite views regarding a film genre: particular genre films can be viewed as conservative propaganda, predictable and grounded in conventions, or as subversive statement precisely because they are predictable and grounded in conventions. How a film is read depends on the use of cinematic elements and the way they are presented. A standard way to subvert a genre is to go a bit "over the top," to create a sophisticated parody, which many directors did (e.g., Sirk's melodramas). In *Film/Genre* (1999), Altman considers the questions of the origin and stability of film genres, and their use by the film industry.[23] Genres speak differently to different groups of audiences, which perceive differently the elements in a movie.

Melodrama is present in many other genres as increased emotionality in response to societal pressures. Usually the conflict involves the spiritual values of humanity against a materialistic consumer society, hence an individual striving with all his or her might, but succumbing at the end to the inevitable forces of

---

[22]   Barry Keith Grant, *Film Genre: Theory and Criticism* (Metuchen, NJ: Scarecrow Press, 1977).
[23]   Rick Altman, *Film/Genre* (British Film Institute, 1999).

the dominant social order. Melodramas serve to remind the audience of the cracks in the order of society by exaggerating the moral polarities of good and bad. As a genre, melodrama had usually negative connotations as an exaggeration of emotions and stereotypical characters, but applied to any genre, it can result in a dull work as well as in a masterpiece.

Aronofsky's films extend the genre of melodrama by presenting complex characters and their transformations alongside ambiguous endings, leaving it to the spectator to decide how pessimistic or not the endings are. Despite working in different times and in different cultures, this melodramatic inclination brings him close to Fassbinder, another auteur who redefined the melodrama genre through his presentation of human psychology, the elasticity of moral convictions, and the elusiveness of satisfying desire, combined with everlasting longing for love and happiness. Both Fassbinder and Aronofsky create ambiguous endings, appearing as utterly pessimistic at first glance, but provoking the spectator to ponder the characters' decisions and the turn of events. Despite the apparent pessimism of the ending, if it is the best of the worst outcomes following the sequence of events leading to it, the ending retains a cathartic feel, a sense of freedom and reconciliation of life and death. *The Wrestler* and *Black Swan* end in a climax insinuating the death of the main character. However, both Randy in *The Wrestler* and Nina in *Black Swan* are driven to their respective final performances as acts of liberation and reconciliation of conflicting forces shaping their lives. They both accept their deaths as the final victory of their lives.

Comparison with some relevant films and directors

Aronofsky is a storyteller and likes to tell a story with a memorable character (Max from π, Sara from *Requiem*, Randy the wrestler, Nina the ballerina, and—of course—Noah). This inclination toward storytelling, involving characters who are caught up in obsessions that develop into extraordinary situations, shows similarities with both Kubrick's and Spielberg's works, despite their opposing sensibilities: Spielberg's sensibility of childlike wonder, emotion, and the sense of adventure, coupled with optimism and redemption; and Kubrick's dissection of humanity's flaws, including obsession, irrationality, stubbornness, and arrogance, and leading to dead ends in life's trajectories. Spielberg's characters are ordinary characters caught up in extraordinary situations created by the outside environment, and they have to find the strength and emotional courage to deal with it. Aronofsky's characters are also initially ordinary characters, but the more or less ordinary challenges of life bring forward their interior weaknesses as if they were predestined to move toward tragic events. His characters exhibit strangeness and otherness from inside; the environment might contribute, but it is not the predominant factor directing their behavior. The characters have strangeness in them, projecting a feeling that they would behave similarly even with less outside pressures, that is, they represent cases of pathological behavior. For example, many people ponder the idea of an underlying order, but would not behave drastically as Max does in π. Many people daydream about appearing on T V, but would not go mad as Sara does in *Requiem*. Many scientists put great efforts in their research, but do not remain fixated on the impossible task as Tommy does in *The Fountain*. Many wrestlers and similar performers age and have to abandon their lifestyles, but do not close all avenues for continuity of their lives as Randy does in *The Wrestler*. Many emerging artists go through painful transformations to perfect their art, but do not end up in psychosis as Nina does in *Black Swan*. Even Noah, the biblical character in *Noah*, behaves as a man who is predisposed toward strong opinions and stiffness in decision-making. Apart from his extraordinary task from "above," he projects a man who would raise his children with an iron hand, strongly convinced that his should be the last word. The extreme behavior of Aronofsky's characters in contradiction with their fragility brings them close to Kubrick's characters who exhibit the duality of human nature. The intertwining of Spielberg's and Kubrick's filmic sensibilities is maybe best articulated in *The Fountain* and *Noah* as will be argued in subsequent chapters pertaining to those films.

In addition to relating Aronofsky's filmic sensibility to directors such as Kubrick, Spielberg, and Fassbinder, it is possible to add Kurosawa and European auteurs such as Kieslowski, Saura, and Polanski. This will be further argued when discussing Aronofsky's films in relation to other films with relevant themes, implicitly acknowledging the importance of cultural conditioning in experiencing a film. Aronofsky's style combines elements of adventure/action movies, testifying to his growing up in the Spielberg–Lucas era of the 1980s, but the action often turns from the exterior environment to the interior psychic space of his protagonists, allowing us to look into the psychical challenges they go through, often visible on their bodies. This inclination to expose his characters from inside out brings him close to art directors and the big themes, such as the meaning of life, sacrifice, death and rebirth, putting his films in a genre of philosophical films.

Relevant philosophical positions

As philosophers would argue, viewing reality in a restricted sense of objectively present entities is incomplete. For example, emotions are real but are not objective things. In addition to triggering an aesthetic response, films stir emotions and move us to reevaluate our ethical and moral stances. In feeling empathy toward a character, I do not identify with that character specifically, but with the depicted state of mind. For example, in feeling empathy toward Sara or Harry in *Requiem*, I am empathetic toward an addict: the character's specificity fades, and my reflection on the state of humanity starts.

Philosophy and film can be related, and there are a number of books dealing with the intertwined relationships between them. One approach to relating the two areas is to go from philosophy to film in applying philosophical thought to analyze film as a complex concept. This amounts to the use of philosophical discourse to define the ontology of film, the epistemology of film (film versus knowledge), the nature of narration, the emotional response to film, and the ethics of film. Noel Carroll and Jinhee Choi edit a collection of papers relating philosophy and cognitive science.[24] Another approach is to use film as a tool to illustrate and explicate a philosophical concept such as emotion, subjectivity, reality. For example, Carl Plantinga and Greg Smith edit a collection dedicated solely to the emotional impact of film.[25] Using various film examples, the papers address a wide range of filmic possibilities for triggering emotions (narrative, music, cinematic techniques). Kevin Stoehr edits the collection *Film and Knowledge: Essays on the Integration of Images and Ideas* (2002) containing essays on individual films, which could elucidate various philosophical concepts (e.g., responsibility, cognition, consciousness) through reflective interpretation, that is, which could increase our knowledge of ourselves.[26] Using insights from cognitive psychology, Ed Tan stresses the impact of filmic narrative structure in provoking spectator emotions.[27] In a subsequent book, Greg Smith argues that films create moods facilitating shared emotional discharge.[28]

---

[24] Noel Carroll and Jinhee Choi, eds., *Philosophy of Film and Motion Pictures: An Anthology* (Blackwell Philosophy Anthologies, Oxford: Wiley-Blackwell, 2006).

[25] Carl Plantinga and Greg M. Smith, eds., *Passionate Views: Film, Cognition and Emotion* (Baltimore, MD: Johns Hopkins University Press, 1999).

[26] Kevin L. Stoehr, ed., *Film and Knowledge: Essays on the Integration of Images and Ideas* (Jefferson, NC: McFarland & Company, Inc., 2002).

[27] Ed S. Tan, *Emotion and the Structure of Narrative Film: Film as an Emotion Machine*, trans. Barbara Fasting (New York: Routledge Communication Series, 2011, Reprint edition).

[28] Greg M. Smith, *Film Structure and the Emotion System* (Cambridge: Cambridge University Press, 2003).

A different direction goes from film to philosophy, that is, starting with film and its capability for triggering philosophical thoughts. *In Doing Philosophy at the Movies* (2005), Richard Gilmore interprets a number of films as being philosophical in depicting characters and actions that invite philosophical reflection behind the narrative.[29] His discussions of specific films and his interpretation of characters and their actions lead to philosophical questions on human existence and the nature of reality. In *Filmosophy* (2006), while discussing the relationship between film and philosophy and referring to philosophers using films to make a philosophical point, Daniel Frampton asks, "If the starting point for these philosophers is 'what can film do *for philosophy?*', how long will it take for them to realize that film *offers* philosophy?"[30] In *Film and Philosophy: Taking Movies Seriously* (2008), Daniel Shaw summarizes different approaches toward the relation between film and philosophy, arguing that "it seems more philosophical to recognize an unintended parallel between a film and a philosophy than to highlight an intended one."[31] Havi Carel and Greg Tuck edit a collection *New Takes in Film-Philosophy* (2011), presenting a number of essays on the interactions between film and philosophy without preferring one over the other, so "they are all prepared to consider not only what philosophy can bring to our understanding of film, but also what film can bring to our understanding of philosophy."[32] This approach resonates strongly with my approach toward Aronofsky films viewed as artistic counterparts to philosophical writings, that is, viewed as triggers to aesthetic experience, provoking new directions of thought. Damian Cox and Michael Levine coauthor a book titled *Thinking through Film: Doing Philosophy, Watching Movies* (2012), discussing ways in which film and philosophy are intertwined.[33] They subscribe to the "moderate thesis," arguing that films sometimes can surpass the written word in explicating a philosophical position. It is neither the case that films have a unique approach to philosophy (a bold thesis), nor the case that films are only mere triggers for philosophizing (the null thesis). The intertwining of film and philosophy contributes to their mutual illumination: philosophical reflection on a film can contribute to assessing its artistic value, and a film can contribute to our understanding of quintessential philosophical concepts, for example, ethics and responsibility, love, consciousness.

---

29   Richard A. Gilmore, *Doing Philosophy at the Movies* (Albany, NY: State University of New York Press, 2005).
30   Daniel Frampton, *Filmosophy* (New York: Wallflower Press 2006), 9.
31   Daniel Shaw, *Film and Philosophy: Taking Movies Seriously* (New York: Wallflower, 2008), 3.
32   Havi Carel and Greg Tuck, eds., *New Takes in Film-Philosophy* (London: Palgrave Macmillan, 2011), 3.
33   Damian Cox and Michael P. Levine, *Thinking through Film: Doing Philosophy, Watching Movies* (Oxford: Wiley-Blackwell, 2012).

Let me turn to Aronofsky's films addressed in this work and clarify my philosophical reading of them. In a sense, every provocative film raising questions about humanity is philosophical in inducing meditation about the state of humanity. All six of Aronofsky's films from 1998 to 2014 are character studies of some extreme behavior. His films depict intriguing facets of human nature, such as the blind spot between desire and happiness, obsession, the process of addiction, meditation about death and rebirth, the quest for perfection, and the sense of responsibility. His characters exhibit contradictory psychic states, from vulnerability, fear, anxiety, resignation, and infatuation with instant fame to hope, promise, and ever-alluring happiness. They project their inner turbulence and psychic states onto their bodies, creating a mixture of horror and melodrama genres. While watching a film and reflecting on it, relevant philosophical positions came into reflection as invited by filmic presentation and were not premeditated. Philosophical interpretation of each film comes out in a metaphorical way, providing philosophical counterparts to the artistic merit of film. In each of the subsequent chapters analyzing Aronofsky's films, I will approach the theme and the questions arising from the film with relevant philosophical writings.

For example, an analysis of the character of Max Cohen in π brings into question the difference between reason and intellect as discussed by philosophers such as Schelling and Jaspers. The addiction of characters in *Requiem for a Dream* relates to the writings of Deleuze and Guattari on the body under the influence of drugs, as the body trapped in habit and unavailable for further development. The use of nonlinear temporality with three intersecting stories and the effort to come to grips with the issue of death as rebirth, as presented in *The Fountain*, resonates with the importance of temporality as stated by Kant and Husserl, and especially by Heidegger in his existential phenomenology describing the being of human being on the road toward attaining authenticity. Next, Randy's final performance in *The Wrestler* invokes the issue of "the gift of death," discussed by Derrida. Nina's psychosis incurred by trying to achieve artistic perfection as presented in *Black Swan* brings into consideration a number of philosophers who write about excess, transgression, and limit experiences, for example, Bataille, Blanchot, Foucault, and Jaspers. Finally, the issue of responsibility and sacrifice, and the inseparable mixture of good and evil residing in humanity, as presented in *Noah*, relates to the writings of Kierkegaard and Schelling.

The themes in Aronofsky's films that treat the extreme behavior of his protagonists, whether provoked by a contemporary social climate (as in *The*

Wrestler) or an ahistorical need for transgression characterizing humanity, provoke strong emotionality, inviting a comparison with the emotionality displayed in ancient tragedies, which brings us to Aristotle and his *Poetics*.[34]

According to Aristotle, a tragic spectacle, as a form of art, can arouse the purifying emotions of pity and fear by introducing a level of cognition into our emotional response. The initial displeasure or pain caused by fear and pity is purposive: it is by means of such painful emotions that we can induce pleasure (i.e., via the catharsis of such emotions). What could be the implication for devising a good tragedy? In order to feel fear, we have to be convinced that with high probability (or even necessity) the evil event could happen to us. Hence, the tragic plot has to include events that are probable or necessary, and ". . . a believable impossibility is preferable to an unbelievable possibility."[35] For Aristotle, virtues are habits formed by certain actions. Actions in general, and habits in particular, are voluntary, but not in the same way: we are responsible for our actions from the beginning to the end; however, for habits we are responsible at the beginning, and the later development proceeds without reflection.[36] Since ethical virtues are habits, we need to acquire them by repeatedly acting in a certain way—but the challenge is to know the right way to act in order to strengthen an ethical virtue. Aristotle writes: "How can we say that men should do what is just in order to become just, and *act* temperately in order to become temperate? For if they do what is just or temperate, they are already just or temperate, just as if they do what is grammatical or musical, they are already grammarians or musicians, respectively."[37] Aristotle's description of the relationship between cognition and emotions stresses the importance of habitual right action in producing ethical virtues as "golden means" between vices as opposite extremes. If we further assume that "the soul never thinks without an image,"[38] it becomes clear that a good tragic spectacle performed by people "acting and not by narration"[39] (i.e., containing a visual reinforcement) can offer an excellent *simulation environment* (to use a contemporary term) for attaining proper habits. Aristotle believed in the positive educational value of good tragedies (or poetry in general) and his analysis is very straightforward. This is the reason that fascination with *Poetics* still persists, and it is relevant for contemporary cinematic spectatorship. We

[34] Aristotle, *Poetics*, trans. Richard Janko (Indianapolis, IN: Hackett Publishing Company, 1987).
[35] Ibid., 61b9.
[36] *Nicomachean Ethics*, trans. H.G. Apostle (Grinnell, Iowa: The Peripatetic Press, 1975), 1114b29.
[37] Ibid., 1105a18.
[38] *De Anima, Book II and III*, trans. D.W. Hamlyn (Oxford: Claredon Press, 1998), 431a16.
[39] *Poetics*, 49b28.

can paraphrase Aristotle by saying that a good film will induce empathy in a simulated environment, providing a clearer outlook on pleasures and pains in our lives, and since "... ethical virtue is concerned with pleasures and pains,"[40] such an environment provides an appropriate ground for acquiring right habits leading to virtuous dispositions.

On one hand, we can argue that Aronofsky's films give testimony to the *power* of hope: his characters are driven to obsession and addiction by the power of hope (e.g., the hope to find the underlying pattern in nature, to achieve the American Dream, to achieve immortality, perfection, and the separation of innocence from evil). But, since it is hope going out of proportion, it loses its power and becomes very fragile, detached from the reality to which it is directed. Hence, we can argue that Aronofsky's films display the fragility of hope. As Aristotle reminds us, virtues going to extreme become vices, and it is difficult to keep the balance. Aronofsky's films do not have pleasant endings, and a spectator does not exit the theater in a happy mood; but his films do provoke reflection, and possibly, reevaluation of priorities in our lives.

[40] *Nicomachean Ethics*, 1104b9.

π: Is Mathematics "The Language of Nature"?

I'm not interested in your money. I'm searching for a way to understand our world. I'm searching for perfection.

Max Cohen, the mathematician in π

Aronofsky's first feature film π (1998), which he directed and for which he served as a screenwriter, introduced originality into the use of camera moves and the ability to tell an interesting story with open-ended implications. π is a story centered around the character of Max Cohen, a talented mathematician who becomes obsessed with the search for the underlying order grounding all seemingly chaotic patterns. Max is convinced that everything in nature—including the stock market as a "natural" organism—has a pattern hidden beneath a seeming chaos and can be represented by numbers. His search for pattern prediction is interesting for predictive strategists from the stock market, and Marcy Dawson from a financial firm is aggressively pursuing him. She tries to bribe him by offering the yet declassified "Ming Mecca" chip, the newest addition to Euclid, the computer he has painstakingly upgraded. His research in number theory is also of interest to Hasidic Jews who are searching for the code relevant to the ancient Kabbalah teaching. Lenny Meyer explains to Max the numerical values assigned to the letters of the Hebrew alphabet and to Hebrew words, and in those numbers Max recognizes the Fibonacci sequence of numbers, leading to the golden ratio discovered by ancient Greeks, and subsequently used in art and science to denote perfect ratios and spirals. This triggers Max's concentration on spirals. However, the input data submitted to Euclid causes the computer to crash right after printing a certain number and predicting an unusual stock pick. Max's visit to his former advisor Sol Robeson, who spent forty years looking for patterns in π, induces a thought on the importance of the generated number of about two hundred digits, since apparently, Sol in his research days came across it as well. Sol tries to persuade Max against further experiments, sensing his dangerous obsession. Max subsequently sees that Euclid's stock pick was correct and

Figure 1.1 Max finds inspiration in a spiral form of a seashell (π, 1998)

frantically tries to recover the generated number from the garbage can where he discarded it. From Lenny Mayer he learns that Hasidic Jews are searching for a number that is 216 digits long, afterward finding that it would represent the "true name of God." The idea of spirals generated via the golden ratio, underlying all natural patterns, including the human brain, leads Max to the following hypothesis: "If we're built from spirals, while living in a giant spiral, then everything we put our hands to is infused with the spiral."[1] Invigorated by his new insights, he accepts the Ming Mecca chip from Marcy Dawson, restarts Euclid, and inserts the disk containing Torah and Jewish words given to him by Lenny Mayer. The words suddenly turn into their number counterparts. Following a dizzying headache sequence intensified by the lovemaking sounds from his neighbor, Max realizes that Euclid produced the number with 216 digits, and he is able to memorize it. The pain in his head intensifies and there is a bulge on his head indicating the area that causes pain, which he circles with a marker. The number seems to be implanted in his head, giving him access to "forbidden" knowledge, such as predicting future stock values, tested by looking at the *Wall Street Journal*. Fearful, Max visits his mentor Sal, who warns him again to stop

---

[1]   Darren Aronofsky, *Π: Screenplay and the Guerilla Diaries* (London: Faber and Faber Limited, 1998), 116.

with this obsession. Finally, after the chase and pressures from both the business world represented by Marcy Dawson's group and the religious Jews around Lenny Mayer and Rav Cohen, he collapses under headaches and hallucinations, and destroys Euclid. Realizing that Sal was right, he drills his head at the point marked for containing the "forbidden" knowledge, subsequently smiling for the first time: outside, peaceful, observing the movement of a tree crown blown by the wind, and conversing with his little neighbor Jenna, not knowing the answer to the number problem she asks him.

Why can the audience "buy" the character of Max Cohen?

The story about a mathematician and the obsession with mathematical regularity as presented in π hits a right note and contrasts two seemingly irreconcilable entities: the imperfect, irrational humanity and the rigor and regularity of mathematics, specifically number theory. A more detailed analysis of Max's character is preceded by a short description of examples with real mathematicians exhibiting mental problems, in turn, providing credibility to Max's obsessions.

Unfortunately, there are some notable real-life stories of outstanding mathematicians who succumbed to madness. *A Beautiful Mind* (Ron Howard, 2001) is based on the life of John Nash, a game theorist whose work on noncooperative games led to the Nobel Prize in Economics in 1994. Despite some divergence from Nash's biography, the film captures his illness, paranoid schizophrenia, and his struggle to overcome it. David Malone produced a documentary for the BBC entitled *Dangerous Knowledge* (2007), presenting four mathematical geniuses who ended tragically, struggling with depression, bipolar disorders, and insanity. They are: Georg Cantor (1845–1918), the "father" of Set Theory; Ludwig Boltzmann (1844–1906), the author of the *Boltzmann equation* dealing with the concept of entropy and the development of statistical mechanics and thermodynamics; Kurt Gödel (1906–78) whose incompleteness theorem discovered a hole in the heart of mathematics, stating that formal systems capable of expressing elementary arithmetic are incomplete because they can originate true statements that are not provable inside the system; and Alan Turing (1912–54), the author of the Turing machine, indispensable for conceptualizing algorithmic computation. Those great trailblazers in mathematics have uncovered knowledge that shatters the very foundations of that science of their time, moving the boundaries, but they themselves could never recover from this "forbidden" knowledge, succumbing to its pressures. Georg Cantor was working on the concept of infinity and discovered that there are many infinities, and died in an insane asylum. Boltzmann undermined the certainty of timeless perfection by introducing the concept of entropy, implying that isolated systems are prone to decay, and that evolution and mortality characterize our physical systems. He hung himself while on holiday in Italy. Gödel studied logic and established the incompleteness of formal, logical systems, undermining the certainty proposed by such systems. Hence, Gödel proved that mathematics cannot provide all answers; that rational certainty is limited, and that there is knowledge beyond logical reasoning, which we cannot establish formally but only via intuition. He suffered from mental instability and starved himself to death. Alan Turing continued on Gödel's work and made it concrete by inventing a computing machine based on logic. Some mathematical problems cannot be solvable on such computers, but we can envision computers based on self-adapting rules, computers that can learn, simulating a human being. This leads to implication for us: are we computers just made of flesh or not? The mental strain required to go beyond visible relations, to ponder concepts such as infinity and transcendence, coupled with pressures from the academic community unprepared for novel discoveries that undermine established rules, probably contributed to the breakdowns of these highly creative personalities. Turing's case is even more drastic: his suicide at the age of forty-two followed his submission to female hormonal therapy (chemical castration) requested by the British authorities because of his homosexuality. The mind who broke the Enigma code used by the Germans in World War II was pardoned by Queen Elizabeth II many years later, on December 24, 2013. Interestingly, *Enigma* (Michael Apted, 2001) is a film that mixes fiction and reality about the code breakers of Enigma, but without ever mentioning Alan Turing. Finally, *The Imitation Game* (Morten Tyldum, 2014) tells the story of Alan Turing based on his biography.

Max Cohen, the mathematician from Aronofsky's *π*, is being consumed by his obsession with the search for the underlying order expressed by numbers, and we can ask how believable such an obsession is. People become obsessive for different reasons, and I am not in a position to speculate about that, but can relate to the allure of logic and order in mathematics. In *The Guerilla Diaries*, Aronofsky writes about the germination of his idea for the main character, developing him from a paranoid schizophrenic to the character of Max who is an obsessive-compulsive math genius, so that the audience can "buy this character."[2] This choice shows Aronofsky's instinct to recognize the proper vector to carry on the story about the incessant search for order behind visible chaos. Indeed, the audience can buy this character since it presents an exaggerated case of a human struggle between the rational and the irrational residing in our human lot, and the consequences when there is gross imbalance. The strong intellect, driven to uncover hidden abstract relations supporting the visible world, is unable to connect emotionally with the outside world because that would pollute the clarity of his thoughts. Or, maybe he clings to the rational obsession as an escape from emotional and sexual insecurity. In any case, the audience can indeed buy this character.

The word *obsession*, stemming from the Latin *obsidere* meaning "to besiege, to occupy," indicates that one dimension occupies the whole being, creating imbalance and resulting in compulsive movements, headaches, and subsequent hallucinations. The obsession with the incessant equation of patterns in nature with numbers is believable when it is applied to a person with a strong intellect and emotional instability. It presents a breaking point between the two poles of humanity: the rational and the emotional. Numbers, as simple unbiased entities complying with the underlying order, are useful for representing the rational vocabulary. We can argue that the alphabet containing a limited number of symbols used to create words and to make sentences, is also a system. However, in language, there is ambiguity: the same word can have different denotations, and even more complicated, a word with unique denotation can have different connotations and can change its meaning based on the context as is well explicated in Wittgenstein's *Philosophical Investigations*. There is no such problem with numbers: they have a unique, unchangeable meaning, regardless of context or usage. And they go to infinity—not one, but multiple infinities, for example the countable infinity of integer numbers or the uncountable infinity of irrational numbers. Number systems are various, increasing in abstraction: *integers* followed by *rational* and *irrational* numbers composing real numbers, then *complex* numbers including the *imaginary unit*. Some numbers are *transcendental* numbers; then there are the so-called *perfect* numbers, *untouchable* numbers, and the list could go on. All real transcendental numbers are irrational and the most famous are π = 3.14..., the ratio of a circle's circumference to its diameter, and e = 2.718..., the base of a natural logarithm. Each set of numbers has a precise definition and is used in attempts to solve various abstract or nonabstract problems.

[2]   Ibid., 6.

When there is something clearly defined, and when a person is overwhelmed by the simplicity, regularity, and timelessness of the number theory, it seems not very far-fetched that the mental strain can turn to obsession, similar to a love obsession. The names given to certain sequences of numbers bear witness to how emotional it is to work with them: *perfection, irrationality, transcendence,* and *untouchability*. Take, for example, the case of number 5, an untouchable number.[3] Number 5 is an odd number, and the question whether number 5 is the *only* odd untouchable number is an open problem in mathematics. Imagine now someone obsessively working to solve this problem, applying his or her complete intellectual powers, being passionately in hold of it, as if being on the brink of understanding the mystery behind the natural world. Why do we have five fingers? Is it a sign of God? ... And the person gets drawn into the allure of pure mathematics, unable to stop thinking about it, unable to resist, sinking into mental delusions and possibly insanity. Luckily, this does not happen often, and a person lets it go, accepting that some knowledge, regardless how simple it might look, is outside his or her reach.

Max from π firmly believes that "mathematics is the language of nature," frantically searching for patterns, and it seems plausible that he finally breaks down after believing that he transgressed the limit of human knowledge. Earlier, he concluded that his computer, Euclid, broke after it became conscious of itself, of its computational structure, so it seems plausible that a human being disintegrates upon de-mystification of its being. We need a mystery of life to be able to enjoy life—de-mystification leads to disintegration of life's impulses. Hence, to end meaningfully, to bring life back to life, Max has to hallucinate about purifying his thoughts, drilling his head, and restoring human balance in unbalance.

Interestingly, the ending of π, with Max drilling his head and afterward sitting on a bench, quietly, with a serene look, at first glance seems somewhat pessimistic: what is left if the mind is devoid of questioning? However, upon more pondering, the interpretation can became more and more optimistic. We can interpret Max as someone who has satisfied his obsession, emerging from a nervous breakdown and hallucinatory hell with a new outlook on life, happy to

---

[3]   Definition of an *untouchable number* is "a positive integer that cannot be expressed as the sum of all the proper divisors of any positive integer (including the untouchable number itself)." The sequence of untouchable numbers starts as: 2, 5, 52, 88, 96, 120, 124, 146, 162, 188, 206, 210, 216, 238.... (Note that the "'important" number in π as "the forbidden name of God" is 216 digits long, which is an untouchable number.)

Figure 1.2 Max about to drill his head (π, 1998)

enjoy the beauty and diversity of natural patterns, as a poet versus the learned astronomer, to allude to Walt Whitman's poem "When I Heard the Learn'd Astronomer." Max's return can be believable because, after all, his obtained number is only 216 digits long. Of course, this is supposed to be ironic, but what would happen if he continued the search for a limit to π?[4] Would he then end as Cantor pondering infinity, as Boltzmann pondering mortality, or as Gödel pondering the flaws of logic?

The optimistic ending is reminiscent of "The Mind and the Matter" (1961), episode 63 from *The Twilight Zone* TV series.[5] The main protagonist gets headaches, annoyed by the people around him, and subsequently reads from a book about the power of concentration. Using concentration, he is able to get rid of all people. Then, due to boredom, he creates a number of people similar to himself. Finally, listening to his conscience, he realizes how wrong all this is, and gets back to the real world, but invested with the capability of relating to

---

[4]   As Cipra observes in 1999, even with supercomputers, we are not able to try every 216-digit number in the foreseeable time (Barry Cipra, "Irrationality Dominates II," *Math Horizons* 6, no. 3 [1999].)

[5]   The title of the episode evokes the title of the influential philosophical treatise by Henri Bergson, "Matter and Memory" (1896) in which he explores the middle ground between idealism and the materialism, arguing about the importance of memory in connecting body and mind.

Figure 1.3 Max's serenity after "purification" (π, 1998)

others. Maybe the awakened conscience, or an epiphany as a sudden leap of understanding when we can see more clearly, acts as a life-changing event. This gives credibility to the character of Max, and a belief in his change. We have to go out of the ordinary world to undergo a radical change. The predilection to transgress, to go beyond, seems to be innate to human nature as argued by various philosophers, for example, Bataille, Blanchot, Foucault, and Deleuze. Max from π was lucky to experience the "forbidden territory" and to come back maybe realizing that what is really important was always in front of his eyes, but he was unable to see it until he satisfied his obsession.

This line of thought brings us to a movie by David Cronenberg, *Videodrome* (1983). The main protagonist in this science-fiction horror movie is Max Renn, the president of a TV station drawn to broadcasting extreme violence (torture, murder, mutilation) for real, subsequently getting involved in events leading to obsession and creating changes in his brain. The changes trigger hallucinations, and his perception of reality is changed. The technological (TV) overtakes the natural (the mind), and the TV screen becomes part of the physical structure of the brain as stated by Professor O'Blivion, the character who is convinced that public life in TV is more real than private life in flesh. At the end, Max from *Videodrome* gives in to his obsession. He sees the TV image of himself, shooting himself in the head, and imitates it, exclaiming, "Long live the new flesh!" His character is infused by the desire for transgression, although nominally stated as a wish for financial gain. But, his desire for transgression, for reaching the limit experience in torture and sexuality, ends in personality disintegration and the inability to recover.

Unlike Max from *Videodrome*, Max from π is able to find peace, to stay in the "old flesh," and live with the mystery of life. While the thematic in *Videodrome* insinuates a critique of media manipulation and inherent fear about technology swallowing humanity, the theme in π seems to be ideologically neutral, dealing with a general human need to ponder the mystery of the world around us, albeit exaggerated by the imbalance between high intellect and deficient emotionality. Max from π is also driven by the desire for transgression, but his hallucinations are concentrated around his brain and his head, leaving the rest of his body intact. Comparing *Videodrome*'s low carnal impulses toward torture and sadomasochistic sexuality coming from a person's interiority, with π's high-intellectual impulses toward understanding exteriority, it seems easier to pull back from a mental than from a bodily obsession, possibly implying that the human body is a prerequisite for a person's individuality. The issue of the body is further addressed in subsequent films by Aronofsky (*The Wrestler*, *Black Swan*), and will be discussed in subsequent chapters.

This rather lengthy analysis of Max's character, and my informal descriptions of some notable real-life mathematical minds searching for transgression of human knowledge and ending tragically, allows us to appreciate the fictional math wizard from π, and his story created by the joint efforts of Darren Aronofsky, Sean Gullette, and Eric Watson. Gullette's fierce performance brought Max's character to life. It would be silly to try to decompose Max's character to pieces, to see if it all fits neatly and logically into place—it would create an obsessive spectator, a bleak equivalent of Max. What gives life to this fictional story is the combination of its textual, visual, and sound effects, creating a *sense* of unity, without proving it formally. While unity is achieved in presentation, the resulting meaning allows plurality of interpretations, contributing to the allure and open-endedness of the story. From the perspective of a filmmaker, as Aronofsky has said, the effort of putting it all together, to tie all parts of a film into a unifying pattern resembles paranoia. Risking some paranoid observations, let me discuss some elements of π that contribute to the main theme of emotional insecurity and intellectual superiority channeled into an obsessive search for a way out.

About visual, textual, and sound elements in π

Max's interior imprisonment in his obsession is visually supported with scenes presenting long corridors, store interiors, subways, and a claustrophobic apartment in which he lives. His living environment mimics a giant computer, a counterpart to his Euclid. There, he becomes a "chip," with the memory of a computer chip. However, regardless of how carefully Max wants to leave outside his system all traces of organic life, life penetrates his habitat. There is organic, lowlife ants, crawling all over the apartment, annoying him, and he squashes them, trying to get rid of them, except at the end, when he gives up. This superposition of ants and technology, and the ants' resilience, invites comparison with Gabriel Garcia Márquez's ants at the end of Macondo society in his masterpiece *One Hundred Years of Solitude* (1967). Interestingly, Aronofsky said that the idea to have ants in Max's apartment came to him when remembering anthills in Mexico, overtaking the remains of the great Mayan civilization. The ants crawling on the computer did not provoke Max's attention, except in the form of frustration, and yet, we can learn a lot from ants, even in algorithmic development and pattern search. Namely, the behavior of ants provides ideas that contribute to a branch of artificial intelligence (*swarm intelligence*), which

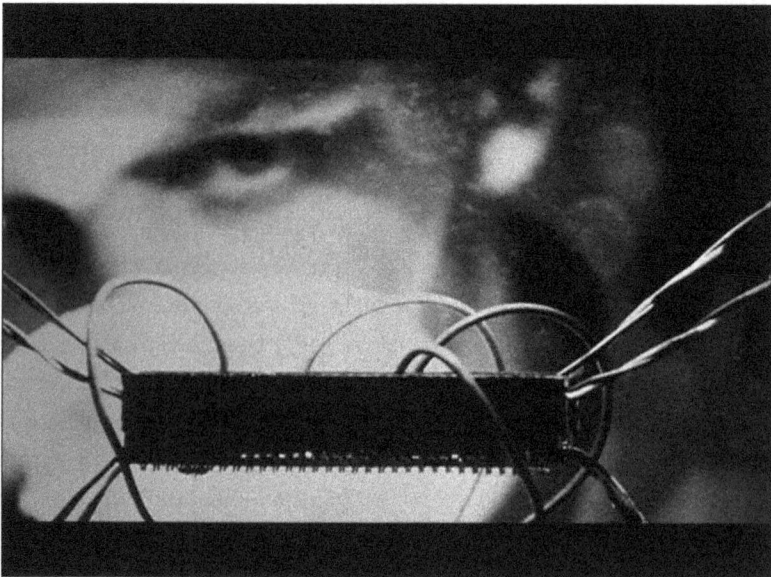

Figure 1.4 Ants crawling on Euclid (π, 1998)

deals with robotic multiagent systems, and to the class of *Ant Colony Optimization* algorithms, which shows success in solving difficult combinatorial problems. But, Max cannot accept the organic nuisance embodied in ants and cannot bring them into the equation. This suggests narrowness of rigorous mathematical fascination.

Then there is another trace of organic life, the lovemaking sound coming from the neighboring apartment, intensifying Max's frustration because he is, in fact, attracted to his sexy neighbor, but is incapable of responding to her touch. We cannot say that Max is emotionally dead; on the contrary, his emotions run very high when working on his hypotheses and trying to understand the underlying pattern to achieve perfection. But he is caught up in his emotional cage when dealing with people, especially the woman he is attracted to.

The contrast to Max's claustrophobic apartment is provided in the scene on the ocean, on Coney Island, when Max observes a spiral of a seashell. This contributes to his search for inspiration and provides a contrast with the confinement of the man-made areas. Aronofsky's visual clues to support Max's obsession with spirals are wider, applying associations and correspondences among visual depictions. By juxtaposing various scenes, the director creates correspondences that might go unnoticed otherwise. For example, the spiral staircase in Max's apartment building provides implicit connection with Max's inner world. Another example: the broken mirror has patterns similar to the wrinkles on Max's shirt, implicitly leading the viewer's visual field into intuition about connectivity of patterns. Superimposing visual similarities of seemingly unrelated entities seems appropriate for the theme of searching for the underlying order and the pattern binding it all together.

This superposition of visual similarities is reminiscent of Vertov's theory of montage, opposed to Eisenstein's "montage of attractions." With his concept of *kino-oko* (camera eye), Vertov wanted to induce a change in the perception of a contemporary man, to sharpen such a perception, to become more like a machine in precision. His masterpiece, *Man with a Movie Camera* (Dziga Vertov, 1929), embodying a cinematic philosophy of "life caught unawares" is in some respect close to π. The camera in Vertov's film bears some correspondence to Euclid, the computer in π. The cameraman, obsessed with trying to capture the reality of life, and his symbiosis with the camera, artistically presented in a close-up of a composite between the camera and the human eye, invokes similarities between the symbiosis of Max's frantic data input to Euclid and Euclid's processing of it. Vertov superimposes diverse scenes to provide a unifying pattern to this cacophony of scenes. The pace is frantic and repetitions are abundant, foreshadowing the hip-hop montage, ending with incessant movement of men and machines. Men's movements resemble the movements of ants, as seen from the camera eye operated by the cameraman—a man with the mission to supply data to this omnipotent eye able to create order, a symphony, out of the apparent disorder. The scenes of a cameraman driving around and filming, the dizzying tempo of movement, the strange positions taken by the cameraman (e.g., lying on the ground while a mining cart passes over, entering the private space of a bedroom, roaming around the city), and trying to encompass it all, project a sense of frenzy, passion, and obsession. Max's passion and obsession with supplying data and code to Euclid bears similarity to Vertov's cameraman. Tree crowns, appearing in both movies, support the theme of unification of disparate parts: the multitude of tiny parts (leaves), but that work in unison—sometimes more, sometime less—conditions the spectator to the idea of an underlying order. Vertov's film was silent and we can only imagine what kind of music would fit it perfectly. This brings me to the sound and music in π.

The voice-over in π, in a style of laboratory findings, works well and supports Max's state of mind, his detachment from his life-world, and his obsession with facts. It invites comparison with some other voice-overs, for example, in

Figure 1.5 Max's symbiosis with Euclid (π, 1998)

A Clockwork Orange (Stanley Kubrick, 1971) and in *The Wolf of Wall Street* (Martin Scorsese, 2013). In Kubrick's film as well as in Scorsese's, the voice-over presents a confessional stance toward the spectator, reinforcing the character who speaks and making the spectator some kind of accomplice. Alex from *A Clockwork Orange* and Jordan from *The Wolf* are despicable characters, with seductive voices, playing with the spectator's morality code: should they be likable, those evil criminals, insensitive to humanity around them? Kubrick and Scorsese push the spectators into the ring, forcing them to reevaluate their moral positions. The voice-over in π starts as if confessional, "When I was a little kid ...," but soon it turns to a description of Max's experiments and his mental condition by describing his headaches and enumerating the drugs he takes, in a precise scientific statement of facts, without mentioning something emotional or something outside his research. The last voice-over repeats exactly the first one, "When I was a little kid my mother told me not to stare into the sun. So, once when I was six I did."[6] This closes the circle of Max's obsession, after which Max drills his head, to reemerge subsequently as a content person, freed from his obsession. Max from π does not sound likable, and he does not need to. He is not a bad guy, so why would he need to charm the people? Having a more likable person would undermine the story. Gullette's performance hits the right note in presenting a detached loner, obsessed with his quest, unable to free himself from his attraction to a woman, projecting nervousness in his voice, prone to migraines and hallucinations. But, he is not an opportunist; he resists pressures from Wall Street and from the religious group, looking to uncover the underlying order and dispense the mysteries of life. His quest comes from inside, maybe as a defensive mechanism for his inability to embrace life in its fullness, to recognize that human perfection is in its imperfection. Aronofsky's choice of the two groups that pursue Max for their own very different purposes, for business and for religion, captures the two poles of instrumental utility. After all, business and religion have similarities: business can assure pleasure in this life; religion, in the other life, and "In God We Trust" is written on a dollar bill.

Clint Mansell's musical score works as an amplifier in its support of the images, adding to the fast pace when needed, adding to the headache and hallucination scenes, calming it down when organic life creeps in, contributing to a thriller feeling when working with Euclid's transformations. The use of electronic music underlines the technological, computer-saturated world. The same applies for the

6   Aronofsky, *Π: Screenplay and the Guerilla Diaries* (London: Faber and Faber Limited, 1998), 65, 152.

black-and-white visual presentation. π is said to be the first narrative feature film using black-and-white reversal film, resulting in high contrasts and image resolution. There are no shades of gray in the movie—either black or white, with sharp contrasts. This is evocative of a computer world, of zeroes and ones, the bits used for representation, and no numbers in-between. It suggests the effort of depicting the reality through simplification, an ordered model starting with initial assumptions and reaching conclusions after some computations.

The musical score and the overall rhythmic quality of π is discussed in "A Musical Approach to Filmmaking: Hip-hop and Techno Composing Techniques and Models of Structure in Darren Aronofsky's π" by Kulezic-Wilson.[7] She observes how different audiovisual elements in the film (the voice-over, diegetic and nondiegetic sounds, techno musical score, the use of various cameras to offer Max's point of view and his state of mind, the hip-hop montage, and fast editing) contribute to the rhythm and musicality of the film. Use of repeated scenic and textual patterns creates the feel of a music score, unifying separate aspects of the film. When Max reports on his experiment, the close-ups with his voice-over alternate with his point of view without sound, all in metrically proportional matter, ending with the camera focusing on a tree crown. This resembles a music score with refrains and a closing line. Kulezic-Wilson observes that hip-hop editing style determines the film's micro-rhythm, and that the techno-music coupled with visual and sound repetitions creates its macro-rhythm. The hip-hop editing creates a sense of urgency and obsession, and of pattern repetitions, while the techno-music situates the story in the technologically saturated environment. The raptures and breaks characteristic of rap music create associations with Max's breaks due to his recurring headaches. Moreover, writes Kulezic-Wilson, "The truth is that, although most aspects of π's external rhythm are the result of a 'hip-hop approach' to editing, the presence of Mansell's score from the very beginning, the electronic drone behind many of its scenes, the frightening noises in the headache sequences, and even some of Max's monologues fit into the 'techno-feel' of the film."[8]

Both the visual elements of π (mise-en-scène, camera moves and setups, cuts, black-and-white coloring scheme) and the audio elements work in unison to provide the viewer with the vehicle to enter the interior of the troubled and

---

[7]   Danijela Kulezic-Wilson, "A Musical Approach to Filmmaking: Hip-hop and Techno Composing Techniques and Models of Structure in Darren Aronofsky's π," *Music and the Moving Image* 1, no. 1 (2008).

[8]   Ibid., 31.

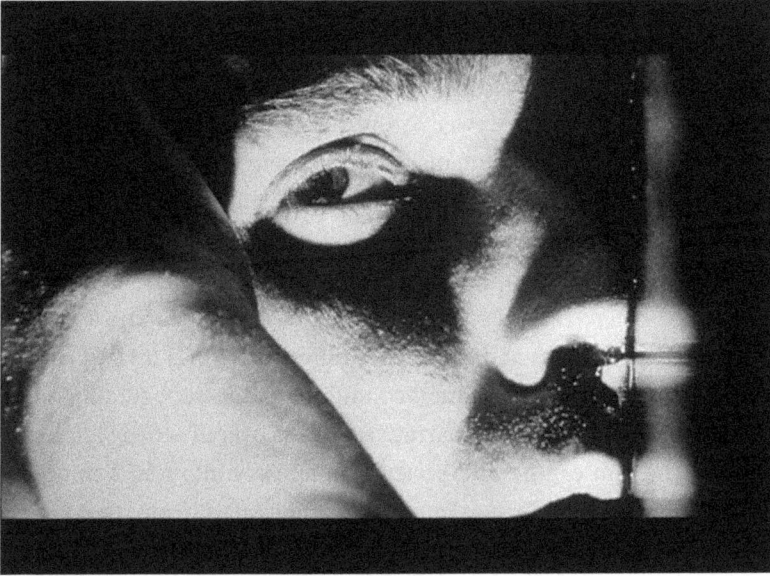

Figure 1.6 Extreme close-up of Max's face (π, 1998)

intense character of Max. The extensive use of extreme close-ups of Max's face, especially his eyes, and the scenes of his hallucinations and his headaches lead viewers to a prereflective bodily identification with Max.

As research in neuroscience related to mirror neurons suggests, a viewer's brain simulates the behavior and the emotions seen on the screen, creating embodied simulation, preceding reflection.[9] The identification simulated via neuronal activity allows the feeling of empathy as the ability to experience the interiority of another being like myself because we share similar biology and neuronal wiring. This precedes my feeling of sympathy or antipathy, or pity, or sorrow. In order to feel sympathy or repulsion, I need to involve judgmental activity, my conscious experience, and cultural upbringing. With diverse camera setups, editing, and extreme close-ups (of faces but also of specific objects, e.g., computer screens, strings of numbers, a finger pressing the return key), a viewer is led to unconscious identification with Max and his inner world. The viewer's sensibility is provoked in its preconscious state before being filtered into separate emotions. When initially encountering a scene with a close-up face of a character (in addition to Max, we can add Sol Robeson and Rav Cohen), a viewer is pulled into a space where there is no subject–object dichotomy, and the viewer and the

[9]   See, for example, Gallese and Guerra, "Embodying Movies: Embodied Simulation and Film Studies."

character inhabit the same body. It is interesting to compare four different scenes
between Max and Sol. In the first scene, the shot reverse-shot between them is
asymmetric in that Max's face is shown in extreme close-up, while there is
distance from Sol, leading a viewer to unconsciously side with Max's view. In
subsequent scenes, as Sol's arguments become stronger and his interiority more
pronounced, the camera moves closer to him, provoking a viewer to experience
a stronger identification with him. The camera eye can provoke various levels of
preconscious bodily identification by emphasizing a detail and distorting
objective space. Afterward, with the beginning of contemplation, a viewer can
make subjective judgments and experience different feelings toward characters.
A viewer's whole apparatus of cultural conditioning can start, guiding reflection
toward judging the character, the narrative, and the overall artistic import of the
movie. Since the film can be interpreted as a journey into Max's mind, let me
offer some additional reflection on his psyche. Apart from the innovative
approach to montage and editing, and the overall artistic merit of π, the intriguing
but timeless story about desire for pondering beyond mere appearances invokes
psychoanalytic questioning of Max's obsession and repression.

A psychoanalytic look at the character of Max Cohen in π

Max believes in the power of rational order, because "everything around us can
be represented and understood through numbers."[10] Such intellectual arrogance
and its difference from reason were analyzed in the existential philosophy of
Karl Jaspers. In *Reason and Anti-Reason in Our Time*, Jaspers argues that *intellect*
and *reason* are essentially different concepts, with intellect employing procedures
and algorithms to prove something, while reason is the will to know, related to
desire. Intellect seeks the totality of knowledge to impose order and be able to
explain everything in analytical terms. This is foreign to the openness of reason,
and Jaspers writes, "Reason has no assured stability: it is constantly on the
move. . . . It leads to self-knowledge and knowledge of limits, and therefore to
humility—and it is opposed to intellectual arrogance. . . . Thus reason works
itself out of chains of dogma, of caprice, of arrogance, of passion. . . . It is in itself
a boundless openness."[11]

---

[10]   Aronofsky, *π: Screenplay and the Guerilla Diaries* (London: Faber and Faber Limited, 1998), 88.
[11]   Karl Jaspers, *Reason and Anti-Reason in Our Time*, trans. Stanley Godman (New Haven, CT: Yale
       University Press, 1952), 39.

According to Jaspers, empirical existence in the world of objective presences is insufficient to characterize an individual's concern for self-knowledge. His concept of *Existenz* indicates a will to go beyond appearances in search of impulses directing our behavior. Jaspers denotes the externality of the world of appearances as the *Encompassing*, the space of transcendence, where we turn when dissatisfied with the world of facts and explanations. Humanity extends beyond intellectual explanations, beyond science and factual explanations. Jaspers writes, "What I feel then is not the impotence of knowledge. . . . Instead I feel a discontent that eggs on me . . . it is my dissatisfaction with existence at large, *my need to have my own origin*."[12]

In considering presence that cannot be represented in the world of appearances, Jaspers was influenced by Schelling's writing regarding the *ground* of existence as residing outside the objectivity of existence and generating desire.[13] Schelling was, in turn, influenced by Aristotle's saying that a touch of madness is necessary to accomplish something new, to digress from a known path. To that end, Schelling proposes that there are three types of people. First, there are "dead intellectuals" who disallow any trace of madness, that is, they govern madness and are totally oriented toward the intellect. The second type are people who are insane, that is, people governed by madness, being completely mad. Both types are obviously deficient, and Schelling proposes the third type, people in between the two drastic poles, balancing intellect and madness, being governed by reason, but with occasional touches of madness. This is the most desirable type of person because, in Schelling words, "where there is no madness, there is also certainly no proper, active, living intellect (and consequently, there is just the dead intellect, dead intellectuals)."[14]

The story of Max from *π* illustrates his "leap of faith" from the existence solely governed by his intellect in pursuit of a fact, a string of numbers, to an authentic existence realizing that there are meanings that cannot be factually explained. He experiences his touch of madness and his lobotomy, followed by his serenity at the end, which illustrates his transcendence. He realizes his *Existenz*, becoming a person able to communicate beyond a presentation of facts. At least, he is able to say "I don't know" to little Jenna and smile for the first time.

[12] "Excerpts from Philosophy (Volume 2)," in *Existentialism*, ed. Robert C. Solomon (New York: The Modern Library, 1974), 139.

[13] F.W.J. Schelling, *Philosophical Investigations into the Essence of Human Freedom*, trans. Jeff Love and Johannes Schmidt (Albany, NY: State University of New York Press, 2006).

[14] *The Ages of the World (Third Version C.1815)*, trans. Jason M. Wirth (Albany, NY: State University of New York, 2000), 103.

Max's obsession with finding the underlying pattern underneath the seemingly diverse natural patterns leads to psychoanalytic analysis and is reminiscent of Lacan's concept of the *primordial signifier*. Max's precise notes of his experiments, including the time and objectivity of observation, point to their formal aspect, to accumulation of facts—but where is the meaning? According to Lacan, the propensity for formal recording of facts goes back to the *primordial signifier*, responsible for starting the subject's entrance into the Symbolic order, but staying outside it and designating the limit of psychoanalysis, escaping the elaboration of meaning. The symbolic order, the order of knowledge and understanding, cannot provide a meaningful analysis of a desire that remains unsatisfied. The need to record a sign, to acknowledge it, starts language, culture, and the subject's desire. If all were understood, desire would cease to exist, annulling the human being as such. Hence, the ambiguity of meaning escapes factual pinpointing, keeps desire alive. Desire to desire is purely formal, objectless, beyond the symbolic order, as absence in presence, yet it is primordial as leading back to the continuity of being, broken by the separation from the mother and with the emergence of the father. Lacan identifies the primordial signifier with the "paternal function." The separation allows the emergence of the subject. The problem arises when we try to endow every sign with a meaning, against the neutrality and indifference of the Real. While in earlier studies, Lacan viewed "communication *qua* meaning," equating communication with creation and transfer of meaning; in later studies, Lacan considers "communication-as-meaning," allowing for communication that is itself meaning, without generating inter-subjective meaning. Efforts in science and mathematical reasoning to provide closed-form formulaic answers to the mysteries of the physical world and the nature of humanity stem from human nature, from the desire to provide meaning. But, such efforts carried to extremes can create psychotic individuals, as is portrayed in π.

In a paper discussing π and Lacan's primordial signifier, Paul Eisenstein elaborates upon Aronofsky's achievement to "isolate the primordial signifier in its purely formal dimension."[15] The primordial signifier is given a formal numeric value via the 216-digit number, followed by the scene of Max drilling his head, in effect, deleting all meaning from the primordial signifier and leaving only its formality. The meaning is gone; Max emerges as a balanced individual with eyes

[15]   Paul Eisenstein, "Visions and Numbers; Aronofsky's Π and the Primordial Signifier," in *Lacan and Contemporary Film*, ed. Tod McGowan and Sheila Kunkle (New York: Other Press, 2004), 11.

that are alive, capable of observing the world around him (the tree crown), and to participate in social communications (with his little neighbor Jenna). Eisenstein credits the end of π with "a kind of imagistic equivalent of the primordial signifier, an antidote of sorts to the psychosis that the film depicts and the antithesis to the lion's share of commercial Hollywood films in which the central images are eventually inscribed within some intelligible and meaningful framework."[16] The ending in π is in contrast with films such as *The Sixth Sense* (M. Night Shyamalan, 1999) or *Signs* (M. Night Shyamalan, 2002) in which the end provides intelligibility to the initially inexplicable phenomena.

The character of Max from π solicits additional psychoanalytic reading, namely following Jungian analytic psychology. In the interview with John Freeman in 1959, when asked about consequences of increased technical efficiency and increased need for people to behave "communally and collectively" leading to "collective consciousness," Jung was very skeptical about the possibility of collective consciousness. He said that his patients show the need to preserve their meaningful existence.[17] According to Jung, we live with the "collective unconscious," but could not live with collective consciousness. The process of individuation, of developing wholeness of the psyche, is a never-ending process of personality development. At the end of Max's ordeal and movement through the phases of exploration, facing adversities, and conversing with his mentor, he finally reaches peace, emerging as the *self*, unifying Jungian fundamental psychological functions of thinking, feeling, sensing, and intuiting. Max's character projects Jungian archetypal structures. His ego directs the search for mathematical order and shows his arrogance in proclaiming that he is the one to get the 216-digit number, "the true name of God." His persona is undeveloped and he does not care to present himself other than what he really is; he is not interested in playing a social role. Euclid, his homemade supercomputer, can be identified with Max's shadow archetype, albeit the relation is not simple. Max consciously searches for the mathematical solution to the unifying pattern, but it seems that unconsciously he wants to be a part of it, a part of this computing machine, which he even tastes at some point and which infiltrates his brain, fusing them. His unconscious wish to become part of a computer serves as a defense mechanism for dealing with his repressed sexual drive. As he gets the desired number, the shadow becomes recognized, moves into consciousness; he becomes conscious of his obsession and is able to free himself from it. His

[16]   Ibid.
[17]   Carl Jung, in *BBC video "Carl Jung: Face to Face,"* ed. John Freeman (1959).

neighbor Devi can stand for the complement of his persona, his anima. She represents the various aspects of emotionality that Max lacks: friendly, motherly, sexual. Toward the end, Max hallucinates about embracing Devi, and in the last scene, he talks with Jenna, the child neighbor, projecting friendliness and a parental look, indicating the reconciliation with his anima. Finally, Max emerges as a self, as the union of his unconscious and his conscious material, balancing various elements of his psyche. After all, Max did find a unifying pattern, unity inside himself, the most important pattern to find.

As previously indicated, π delivers intriguing visual and audio elements, all working in unison and leading the spectator along an uncharted path, provoking him or her to try to make sense of the story, to understand the details, triggering impatience to figure it all out. Hence, the spectator is led to unconsciously identify with Max, the seeker of a unifying pattern, but not in the classical sense of identification with a desirable hero. If we reflect afterward on Max's character, his obsession and driving force, it appears that Max is not a likable hero and his quest for answers is exaggerated to the point of paranoia. However, he is not colored by a certain ideology or a religious belief, he is not hungry for money, he is not pretending to be what he is not—he resonates with many desirable human characteristics. His paranoia and emotional inability work against him throughout the film, but he gets full redemption at the end. The end is unexpected and a spectator might need some time to digest it. As already stated, the end could initially seem pessimistic as insinuating a character devoid of search, that is, dead inside (after the scene of his lobotomy). It might take additional viewing and analysis to interpret the ending as utterly optimistic. But, on another thought, can Max be able to desire again, to put his inquisitive mind to a new task, though one less obsessive?

Supporting the narrative plot in π and the main character's obsession with an underlying pattern in nature, Aronofsky's direction and audiovisual elements (the cinematography of Libatique and the musical score of Mansell) lead to an implicit unity connecting all elements in π.

Requiem for a Dream: Addiction and Broken Dreams

You know who's somebody now? Who's no longer just a widow in a little apartment who lives alone? I am somebody now, Harry. Everyone likes me. Soon millions of people will see me and like me.

Sara Goldfarb in Requiem for a Dream

Aronofsky's theme of a unifying pattern continues in his subsequent film, *Requiem for a Dream* (2000), restricted to a psychologically intriguing facet of humanity: *addiction*. The screenplay, written jointly with Hubert Selby, Jr., and based on Selby's 1978 book of the same name, follows four protagonists as they succumb to addiction, each with his or her own dream, all pointing to the elements of the same dream—the American Dream, according to Selby, Jr. The story follows a widow from Brooklyn, Sara Goldfarb, her son Harry, his friend Tyrone, and his girlfriend Marion.

Using similar cinematic language as in π when presenting obsession (hip-hop montage, extreme close-ups, repetitive scenes), Aronofsky and his team created an audio/visual illustration of addiction in *Requiem*. Both obsession and addiction are extreme mental states characterizing distorted interiority that can lead to external bodily distortions. As in π, the audio/visual style provokes unconscious and prereflective bodily simulation finding a viewer in the challenging position to experience the events as being objectively present. A viewer can feel the initial rush of adrenaline and subsequent bodily changes as if his or her body is being engulfed in the pawns of addiction, all on a subconscious level. As stated earlier, the experimental work on neuronal activity of the brain provides a plausible explanation for such embodied simulation, for consciousness of the body.

Let me first present an outline of the narrative and an interpretation of the characters as unexceptional, everyday characters in contemporary American society. The selection of characters underlines a wide terrain for the beginning of

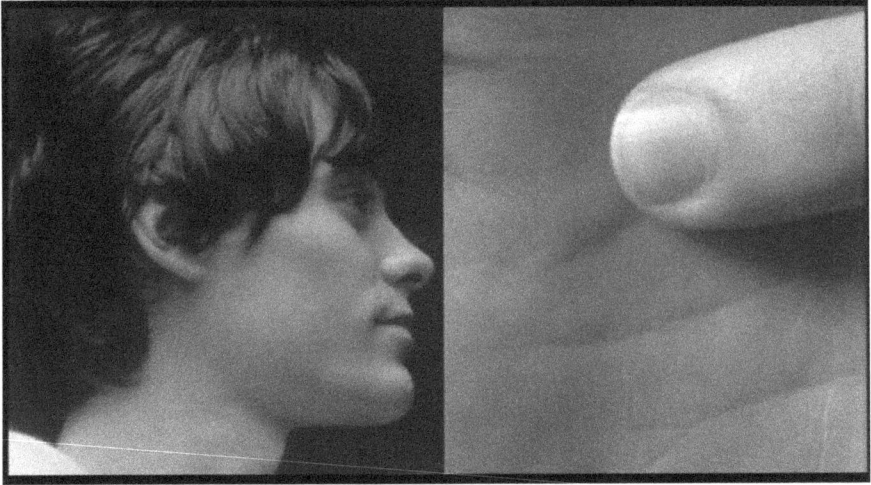

Figure 2.1 Use of split screen and extreme close-ups (*Requiem for a Dream*, 2000)

addiction, not restricting it to race, gender or age. The diversity of characters united in addiction is in line with the theme of pattern unification. Since addiction can be so prevalent, it is possible to consider it as an existential determination of humanity, and it is not surprising that philosophers pondered both the issue of transgressing the limits of everyday existence by opening experience to new levels and the possible consequences of such practices. Various films about addiction have been made based on autobiographical works, often casting real addicts. In *Requiem*, the scene of the supermarket rush presents real addicts. Although *Requiem* is wider in its consideration of different instances of addiction, it is interesting to compare it with some other films dealing with addiction because the majority of films on addiction objectively emphasize the impact of environment and the deterioration of a character, while *Requiem* takes a predominantly subjective approach leading the viewer into the mind of a character. *Requiem* offers not a visualization of an addict (or a group of addicts), but a visualization of addiction as such. Addiction is visualized with camera moves and extreme close-ups, with the sound track and the color scheme that support the protagonists' initial euphoria, climax, and downfall, appropriately labeled with three inter-titles: summer, fall, and winter.

There are four main characters in *Requiem*: Sara, Harry, Tyrone, and Marion. Sara's dream is to be somebody, to distinguish herself from the suffocating anonymity of existence, plagued as she is by loneliness and physical decay due to aging. Although she lives in a community with similar women, she is not satisfied

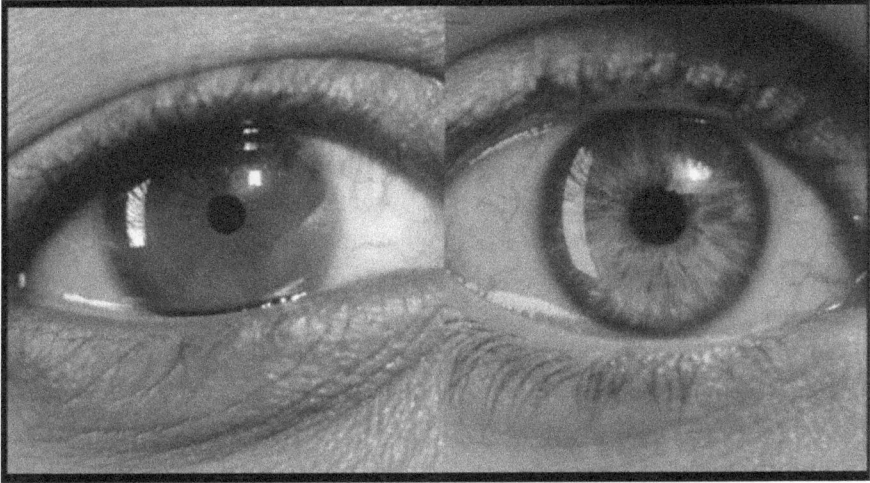

Figure 2.2 Different characters united in addiction (*Requiem for a Dream*, 2000)

and jumps obsessively to the perceived opportunity of appearing in a TV show, one of those shows that "can teach you" how to live your life to the fullest, entitled *Join Us in Creating Excellence (JUICE)*. Convinced that she will appear on the show, she explains her reasons to Harry, "I'm somebody now, Harry. Everyone likes me. Soon millions of people will see me and like me."[1]

Her son Harry dreams of making it in the business world. His girlfriend Marion is from a wealthy garment business family and Harry asks her why she is so hard on her parents who give her everything: an apartment, a shrink. . . . Marion answers that this is great, but, "Money isn't what I really wanted from them. That's pretty much all they had to give."[2] Harry suggests that she should design clothes and open her own store with him. His dream is to have a loving relationship and monetary independence. He says, "You remember when I told you about the store. Well, I've been thinking about it. I put together some numbers and it's not impossible. I think you can do it. You should do it. I mean, we can do it together." His friend Tyrone dreams of making something significant out of his life, to deliver on a promise he gave to his mother as a young child. We see his fantasy as a little boy talking to his mother, "I told ya', Ma. One day I'd make it."

[1]   Darren Aronofsky and Hubert Selby, Jr., *Requiem for a Dream* (London: Faber and Faber Limited, 2000), 58.
[2]   In the published screenplay, Marion answers, "Like they're in that big house with all their cars and money. They pay me off so they don't have to deal with me. They pay off charities to deal with their racism. Then we'll see how liberal they are when I come home with a black guy." Ibid., 14.

The elements of their unifying dream (to be somebody worthy of admiration, to be in love and to have financial security, to fulfill parents' hopes) seem universal, independent of geography or time. What makes these elements contemporary and American, that is, specifically positioned in time and geography, are the means of achieving them.

Sara's fascination with appearing on a TV show and her wish to look "perfect" starts her addiction to the weight-loss amphetamine pills, leading to a full-blown psychosis and institutionalization in a mental hospital. Through this character, the movie projects a social critique of spectator manipulation via programs designed to strike upon their viewers' weaknesses, such as the obsession with perfect appearance and instant fame. It also critiques the healthcare business, through its representation of indiscriminate drug prescriptions by careless doctors (the doctor does not even look at Sara when she comes to his office for the first time). In this sense, the character of Sara approaches the cliché of a contemporary person obsessed by superfluous gratification grounded in physical appearance and success based on no criteria other than appearing on TV. In the contemporary world full of stars of reality shows whose popularity is orchestrated by TV networks in order to generate profit, it is not unusual that a vulnerable spectator gets infected with the virus "I can appear on TV and become famous just by being seen, regardless of what I can or cannot do, as long as I look good."

A generous view toward Harry is that he seems to be a good person. He feels for his mother, eventually buying her a present when he thinks he can afford it. He is in love with his girlfriend and really wants to help her to establish independence from her parents, although he does not understand why she needs to be so hostile toward them. He is creative and likes to take the initiative as when he presents an initial business plan for a joint store with Marion. He is not a dropout; his graduation photo shows him with his proud parents. He is a loyal friend as when he gives their mutual savings to bail out Tyrone from jail. The only problem is that Harry is a junky, a heroin addict, and his business plan is based on drug dealing. There is not a trace of remorse about the possible harm that it can create, only a fear about being busted due to the illegality of his business plan. Yet, he seems to be aware that drugs are not that healthy as when he tries to convince his mother, "Hey, Ma, ya' gotta cut that stuff loose. I'm telling you it's no good." The old Machiavellian doctrine that the end justifies the means seems to be embedded firmly in his dream of success and happiness. The addiction and financial loss result in the final moral debasement when he asks his girlfriend to prostitute herself for needed money. Both the most demanding entity (in the grip of addiction) and the last resort to achieving something (by selling it for money or perfecting it for fame), the human body serves as the link to a state of mind when ethics and morality are overwritten.

Tyrone is like Harry, a loyal friend, a personality driven to get out of the streets, to do something with his life, as he promised his mother. In his fantasy, she tells him, "You don't have to make anything, my sweet. Just have to love your momma." This dubious request calling for psychoanalysis, and the fact that he is black, adding another layer of difficulty, diminish Tyrone's chances of making it. Like Harry, he does not see anything wrong with the drug-dealing business, just an opportunity to make it in this world: If you make it, the result is important, but how you get there is irrelevant. In his environment, this seems to be the most realistic business plan because it seems unlikely that he could base his plan for financial independence on education or some other type of entrepreneurial opportunity. His addiction and bad luck when caught in a drug-gang killing lead to the crumbling of his dream and his spiral downward.

Marion, Harry's girlfriend, is also a cocaine addict and approaches the cliché of a rebellious rich kid who has to differ from her parents, though she is unable to measure up and assert her own individuality. Her parents are successful in the garment business; she believes she has talent for designing clothes, but when Harry asks her why she does not open her own store, she responds, "And when will I have time to hang with you?" Marion appears hypocritical, stating that she does not need money from her parents and then explaining to Harry that she needs to see a shrink, fearing that her parents might cut her off. Moreover, the way she prepares herself for visiting the shrink indicates there is a relation between them. Later on, when Harry asks her to see the shrink again to get some money, she insinuates that she'll have to have sex with the shrink for the first time, while afterward in the shrink's bedroom when she wants him to turn off the lights, he says, "You never did before." Despite her past and her possible future, it seems that Marion at some point falls in love with Harry and tells him that. But, the love disappears as the addiction and the inability to get hold of drugs grow. Marion is the only character who does not have any daydreams or hallucinations, so that the spectator can "read" her thoughts. Her first appearance in the film is when she is looking at a pair of high-rises from below, possibly indicating high ambition. Afterward, she sets off the alarm, indicating her need to create excitement, to experience an adrenaline rush. She suggests to Harry and Tyrone that they "waste some time" by having a party in her apartment. These few initial brush strokes paint the character of a reckless rich girl who does not know what she wants, or even if she knows what she wants, does not know how to get it. Later in the story, after Harry prompts her to open her own business, she seems to be on the right track for the first time, starts working on her designs, and proclaims her love for Harry. She needs love, but she also needs a fix. In one scene, she is naked in front of the mirror but does not look at herself, possibly indicating her self-disgust. She needs a fix to enter a different reality, lifting her arms as if embracing the world. When she engages in sex with the shrink (presumably not the first time), she vomits afterward, indicating that this was a painful and filthy experience. Although Marion is the only one of the four characters without daydreams, her dream is narrated through her behavior and through what she says. We get to know the other three characters by what they do and imagine, not only by what they do and say.

Initially, the four main characters seem familiar, exhibiting predictable behavior and resembling clichés to some extent: a lone widow in front of a TV, a couple of friends doing drugs and starting to think how to do some business with it, a young couple in love, with adrenaline for some action and drugs. Together, they cover different parts of American society. They are old (Sara) and young (Harry, Tyrone, Marion), black (Tyrone) and white (Sara, Harry, Marion), male (Harry, Tyrone) and female (Sara, Marion), rich (Marion), middle class (Sara, Harry), and poor (Tyrone). Even their last names invite interpretation of some general meaning: Goldfarb (Sara and Harry) translates as "gold color"

Figure 2.3 High-angle shot of Harry and Tyrone getting high (*Requiem for a Dream*, 2000)

insinuating *appearance* of something valuable and a wish to achieve perfection and financial stability; Silver (Marion) denotes richness; Love (Tyrone) implies emotional triggers. The last names coincide with the characters we get to know as the story evolves and they develop into recognizable individuals. None of them is an extraordinary character; none has any special talent, or leadership capabilities to fill the role of a hero. No, they seem to be average in their age and/ or gender group. Even in materialistic terms, they do not differ drastically: we do not see how poor is Tyrone, nor how rich is Marion (actually, her parents). But, they all want to participate in the American Dream. They all fall prey to addiction with endings that are unhappy, bleak, and offer little hope. Such endings follow naturally from the story because, as we get to know the characters, we do not see a possible source of power to free any of them from addiction. Now, suppose that the story ends differently: that the power of love saves Harry and Marion and they start their hopeful future together, or that the power of friendship saves Harry and Tyrone and they go off the drugs, or that the power of motherly love saves Sara who comes to her senses and accepts her environment and ladies around her. Suppose that at least one of them succeeds in freeing himself or herself—the movie would then convey the standard type of movie magic: there are problems and obstacles; not everybody can make it, but somebody can, so keep trying. This would approach a standard ending shown in many movies, and the audience would be satisfied because such a feel-good ending would be soothing for the audience. However, Aronofsky is not that kind of director, and before him, Selby, Jr., is not that kind of author, although it seems easier to publish a novel with strong content and an ambiguous ending than it is to make an analogous film, an expensive undertaking.[3] The ending, regardless of how pessimistic it is, follows naturally from the seemingly everyday, average characters and the grip of addiction to which they all fall prey.

When talking about addiction and its widespread appeal for humanity, the everyday characters seem to underline the grimness of it. A clichéd character acts predictably, as already seen and expected. But, clichéd behavior also expresses some truth of human behavior. Jung defines archetypes as character templates residing in the collective unconsciousness and attaining objective representations when individualized in our character. Archetypes provide common grounds for character development, for the development of our psyche.

---

[3]   The rating for *Requiem* was NC-17, restricting the distribution and diminishing the revenue. Aronofsky's appeal was denied. Some years later, he appeared in "*This film Is Not Yet Rated*" (Kirby Dick, 2006), a documentary about how films are rated.

In an individual consciousness, the archetypal forms from the collective unconscious become enriched with the content, depending on our environment and physical structure. In this respect, an archetype can provide grounding, a justification for predictable behavior, and hence, can justify some clichés. The approach of introducing more-or-less predictable and already-seen characters works well for the story since it allows the four main characters to rise from the ground (the two-dimensional space populated with paper-thin stereotypical characters) and become individuals. Through the camera moves emphasizing the subjective view of the characters and through scenes of their daydreams and hallucinations, they become acquaintances, and we, the spectators, are drawn to them and are forced to see various situations through their eyes. Even the minor characters in *Requiem* are lifted from a cliché or a stereotype: Marion's shrink does not act as a stereotypical shrink, but as an unprofessional, cold neurotic (the way he eats and negotiates sex with her); Sara's doctor does not even look at her, unusual for a doctor; Tyrone's drug boss can hardly speak, so it is peculiar how he could be a leader. The story starts as something already seen, implicitly bringing the notion of repetition (Harry taking the TV, Sara getting it back), characterizing both the everyday environment and the addiction. Then, the story progresses in different dimensions: narratively as the seasons change from summer to fall to winter; visually (camera moves, changing tonality of colors, speed of cutting) as the addiction becomes more and more gripping; and aurally as Mansell's score and the Kronos Quartet's performance intensify in tonality.

The need for transgression and the habit of addiction

A stereotypical view of an addict presents somebody unable to control his or her behavior, a problem for the person's immediate circle and for society overall. Treatment of addiction is the matter of societal institutions (medicine, law), but why and how does someone become an addict? How does he or she get out of addiction? Many sociologists, philosophers, and artists have attempted to answer these questions. A number of philosophers and artists have written about the human need for *transgression*, for overstepping limits (e.g., Bataille, Foucault, Deleuze). Humanity cannot be constrained by a well-ordered set of rules due to the duality of the rational and irrational forces shaping our subjectivity. As Bataille puts it, "human life cannot in any way be limited to the closed system assigned to it by reasonable conceptions."[4] This is a blessing and a curse of the human race: the desire for an open existence, for possibilities leading to the augmentation of experiential space. Foucault connects the view of excess and transgression with the death of God because in the presence of God (a transcendent being), a human is a finite creature, with defined limits, and transgression has a negative connotation. The "death of God" frees transgression from negativity, affirming its value in pointing to human limitlessness. Foucault senses the danger as well as the benefit of going overboard.[5] Speaking from a personal experience with alcohol, Marguerite Duras concurs with Foucault.[6]

Deleuze's "philosophy of becoming" stresses the need for escaping routine, the closed existence that is guided by rules and that prevents improvisation. His concept of "lines of flight" indicates a possibility to free our thought from entrenched structures and to achieve "deterritorialization," to go to new territories, to augment our experiential space. He distinguishes between two structures of thought: arborial and rhizomatic, and two spaces of movement: striated and smooth. Arbor (or tree) structure has a root and branches following from it, and it is organized, appropriate for movement in striated space. Rhizome (or stem) structure appears freely, pops up outside composition, moving in a smooth space. Smooth space is nomad space, which allows movement without prescribed boundaries. Striated space is sedentary space, including obstacles that arise due to habit and organization. Deleuze and Guattari stress the importance of rhizomatic thought for new beginnings, and for perceiving a subject always in the process of becoming, of spilling over the structured organization. However, the two poles are extreme and the most interesting developments happen in the passages from the arboreal to rhizomatic thinking and back, and from the striated space (via a line of flight) to a smooth space and back. For example, improvisation in music happens when free moves are incorporated in a theme, when the rules provide meaning, but leave freedom for expression.

---

[4]   Georges Bataille, "Visions of Excess," in *Theory and History of Literature* (Minneapolis: University of Minnesota Press, 1999), 128.
[5]   Referring to the affirmation of the value of transgression pointing to human limitlessness, Foucault writes, "This affirmation contains nothing positive: no content can bind it, since, by definition, no limit can possibly restrict it." Michel Foucault, *Language, Counter-Memory, Practice*, trans. Donald.F Bouchard and Sherry Simon (Ithaca, NY: Cornell University Press, 1977), 35.
[6]   Duras writes, "Alcohol doesn't console, it doesn't fill up anyone's psychological gaps, all it replaces is the lack of God. It doesn't comfort man. On the contrary, it encourages him in his folly, it transports him to the supreme regions where he is master of his own destiny." Marguerite Duras, *Practicalities (Alcohol)* (New York: Grove Press, 1990).

In *A Thousand Plateaus*, Deleuze and Guattari consider the term *body* in a wider sense, referring not only to a physical body, but to any entity representing a part of reality (e.g., a book, an artwork, a political system). In the smooth space, bodies are perceived as *assemblages*, free to make connections with other assemblages. Deleuze and Guattari give an example of a book as an assemblage. A book can contain various elements allowing multiple interpretations, and can provide various effects, from aesthetic to creative to machinic. A body with machinic assemblage resides on the limit of the boundary between organization and freedom.[7] Deleuze's concept of the "body without organs" indicates that there is more to a body than its functionality following the organization of its parts.

In order to connect Deleuze's philosophy with Aronofsky's characters from *Requiem*, we are interested in descriptions of the body under the influence of drugs. The drugged body as a machinic assemblage is discussed by Peta Malins.[8] She proposes that the body viewed as a machinic assemblage becomes a body that is multiple, meaning a body that changes its meaning as it forms assemblages with other bodies. Arguing against labels such as "drug user" or "addict," Malins proposes "to rethink the drug using body as an ephemeral entity: a machine that exists only in the event, in its moment of connection with the drug and the specific affects it enables."[9] She asks us to consider the term *drug user* as a classification imposed by social institutions, arguing that a body can never be fully addicted, but only in the process of addiction. The need to free ourselves from the habitual environment, to transgress the boundaries, and to unleash creative potential, might lead to the use of chemical substances. A drug-use assemblage (connecting a physical body, drug, environment, subculture) initially creates the flow of desire, a new kind of openness to and connectivity with the outside, but eventually leads to stratification, to repetition and habit, to the inability to desire anything else apart from the fix, and to the inability to connect with the social world.

Christopher Moreno describes Deleuze and Guattari's philosophy of becoming as relevant for the development of the characters from *Requiem*.[10] The characters

---

[7]   Deleuze and Guattari write, "One side of a machinic assemblage faces the strata, which doubtless make it a kind of organism, or signifying totality, or determination attributable to a subject; it also has a side facing a *body without organs*, which is continually dismantling the organism. . . ." Gilles Deleuze and Felix Guattari, *A Thousand Plateaus: Capitalism and Schizophrenia*, trans. Brian Massumi (Minneapolis: University of Minessota Press, 1987), 4.

[8]   Peta Malins, "Deleuze, Guattari and an Ethico-Aesthetics of Drug Use," *Janus Head* 7, no. 1 (2004).

[9]   Ibid., 88.

[10] Christopher M. Moreno, "Body Politics and Spaces of Drug Addiction" in Darren Aronofsky's *"Requiem for a Dream," GeoJournal: New directions in media geography* 74, no. 3 (2009).

show desire and adrenalin rush during summer, which transforms into restricted desire toward drugs in the fall, and ends in full addiction and despair during winter. The promise of freedom changes to habit and to the inability to deal with the physical needs of the body addicted to a substance. Drug usage during summer shows the potential for self-improvement (Sara trying to improve her appearance, the young protagonists excited about new business opportunities and socially engaged in parties). During fall, the addiction starts to get hold of the characters; summer euphoria dies out; habit kicks in; and they start distancing from each other. Deleuze and Guattari's description fits well with the characters' progression into addiction: "Drug addicts continually fall back into what they wanted to escape: a segmentarity all the more rigid for being marginal, a territorialization all the more artificial for being based on chemical substances, hallucinatory forms, and phantasy subjectifications."[11] Winter presents a breakdown of their bodies, indicating a breakdown of their dreams. The three parts of the film (summer, fall, winter) suggest the inevitable progression toward the end, while the subsequent spring may only be felt implicitly, offering a glimpse of hope, if a spectator is so inclined. The characters' addictions as a way out, full of hopes for acting in order to change their living habitat, turns into bodily reactions confined by restricted spaces, in fetal positions, as if contracting into a hole, a mother's womb, prior to being born as an individual. Their American Dream of a fulfilling life dies as their bodies succumb to addiction. Three characters (Sara, Harry, and Tyrone) end in institutionalized spaces (mental institution, hospital, jail), indicating the needed intervention of society. There is no hope for Sara, but Tyrone and Harry might have a chance. At the end, Marion is the only one shown in her own apartment, and her future can go either way: She can continue her downfall or change with the intervention, possibly from her wealthy parents. One of the film's strengths is the ending's ambiguity: predominantly bleak, but there is still hope—this potent "drug" that remained at the bottom of Pandora's Box. Since all characters show their humanity and their need for love, which erodes as the story of addiction progresses, they invoke compassion and a hope for something positive to happen to them in the future. Selby's storytelling about compassion for people shows through in the film.

[11]   Deleuze and Guattari, *A Thousand Plateaus*, 285.

Visualization of addiction in *Requiem for a Dream*

In *Requiem for a Dream*, Aronofsky brings a new angle to films about addiction: a strongly *subjective* view with innovative camera moves and editing. His camera serves as a vehicle for exploring the characters' states of mind, hallucinations, visual distortions, and corrupted sense of time. The intertwining of narrative sequences with hallucinations pulls a spectator into the interval between objectively and subjectively perceived realities, making it unclear when the hallucination or dream starts.

In *Deleuze, Altered States and Film*, Anna Powell applies Deleuze's philosophy to a number of films that present extreme states (hallucinations, dreams, chemical influence) and argues that cinematic experience can provoke "altered states" in viewers, namely, states that lead to previously uncharted experiential domains.[12] Deleuze's philosophy of becoming stresses the importance of new beginnings, new "lines of flight" or new experience enriching our experiential space: "becoming-otherwise." Altered states of mind bring possibilities for reaching new experiential territories. But, how (if possible) can this be experienced without reaching a dead end, or apart from the impossibility for recuperation? This wish for limit experiences is reminiscent of Bataille's wish to come as close as possible to the experience of death, but to still be alive.[13] Deleuze states that cinema has the potential to lead a viewer in virtually experiencing the story and characters' emotions as seen on the screen. Such an experience is on a preconscious level, involving bodily reactions that precede the invocation of mental cognition and that create affects. Deleuze's affects as occurring in a gap between perception and action point to a break of our consciousness and the annihilation of subject–object polarity, bringing him close to Merleau-Ponty's notion of the commonality between seer and the observed. Without going into their similarities and differences, it seems that Deleuze's writings on affects and altered mental states induced by watching a film prefigure the discovery of mirror neurons and the subsequent work on the neuronal approach to understanding spectatorship. In fact, in the interview titled "The Brain is the Screen," Deleuze says:

---

[12] Anna Powell, *Deleuze, Altered States and Film* (Edinburgh: Edinburgh University Press, 2007), 1.
[13] Georges Bataille, *Erotism: Death and Sensuality*, trans. Mary Dalwood (San Francisco, CA: City Lights Books, 1986).

Cinema not only puts movement in the image, it also puts movement in the mind. One naturally goes from philosophy to cinema, but also from cinema to philosophy. The brain is unity. The brain is the screen. I don't believe that linguistics and psychoanalysis offer a great deal to cinema. On the contrary, the biology of the brain—molecular biology—does.[14]

Thus, film theory should consider cinematic experience as related to the mutual intertwining of bodily and mental processes, combining consciousness of the body with consciousness of the mind.

Powell offers an analysis of *Requiem* by employing concepts from Deleuze and concludes that, despite "harrowing subject matter and downward-spiralling narrative," the artistic import of the film can trigger an enriching experience, in line with Deleuze's wish to go further in productive delirium, sensing the truth of the event without the need for its actualization. In watching a film that depicts extreme emotional states, my neuronal activity simulates the behavior on the screen and allows me to experience such an event in reality surpassing the actual objective world. My body reacts physically, and yet, I am at a safe distance, can recuperate afterward, and start processing the encounter in reflection.

The fact that I can achieve bodily simulation with a character on the screen implies that I can feel emotional empathy with that character. Writing about *Requiem*'s visual style and the use of the Snorri-Cam, Powell argues that such use of the camera depersonalizes and diminishes empathy, which is further provided by the use of inter-titles. She writes, "Rather than revealing personalized emotions, the Snorri-Cam expresses the affects of opiated consciousness, such as the addict's tangential relation to environmental context."[15] While this seems a plausible interpretation, on the other hand, we can argue that centering the motionless character inside the moving background provides even easier bodily identification with that character because of its centrality. As the background moves out of focus, becoming abstract, a viewer clings to the character in increased empathy.

Let me offer some additional comments regarding the visualization of addiction in *Requiem* in scenes that invoke emotional empathy.

When Harry sees Marion on a dock of Coney Island for the first time, and later on when his dream is broken and he falls into the abyss, his state of mind is presented with camera moves, lighting, and atmosphere appropriate for a lyric

---

[14] Gregory Flaxman, ed. *The Brain Is the Screen* (Minneapolis: University of Minnesota Press, 2000), 366.
[15] Powell, *Deleuze, Altered States and Film*, 76.

Figure 2.4 The use of a Snorri-Cam (*Requiem for a Dream*, 2000)

moment when dreaming of a future with a beloved one. Harry's dream images illustrate his character as somebody who has a vision and a plan for the future.

Sara's hallucinations, presented through fisheye lenses, provide the opportunity for the audience to see through her distorted view, and to hear through her distorted sense of hearing. Her dream turns to a full-blown hallucination when TV characters, including her younger self, invade her living room in a scene reminiscent of Fellini's movies. Her psychological distortions and induced fears are displayed through images of the threatening and moving fridge, indicating her struggle to persist on a diet. The changes in her behavior due to pills are depicted through fast movement as when she cleans the apartment (fast shots of 1 frame/sec).

Tyrone's daydream of his childhood and his mother, especially before he is called by his girlfriend to engage in sex, provides his motivations and an insight into his emotions. This narrative element points to Tyrone's source of unquenched desire, and his arrested development between the imaginary and the symbolic order. The imaginary order of pre-Oedipal unity with the mother intrudes into the symbolic order characterized by a lack, by unsatisfied desire.[16]

As already stated, there are no scenes of Marion's daydreaming. She accepts Harry's idea of a joint store and works on some designs, but it does not look as if

---

[16] A psychoanalytical reading of *Requiem for a Dream* is given in Paul Eisenstein, "Devouring Holes: Darren Aronofsky's *Requiem for a Dream* and the Tectonics of Psychoanalysis," *International Journal of Žižek Studies* 1, no. 3 (2007).

Figure 2.5 Sara's distorted view presented through a fisheye lens (*Requiem for a Dream*, 2000)

Figure 2.6 Sarah's hallucination, reminiscent of Fellini's scene (*Requiem for a Dream*, 2000)

she has the interior strength to pursue it. She seems to be the least driven character of the four of them. The last scene when she lovingly takes and caresses the fix she earned after the orgy scene, cuddled in a fetal position, indicates a peculiar "enjoyment" and possible continuity in the future.

Selby's book presents a tragic narrative intertwining of the four main characters and is important in its own literary merit. The dialogue in the screenplay of

Requiem works well, but the visual and musical effects carry the narrative almost exclusively. Even not hearing what the characters say, and just watching the film and hearing the music, would be enough to tell the story. The music is the fifth main character in the movie: listening to the Kronos Quartet, even without the film, produces a sense of impending doom. Maybe it is a coincidence, but Kronos in Greek mythology is a Titan usually presented with his symbol, a scythe. A scythe is also a symbol of the personification of death, the Grim Reaper, and of the Fourth Horseman of the Apocalypse, Death on the Pale Horse. When the four musicians from the Kronos Quartet perform Mansell's *Lux Aeterna*, it is tempting to envision deathblows with a horrible scythe: merciless, progressive, entering our system, and at the same time fearsome and awesome, eliciting lamentation, leading to the imminent tragedy. That is why the music acts as the fifth addict in the film—it is an audio illustration of the addiction.

The dialogues in *Requiem* are, to some extent, banal: after all, the characters start as clichés, and we get to know more about them in visual terms. Although unrelated in subject and style, the visual strength of *Requiem* to present addiction reminds us of the visual strength of *2001: A Space Odyssey* (Stanley Kubrick, 1968) in its presentation of the mystery of human evolution. In Kubrick's film, dialogue is very sparse, with no speech in the first or in the last twenty minutes. The existing dialogue is quite banal, and the movie becomes a visual poem, helped by the fitting soundtrack. Likewise, *Requiem for a Dream* is a visual poem about addiction, helped by the fitting soundtrack. In fact, we could watch *Requiem* as a silent movie, with only the three inter-titles denoting both seasons and the phases in the process of addiction.[17] The characters are defined by their actions and hallucinations, and the story is told with the vocabulary specific to film (camera moves, focus, cuts, tracking shots, close-ups, editing, lighting and color tonality, etc.). To a certain extent, this reliance on cinematic elements accords with the filmic credo of Dziga Vertov, as stated in his essay "The Man with a Movie Camera" (1928), justifying his film. He writes about the need "for a decisive cleaning of film-language, for its complete separation from the language of theater and literature."[18] Vertov was strongly opposed to narrative cinema,

---

[17] André Bazin analyzed the development of cinema language and style in the essay "The Evolution of the Language of Cinema," stating that the introduction of sound initially created only an aesthetic revolution based on technical achievement, and that the real change came in the beginning of the 1940s. Andre Bazin, *What Is Cinema?, Vol. 1* (Berkeley, CA: University of California Press, 2004), 23.

[18] Dziga Vertov, Kevin O'Brien, and Annette Michelson, *Kino-Eye: The Writings of Dziga Vertov* (Berkley, CA: University of California Press, 1984), 83.

calling it the "opiate of the masses."[19] However, he argued that we do not need to follow visual elements literally in order to present the reality of life, and that the proper montage creates a work of art without distorting information or the factuality of the filmed scene.

Abstracting the issue of narrative versus documentary film, or fiction versus "life caught unawares," *Requiem for a Dream* narrates the story of addiction, and the correspondences among different types of addiction in visual terms. In addition to providing the narration, the cinematic language, supported by the musical score, creates the mood that at the same time pulls spectators close to the characters and pushes them away. The close-ups lead to uncomfortable closeness, but then scenes filmed from above indicate the characters' vulnerability and insignificance, prompting spectators to distance themselves from the unfortunate characters. The objective reality of the progress of addiction is seen through changed social interactions, repetition, different camera moves, close-ups, and split screens. Split screens either divide characters unable to communicate or connect different yet corresponding scenes. The correspondences between different aspects of addiction and different situations are presented through editing and cutting, with increased speed as the ending climax approaches, for example, when we see Marion at the orgy surrounded by men or Sara in the hospital surrounded by doctors. Long corridors (as when Marion leaves the shrink's apartment or when Harry, Tyrone, and other junkies rush down a supermarket aisle) emphasize the framing of the characters, their inability to move freely and their being caught in the objectively narrow space, and the subjective imprisonment of addiction. The subjective reality of characters and the changes they undergo due to addiction are visualized in daydreaming and hallucination scenes. Distorted lenses present hallucinatory states and distorted reality. The use of handheld cameras project unsettled feelings and personal disintegration. Changing colors, from warm summer to colder fall and winter, reinforce seasonal climatic changes, but also visualize the characters' degradation and the chilling reality of their addictions. The only color that stands out is Sara's red dress and Marion's red dress in Harry's dream. In both cases, the color projects desire: Sara's desire to look perfect and Harry's desire for Marion. Because of the richly used cinematic language, a spectator would understand Sara's obsession and her story, Harry and Marion's love and desperation story, and Tyrone's emotional story in purely visual terms.

---

[19] Following the publication of the *Manifesto* in 1922, Vertov started the *Kino-Pravda* (Film-Truth) series to capture realities of everyday life, sometimes with a hidden camera, convinced that the camera eye (*kino-oko*) can probe into deeper reality than what can be observed with the naked eye.

Figure 2.7 Sara in a mental institution (*Requiem for a Dream*, 2000)

At the end, Sara is gone, lost to madness, so she is in a "happy place," and can continue dreaming all the time. The two old ladies, Sara's friends, sitting on a bench and hugging each other after a shocking visit to Sara, project the need to hold together, to support each other. We need social support, hopefully given voluntarily out of love, by family or friends, or involuntarily by an institution. Tyrone, in a fetal position in a prison bed projects a sense of inability to ever recuperate and satisfy his dream, but he can still have it as a daydream to improve his suffocating reality. Maybe he has a chance after getting out of the prison. Harry's last dream of falling into an abyss, and subsequent wakeup to an amputated arm, and his understanding that Marion will not and cannot come to see him, leaves a trace of hope that he can start thinking more realistically, and maybe, bring some order to his life. Marion in all likelihood will continue along the same path.

Reality and fiction in stories about addiction

While there are countless stories about drug victims, there are also examples of writers and artists producing creative works in periods of drug use. Some overstepped the limit (e.g., Joplin, Hendrix, and Fassbinder), some continued fulfilling careers (e.g., Bowie who, at the age of 67, was recipient of the *Best*

Male Solo Artist BRIT Award in 2014, and Scorsese who, at the age of 71, was a nominee for the *Best Director* Academy Award in 2014). Transgressing a limit and being able to come back is a heroic undertaking, and it is certainly easier for a strong and creative character to replace the high from a fix with the high from a creative work. Films dealing with addiction are often based on literary sources written as autobiographical or semi-autobiographical stories by former addicts or protagonists, projecting sincerity: some end happily, while some don't.

In *Leaving Las Vegas* (Mike Figgis, 1995), an alcoholic screenwriter and a prostitute experience a hopeless love story in Las Vegas, contrasting the reality of their need for each other, with both the artificiality of the environment and his inability to deal with alcoholism. The screenplay is based on the autobiographical novel *Leaving Las Vegas* (1990) by John O'Brien, who committed suicide in 1994 a few weeks after learning that the novel was to be adapted for film.

In 1971, Larry Clark published *Tulsa*, a photography book depicting young people shooting drugs, having sex, and playing with guns. It was mostly autobiographical, depicting the circle to which Clark belonged. In 1995, he directed a feature movie *Kids*, adding into the equation the HIV epidemic from the 1990s.

Drugstore Cowboy (Gus Van Sant, 1989) is based on an (at that time) unpublished autobiographical novel by James Fogle, who spent thirty-five years in prison. The film is narrated by a main protagonist Bob, who proclaims, "I'm a junkie. I like drugs. I like the whole lifestyle. Just didn't pay off.... Nobody, I mean nobody can talk a junkie out of use. You can talk to them for years but sooner or later they'll get hold of something."[20] Bob seems to be a nice guy, but he is a junkie, which erodes his positive side, and he is addicted to the adrenaline rush when stealing drugs. With a touch of humor coming out of cluelessness and warmth of the characters, but without moralizing or glamourizing drug culture, the film shows the arbitrariness of actions when under the influence. The look of the character from the early 1970s was inspired by Clark's photography collection *Tulsa*, and the further intrusion of reality into fiction is achieved with the appearance of William S. Burroughs as Tom the Priest, an old junky priest. In the novel, the main protagonist Bob dies; while in the movie, he gets redemption at the end, unlike his wife who continues with the drug-related lifestyle. Yet, we are not sure about Bob's future, seeing him in an ambulance car. He can die soon, or

[20]   Gus Van Sant, *Drugstore Cowboy* (1989).

he can get better and either can stay clean or get back to the old lifestyle. The ambiguity of the ending leaves space for the spectator's individually created ending.

Another film based on a literary work is *Jesus's Son* (Alison Maclean, 1999), based on a collection of short stories by Denis Johnson, himself a former addict. Johnson appears in a small role, adding a layer of reality to the story. In addition, the appearance of the legendary easy rider Dennis Hooper, talking about a dream he has over and over, provides reality to the drug culture.[21] The film employs a voice-over, narrated by the main protagonist, FH, recollecting his drug-ridden past, travels, and love. Again, he seems to be a nice person, except he is an addict and disoriented, with no specific plans for the future. Eventually, he settles with a job as an orderly in a hospital, and finally, finds redemption, getting his life in order. The last scene shows him on an open country road, walking toward an open future, reminiscent of western movies with a lone cowboy leaving a town and finding his peace. The unequivocal happy ending and redemption is uplifting (following the redemption of the author Johnson), making the audience feel good, but does not have the ambiguity that would provoke a spectator to make his or her own ending. However, the movie's cinematic style—with repetitive scenes, scenes of hallucinations evocative of a drugged mind mixing humor and tragedy, and a split screen to highlight the correspondence among the fates of the related protagonists—works well in giving an objective and a subjective view of addiction.

Trainspotting (Danny Boyle, 1996) takes an ironic stance toward heroin use, following Kubrick's steps in depicting the violence of *A Clockwork Orange* (Stanley Kubrick, 1971). The movie is based on the novel by Irwin Welsh, who appears in a small role. The style and sound of Renton's voice-over in *Trainspotting* is reminiscent of Alex's voice-over in *A Clockwork Orange*, and the themes of group dynamics in both movies are comparable. Renton's heroin usage and his attempts to deal with it, as well as the ending and some scene references and similarities, point to the influence of Kubrick's film in *Trainspotting*. The ending in *Trainspotting* approaches the stereotypical view of someone accepting everyday, normal life with repulsion, sounding disingenuous. In the end, Renton laments about why he did it, concluding that he is a bad person, but that he is going to change, addressing the spectator:

---

[21] A book by Tom Folsom, *Hopper: A Journey into the American Dream* (2013), provides a biography of Dennis Hooper.

I'm going to be just like you: the job, the family, the fucking big television, the washing machine, the car, the compact disc and electrical tin opener, good health, low cholesterol, dental insurance, mortgage, starter home, leisurewear, luggage, three-piece suite, D.I.Y, game shows, junk food, children, walks in the park, nine to five, good at golf, washing the car, choice of sweaters, family Christmas, indexed pension, tax exemption, clearing the gutters, getting by, looking ahead, to the day you die.[22]

The enumeration of various elements of our life, from family, good health, and children to a number of useful tools and entertainment, begs the question: So what's bad about that? Renton's statement, directly addressed to the spectator, "I'm going to be just like you," followed by an enumeration of issues and things in the spectator's life sounds pessimistic and accusatory, but lacks intuitive credibility. It presents a dubious understanding of what is and is not important in our life. Even the fact that Renton left some money for one of his friends does not redeem him. And he does not need to be redeemed; that is the point of his character and its role in the theater of humanity. In *A Clockwork Orange*, Alex ends with, "I was cured, all right," and it leaves the spectator to make a judgment. In *Trainspotting*, Renton's direct monologue addressed to the spectator sounds overly didactic. In contrast, the characters in *Requiem* do not state their views *ad litteram*, as Bob does in *Drugstore Cowboy* when defining a junkie or Renton does in *Trainspotting* in his ending monologue. A viewer gets to know them from inside, through the visualization of their hallucinations.

Christiane F. (Ulrich Edel, 1981), a movie based on the autobiographical novel by Christiane F., *We Children of Bahnhof Zoo* (1979), presents a drug culture of West Berlin in the mid-1970s. The downfall of a thirteen-year-old girl into addiction, and subsequently prostitution to get money for drugs is presented with brutal sincerity in a documentary style. The group of young drug addicts and their behavior can be compared to some extent to the protagonists of *Requiem for a Dream*. The main difference is their initial motivations. The heroin addicts in *Requiem* are older and have business inclinations; they want to use drugs as a vehicle to a better life, even though they are unable to deal with their drug habits. Christiane F. is too young to have already developed dreams of her future life. She is from a not-so-dysfunctional family and starts using drugs out of curiosity, following others in her environment. Christiane goes to a David Bowie concert, and fascinated by the atmosphere, tries heroin for the first time. Identifying with

[22] Danny Boyle, *Trainspotting* (1996).

a rock star who, at the time of his Berlin years, was a heavy cocaine addict, and listening to his *Station to Station* in a crowd of many drug users, Christiane F. comes to find drug addiction irresistible. Bowie's perfection and allure, his undisputed talent and sincerity are contagious and the crowd goes wild, ready to follow. The lyrics are contagious.[23] The scene of a concert, with David Bowie in his red jacket dominating the spectacle, the idol for his spectators infatuated by desire to identify with him, has some correspondences with the Tappy Tibbons JUICE show in *Requiem*. However, the Tappy Tibbons show is fake, a lure for insecure and lonely spectators looking for a way to improve their lives. Sara's hallucination of being in the show in her beautiful red dress, the star of the show, presents an element of the American Dream: to be somebody important. When in *Cristiane F.* the protagonists talk about possibly quitting heroin, they do not see a reason for doing it; the future does not show any promise. When they do business with drugs, it is prostitution for getting money for their own drug use and not for making a profit with a drug-dealing business. In this respect, *Christiane F.* is a completely different story than *Requiem for a Dream*; it is a "Requiem for No Dream," a consequence of delusion, loneliness, and a need to be accepted, unfortunately based on a true story. The film depicts young protagonists with no dreams, with the initially innocent wish to "be like everybody else" and experience something new, followed by a full addiction when the body needs a fix, regardless of the price. In *Christiane F.*, drugs are a vehicle to *get in* the group, to belong to the group, and to be as the rest of them; while in *Requiem,* drugs are a vehicle to *get out* of anonymity, to individualize ourselves, to become "somebody." Eventually, both films depict the same, unfortunate end. Edel's film, with its dark scenes of countless city lights projecting outside indifference, the scenes at the Zoo station with empty faces and zombie-like protagonists desperate to get money for a fix, puts a spectator in a position to experience the *objectivity* of the protagonist's fall into addiction. In both films, *Christiane F.* and *Requiem*, close-ups of faces show progressive disintegration of their owners' humanity, creating a strong emotional context and inviting viewers to experience the downfall of the characters on a preconscious level, in embodied simulation.

---

[23] Some lyrics from *Station to Station*, "It's not the side-effects of the cocaine / I'm thinking that it must be love. . . ."

The Fountain: Death and the Authenticity
of Existence

Death is a disease. It's like any other. And there is a cure. A cure. And I will find it.

Tommy Creo from *The Fountain*

The Fountain (2006) was Aronofsky's third feature film, and while it differs in visual effects from his previous films, the underlying search for unity continues. In *π*, Max Cohen searches for a unifying pattern behind all visible phenomena (both natural patterns and man-made patterns such as financial data), and *Requiem for a Dream* presents a unifying pattern of the process of addiction connecting the four main characters. *The Fountain* presents a search for a personal unity, a unifying pattern supporting our inner world, that is, for achieving wholeness of existence by coming to grips with mortality and realizing that the continuity of life is preserved when death is viewed as a rebirth. Viewing birth and death as two sides of the same coin amounts to understanding life as the unity of all dualities facing humanity, for example good versus evil, rational versus irrational or emotional, sorrow versus joy, victory versus defeat, and so on.

In *The Fountain*, Tommy Creo's search for the cure for death viewed as a disease follows the pattern of *π*'s Max Cohen searching for the numerical sequence that would dispense the mystery of the visible world. Max finally realizes that the problem he is pursuing so passionately and obsessively is the wrong problem, and that its "solution" is a deathblow to humanity. (What will be left of a life in which all is known with certainty?) Tommy Creo finally realizes that the cure for death he is searching for is the wrong search direction, and that the only immortality we humans can comprehend is by understanding immortality as the continuity of life when death is understood as a rebirth. Accepting death as a natural part of life brings the solace needed to endure the pain and sadness of witnessing the death of a loved one, and brings a comforting thought when thinking about our own death.

The story in *The Fountain* introduced the collaboration with Ari Handel, a neuroscientist turned filmmaker, and subsequent Aronofsky's collaborator as a writer and producer. The problems with initial production, cost overruns, and a change in lead actors in 2002, necessitated the rewriting of the story and the film was finally released in 2006. The graphic novel preceding the film was released in 2005, written by Aronofsky and illustrated by Kent Williams. According to Aronofsky, the graphic novel is based on the original script of the initially envisioned film, that is, it can serve as a director's cut.[1] There are some differences between the novel and the film, but the main plot remains. The narrative of the film contains a number of facts, historical and scientific, combined with fictional characters, and the plot develops in nonlinear style, combining the three related stories. The past story spans the years 1532–35, following a Spanish conquistador Tomas who, on behalf of Queen Isabella of Spain, searches for the Tree of Life in the jungle of New Spain, in the midst of the Mayan civilization. The present story spans 1997–2005, following the couple Izzi (Isabel) and Tommy Creo; she is dying from an incurable brain tumor, and he is a scientist trying to find a cure for cancer. The future story in year 2463 shows the last man, Tom, traveling through space in a biosphere bubble together with a dying Tree of Life, set to reach the nebula of a dying star as the place of rebirth. The plot seems very complex, questioning how the three stories are interrelated with various possibilities in doing so: Is it a story told by Tom, the last man from the future, or Tommy, the current-day scientist? How do these two stories relate to the past story coming out of Izzi's unfinished manuscript? Let me offer an interpretation that actually is quite simple as a story of coping with grief and fear in the face of death.

Izzi and Tommy met and fell in love in 1997 and happily married, but she is diagnosed with a brain tumor, which in 2005, progresses and now she is dying. Tommy, a scientist working in a medical lab, is part of a team of doctors experimenting with live monkeys and trying to find a cure for cancer. Both Izzi and Tommy have to deal with the issue of dying: for Izzi, her own dying, and for Tommy, his beloved dying.

Izzi finds a way to cope by writing a book entitled *The Fountain*, based on Mayan mythology of death and rebirth, viewing "death as an act of creation," or "death as a road to awe." The Mayan myth of creation describes the First Father

---

[1] Aronofsky used the same tactic with *Noah* (2014), where the graphic novel illustrated by Nico Henrichon preceded the film.

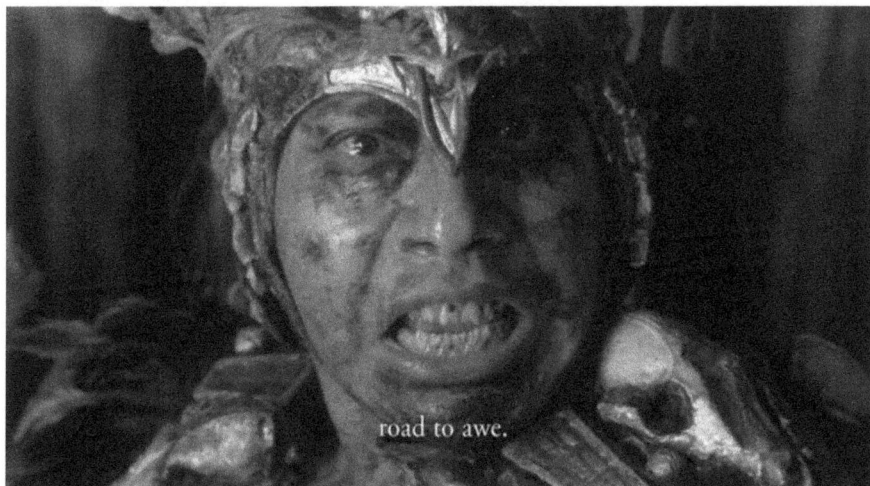

Figure 3.1 Mayan priest welcoming death (*The Fountain*, 2006)

who sacrificed himself, and from his sacrifice grew a Tree of Life; his soul evolved into the skies with its upward branches, and his body into Earth with its roots, while his head became Xibalba. Xibalba is the Mayan underworld where souls go to be reborn, and which is visible in the sky as a nebula around a dying star, as the birthplace of new stars. Izzi's book connects the Mayan myth with the story from Genesis: Adam and Eve took from the Tree of Knowledge of Good and Evil, entering into the world of opposites and duality, and did not have a chance to try the Tree of Life before being expelled from the Garden of Eden. Hence, immortality is left outside of reach for humanity, leaving only a desire for it. Izzi's book starts in sixteenth-century Spain and Central America during the time of Mayan civilization and Spanish conquistadors. Tomas, a conquistador for Queen Isabella, is sent to Central America in search of the Tree of Life, fighting against the politics of the Grand Inquisitor back home in Spain, and against Mayan warriors protecting their temple and the Tree of Life. If he finds it, he and Queen Isabella will be reunited and will live forever. Izzi, realizing that she does not have the time to finish the book, stops at the last chapter. The last sentences in her manuscript describe the relation between the Mayan priest about to sacrifice Tomas and Tomas's fear: "The Mayan stares serenely. Tomas' fear paralyzed him. All he could see was the deathblow."[2] She gives the unfinished

---

[2]   Darren Aronofsky and Kent Williams, *The Fountain* (New York: Vertigo, 2005), 135.

book to Tommy, asking him to finish it and to continue writing it with a dip pen and ink, which she gives him as a gift at her deathbed.

Tommy's way of coping with Izzi's dying is to immerse himself frantically in his laboratory work to find the cure for cancer. In the process, he is unable to understand Izzi's need to spend time with him, convinced that he has a chance

Figure 3.2 Symmetry in the scene with Tomas and Queen Isabella (*The Fountain*, 2006)

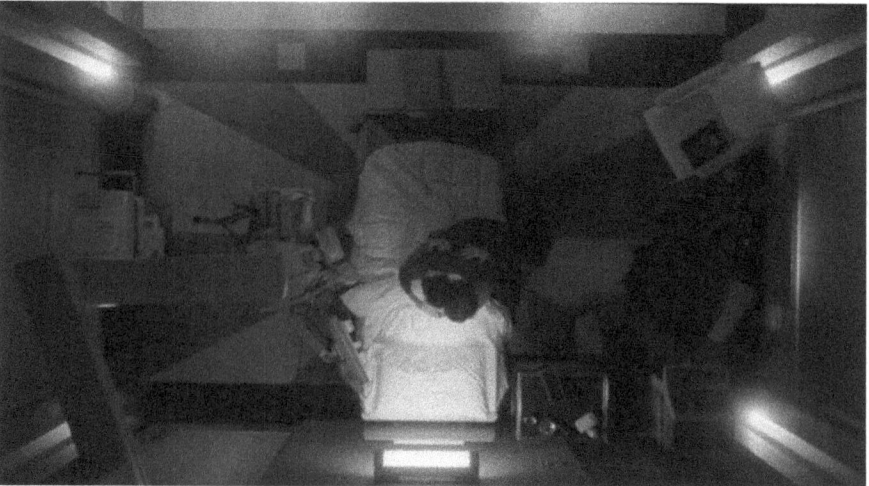

Figure 3.3 Tom and Izzy faced with death. The floor tile is similar as in the past story (*The Fountain*, 2006)

to fight the disease and cure Izzi. His reasoning and behavior is believable for a scientist entrenched in the conviction of scientific omnipotence and who sees no other way out. There is progress at the lab, and Donovan, the monkey in the laboratory, shows signs of rejuvenation of cells, due to an ethno-botanical compound from Guatemala used as medicine by indigenous people. The medicine subsequently leads to the shrinking of the tumor, indicating that cancer can be cured. Tommy runs to the hospital, but Izzi is dead. Grief-stricken Tommy reads her unfinished book, unable to do anything else. He takes Izzi's pen and ink and makes a tattoo wedding ring in place of a missing one, possibly feeling remorse for having lost it. His lost wedding ring suggests distance from Izzi, when he could not feel that all she needed from him was his presence, to be close to her. He was convinced that there was enough time and that he needed to work on finding the cure. Now, after her death, he resorts to the tattoo ring as a symbol of everlasting love. At Izzi's funeral, Tommy still cannot accept death and is convinced that "Death is a disease. It's like any other. And there is a cure. A cure. And I will find it."

The stress of a dying Izzi, the discovery and reading of her book, the progress in the lab with its "promise" to cure incurable diseases—all this justifies Tommy's inner turbulence and hallucinatory dreams. The historic fictional story from Izzi's book that he reads, and the tragic present and Izzi's wish for him to finish the book, create a dream of a future in which he travels centuries, prolonging his life by the sap of the Tree of Life. He is in the twenty-fifth century in the future, as Tom, the last man, traveling in space in a bubble with a dying Tree of Life, set to enter the nebula of a dying star in order to revitalize the tree, and his own life.[3] He is accompanied by apparitions of Izzi asking him to finish the book, and sometimes with apparitions of Queen Isabella. Tommy's hallucinatory dream mixes the past and the present in his future. The past protrudes from Izzi's book combining Mayan myth and the biblical Tree of Life, the love story between Tomas the conquistador and his Queen Isabella. In the future, Tom's past is Tomas, and Tom feels the wound of Tomas the conquistador. Tommy's present enters through apparitions of Izzi, and the first tattoo ring on his finger. Subsequently, tattooing circles around his arms, Tom measures the passage of time. Tommy's dream (or his inner space travel) narrated throughout Tom's space travel, reaches the end when the Tree of Life dies, but with the exploding

[3]   In Aronofsky's words, Tom, the last man, is an homage to David Bowie's Major Tom from "Space Oddity" of the album (1969) of the same name; here are some of the lyrics: "...Am I sitting in a tin can/ Far above the world..../ Tell my wife I love her very much...."

star new life is about to begin. Finally, Tommy the scientist, is able to understand Izzi's book, and he knows how to finish it. In the end, the Mayan priest sacrifices himself. Tomas is allowed to drink from the Tree of Life, and he transforms into organic life; eternal life equals eternal death. Tom transforms into a part of cosmic eternity, finally allowing Tommy to understand what the meaning of immortality is. Eternity is not a linear sequence of clock time units; it is beyond time, unlike the time "everlasting" that is a very, very long time. Immortality as related to eternity is out of time, unlike everlasting life. Hence, immortality is *not* everlasting life; it is a transcendental concept pointing beyond objectivity of presence. A glimpse of immortality can be sensed in a moment that lasts as long as we live. Such a moment might be short when measured in clock time, but persistent in memory as long as we can remember.

At the end, Tommy is finally at peace with the physical consequence of Izzi's death; he understands that the real "cure" for Izzi's incurable situation is simply to be there for her when she needs him. He also comes to terms with the inevitability of his own death. In the last scene, Tommy plants a seed on Izzi's graveyard, acknowledging the cycle of life (or the ring of eternity) in which death leads to a rebirth.

There are various films dealing with the issue of death and the nature of reality. For example, *Big Fish* (Tim Burton, 2003) explores changing personal relations (father and son) in the face of death, testifying to the need for achieving

Figure 3.4 The future with Tom and the dying Tree of Life (*The Fountain*, 2006)

some kind of closure before the final hour. *Big Fish* presents a mix of realism and fantasy, challenging the view that reality is restricted to objective representations; feelings are also very real, and yet, we do not see them. Burton's rich visual style, approaching Fellini's surrealist images, presents a poetic stance toward the nature of truth and our approach to life. The love story between Ed Bloom and Sandra, his wife, narrated through his life adventures, when seen in the present time is given in visual terms, through looks. Their closeness is sensed when Ed is dying of cancer, and she joins him in a bathtub for a moment of intimacy. The scene has similarities to the bathtub scene between Izzi and Tommy in *The Fountain*. In both cases, the immersion in the bathtub water of the one dying from cancer alludes to the unconscious reconciliation with death, the acceptance of the continuity of the birth-death-birth cycle. Water often contains a symbolic meaning as the origin of life, a rebirth. In Jungian psychoanalysis, water "is the commonest symbol of the unconscious," with oceans symbolizing the collective unconscious, while smaller amounts (e.g., in a bathtub) might represent a personal unconscious. The spouse joining in the bathtub represents the desire between them. In *Big Fish*, Sandra takes the initiative and joins Ed in the bathtub, demonstrating their closeness and her understanding and acceptance of his condition, regardless of how painful it is. However, in *The Fountain*, Izzi pulls Tommy to her, and he is at first reluctant, saying, "I don't think this is ...," but finally gives up, and the scene ends in a depiction of transcendence, with the white screen.

The suggested interpretation of *The Fountain* is simple: the intimate journey of initial denial and final acceptance of loss due to the death of a loved one, and the acceptance of the inevitability of our own death. But, the issues of love and death are the most complex issues for humanity. The thought of our death contributing to some future life by fertilizing the soil with decomposing organic remains seems optimistic as the last resource to deal with the annihilation of existence.

Myths and symbolism in *The Fountain*

The (proposed) simplicity of the underlying theme, coupled with the complexity of the underlying concepts, allows Aronofsky and Handel to create an intricate story with various symbols, challenging the concepts of time, causality, and connectivity. The film allows many avenues of analysis, from mythology presented in sixteenth-century Mayan civilization and related to the story in Genesis to obsession with scientific discoveries in the present time to speculation about future life and life on Earth as related to life in cosmic terms. All three stories are united with the same desire: to achieve victory over death and to achieve immortality, until the realization of impossibility to defeat death, finally leading to the acceptance of death, but with hope: death as rebirth.

In *The Power of Myth*, Joseph Campbell states, "The secret cause of all suffering is mortality itself, which is the prime condition of life. It cannot be denied if life is to be affirmed."[4] Campbell's interview with Bill Moyers for the PBS series in 1988, titled *The Power of Myth*, presents his ideas connecting myths, consciousness, dreams, and bodies. There is a common ground to all myths— the archetypal collective unconsciousness as proposed by Jung. Archetypes provide common forms to images and themes occurring in different cultures and their myths. Against the Cartesian view that consciousness resides in our brain, Campbell argues that consciousness as energy belongs to the body as well, and it is not restricted to humanity: a plant exhibits consciousness when it turns toward sun. Myths provoke our *spiritual* consciousness, awaking strong emotions and pointing to the spiritual potentiality of humanity, to the experience of being alive. How did mythology start? Campbell relates the birth of mythology with the image of death: the first burial sites distinguished humanity from the animal kingdom. In different myths, death is viewed as necessary for rebirth. This follows from observing the botanical world: a plant dies and new sprouts start. The moment of becoming, connecting death and rebirth at the same time, is presented in Indian religion in the deity Shiva, the creator and destroyer, surrounded by a ring of fire—a dance of the world symbolizing the eternal cycle of death and rebirth, or of destruction and creation. Campbell recalls a myth of an Algonquin boy who needs a plant to find a food source other than hunting to save his old father. The boy kills the man and buries him so that the corn can grow on top of the mound or so that the plant grows from his body. This myth has similarities to the Mayan myth of creation presented in *The Fountain*.

The sixteenth-century story in *The Fountain* relates the Mayan ancient myth of creation and the Biblical story of the Tree of Life. The future story, from the twenty-fifth century, with Tom in a bubble traveling through space, contains additional symbols supporting the main themes of death and rebirth. Tom picks up the ring left after Tomas the conquistador is transformed into the world of

---

[4] Joseph Campbell and Bill Moyers, *The Power of Myth* (New York: Anchor Books, Doubleday, 1988), xi.

Figure 3.5 Tom in a cosmic circle, in a lotus position (*The Fountain*, 2006)

plants, symbolizing the circularity of ending and beginning, death and rebirth. The ring or the circle is one of the most important mythical and religious symbols. Campbell references Jung's statement that with the symbol of the circle we are analyzing the self. For Campbell, "Everything within the circle is one thing, which is encircled, enframed. That would be the spatial aspect. But the temporal aspect of the circle is that you leave, go somewhere, and always come back. . . . The circle suggests immediately a completed totality, whether in time or in space."[5]

The title of the film supports the symbolism and the main theme of death and rebirth. The fountain is often used as the symbol of regeneration, indicated by the clichéd expression "the fountain of youth." A fountain works by using a pump that recycles water, in a constant movement of new water spouting from water accumulated by past spouts; hence, a spout of water has to "die" to allow a new spout, in a constant cycle.

Philosophical views of existence, temporality, and death

As the three related stories from *The Fountain* are presented in nonlinear narrative, Aronofsky provokes a spectator to search for the connecting pattern, to try to piece the stories together, and to construct a meaning in it. It is definitely

[5] Ibid., 269.

not a film served on a platter, ready to be consumed without questions. In addition to the two prevalent drives for humanity stated in clichéd expressions such as "the power of love" and "the fear of death," we can ask: Why desire immortality? Immortality makes the concept of death irrelevant—but that is outside of human reach because we are characterized by mortality. Futurists propagating the so-called h+ (transhumanism and posthumanism), achieving immortality due to technological advances and separation from biology, envision a different entity. We humans with biological bodies prone to aging, decay, and death have to come to grips with mortality. Accepting death as a part of life, that is, acknowledging death, not as a disease, but as an integral part of our life, makes it easier to endure loss and leads toward unity of various concepts that disorient our life (good and bad, positive and negative, courage and fear, etc.).

The issues of temporality and death are important philosophical issues. Let me give description of positions by Kant, Husserl, Heidegger, and Arendt as relevant for the thematic in *The Fountain*, in the process risking misrepresentation of these complex philosophical positions due to the terseness of my descriptions; however, engagement with a more detailed analysis is outside the scope of this book.

The consideration of nonlinear time in *The Fountain* relates to philosophical writings on the concept of experience and its relation to consciousness and temporality. In *Critique of Pure Reason*, Kant's temporality presented via the schema of "*transcendental time determinations*" is central to the unity of experience.[6] The consideration of time is also addressed by Husserl, who distinguishes among three levels of temporality: the level of *objective or clock time*, the level of *internal or experienced time*, and the underlying level of *the consciousness of internal time*.[7] Husserl defines *experience* as a flow, a stream in internal time-consciousness, terming it "concatenations of experience." In order to be meaningful, the stream of experience has to be synthesized, and this synthesis is evoked by an "intentional

---

[6]   For Kant, experience starts with intuition induced by sensibility. Intuition is characterized by both its outer sense (space) and its inner sense (time). Sensibility allows the receipt of outside stimuli, but these stimuli have to be combined into a unity to qualify as experience. The unity can be achieved only under the subject's self-activity (*I think*). This starts understanding that produces thoughts employing concepts. Kant defines *categories* as pure concepts of understanding that, through respective schemata, reach down to sensibility (albeit sensibility as exhibited by imagination). *Transcendental determinations of time* (as affects of inner sense) connect our subjective conditions of thought and their objective validity. Immanuel Kant, *Critique of Pure Reason*, trans. Werner S. Pluhar (Indianapolis, IN: Hackett Publishing Company, Inc., 1996).

[7]   Edmund Husserl, *On the Phenomenology of the Consciousness of Internal Time (1893–1917)*, ed. John Barnett Brough, trans. John Barnett Brough (Dordrecht, The Netherlands: Kluwer Academic Publishers, 1991).

subjective process" as *consciousness-of*, according to Husserl, our consciousness is intentional.[8] The fundamental form of synthesis includes temporality on the level of the *consciousness of internal time*.[9] While internal time gives a sense of endurance, the *consciousness* of internal time provides the sensation of *duration as such*; hence, it provides the grounding of any specific endurance. [10]

In *Being and Time*, Heidegger describes the being of a human being, *Da-sein*, and proclaims that its essence is existence.[11] Existence is characterized by existential determinations (*Attunement, Understanding, Discourse*, and *Falling*), and can be either authentic or inauthentic, depending on whether the determinations are primordial or derivative. Primordial attunement, understanding and discourse, take into account all potentialities of my being, while in their derivative state these potentialities are restricted by the commonalities of others. When I think for myself, or when I am open for various possibilities, I approach authenticity of existence. When my understanding is limited by what others tell me, I am in an inauthentic mode of existence. Heidegger states that *Da-sein* is "initially and for the most part" in the inauthentic mode of existence, which is everyday existence. Existential determinations of discourse, understanding, and attunement are combined in the unifying existential phenomenon of *care*.[12] *Care* should not be understood in its everyday meaning as "taking care of something," but as a way to achieve the structural wholeness of *Da-sein*.

Initially, we are "thrown" into the world, into everyday existence—this is how we start, as inauthentic beings. The challenge is to find a way for authenticity of existence, and Heidegger proposes the *mood of anxiety* [*angst*] as a type of attunement pointing away from the commonality of men. Unlike fear, which is related to a specific objectively present thing, anxiety is a feeling unrelated to something specific; it indicates that something is missing. The intuition that something is not there provokes a feeling that something should be there in the

8   Edmund Husserl, *Cartesian Meditations*, trans. Dorion Cairns (The Hague, The Netherlands: Martinus Nijhoff, 1977), section 17.
9   Ibid., section 18.
10   Husserl proposes the relation between the consciousness of internal time and intentionality via *retentions* (primary memory) and *protentions* (primary expectations). Due to continuity of experience, an impression just happening now has its impressions of "just-past," and "just-about-to-happen," and these are impressions of duration *as such*, unrelated to any specific matter of either memory or expectation. These impressions are followed by the *reproduction* or *secondary memory* containing the recollection of past events, and by *secondary expectations* containing the specific matter of expectations. Husserl, *Consciousness of Internal Time*.
11   Martin Heidegger, *Being and Time*, trans. Joan Stambaugh (Albany, NY: State University of New York Press, 1996).
12   Heidegger formally defines the phenomenon of *care* as "being-ahead-of-oneself-already-in (the world) as being-together-with (inner-worldly beings encountered)." Ibid., 180.

first place, something primordial. While the phenomenon of *care* allows unification of existential determinations of *Da-sein*, it is insufficient to unite the inauthentic and authentic modes of existence, prompting Heidegger to turn to temporality. Heidegger's model of *primordial temporality* employs a notion of time different from the everyday interpretation of time as the succession of the "now" without beginning or end. His "temporal ecstasies" of future, present, and having-been, are *equiprimordial* rather than successive. He defines the meaning of *temporality* as follows: "Temporalizing does not mean a 'succession' of the ecstasies. The future is *not later* than the having-been, and the having-been is *not earlier* than the present. Temporality temporalizes itself as a future that makes present, in the process of having-been."[13]

Heidegger's analysis of temporality considers death, conscience, and resoluteness; hence, we come to *the issue of death and its importance for achieving authenticity*. In existence, *Da-sein* has potentialities and as long as all potentialities are not exhausted, *Da-sein* exists as the being of human being; without any potentialities, its very existence would be annihilated. Death presents the ending of *Da-sein* and it has a special place in the set of *Da-sein's* possibilities. Heidegger defines *death* as *Da-sein's* own-most possibility, which is nonrelational and unavoidable, stating, "*No one can take the other's dying away from him.*"[14] The possibility of *my* death individualizes me, and serves as a testimony to my potentiality for achieving the *authentic mode of existence*. However, my death is my special possibility, the *possibility of my absolute impossibility*,[15] and I cannot experience it. I know it is unavoidable, and I see others dying, but I can only anticipate my death. My existence spans from being thrown into the world in an inauthentic mode to the ending with my authentic death.[16]

Heidegger associates death with authenticity of the human being, but does not consider the importance of birth as a new beginning. However, death and birth have something in common: if nobody can die for me, nobody can be born

---

[13] Ibid., 321.

[14] Ibid., 223.

[15] Heidegger writes, "Death is the possibility of the absolute impossibility of *Da-sein*." Ibid., 232.

[16] Heidegger's view of death as one's own-most possibility and the way to achieve authenticity is challenged by Blanchot, who defines *death* as the "impossibility of a possibility," referring to the possibility of the process of dying. Death stops the movement of the process of dying, implying that *I* cannot die: death is *not* my own; it is anonymous, belonging to impersonality and loss of subjectivity. Hence, I never achieve a closure. Blanchot relates this line of thought to a work of art that is never completed, and argues that writing is akin to the process of dying as the finished book implies the impossibility of further writing. He states: "The book is to writing what death would be to the movement of dying." (Maurice Blanchot, *The Step Not Beyond*, trans. Lycette Nelson (State University of New York Press, 1992), 104.)

for me as well, which indicates a potentiality of an authentic beginning. Our understanding has the capacity for augmentation, for acknowledging something new. Heidegger's *hermeneutic circle* as the structure of understanding provides a shape in which a movement forward is at the same time a movement backward, fit for understanding based on projecting forward, but taking into account what is already understood. He writes, "What is decisive is not to get out of the circle, but to get in it in the right way."[17] Getting into the hermeneutic circle in the right way implies that something new enters our understanding, not a derivative of something already encountered. Such a situation can be viewed as a "birth" and in order to traverse from an initially inauthentic existence toward authenticity, such experiences of newness or rebirth have to be encountered.

In an answer to Heidegger, Arendt argues for the importance of birth and "the human condition of natality."[18] Our factual birth signals a new beginning in the world. We are endowed with the capacity to act, which implies the *capacity for beginning*, and Arendt says, "It is in the nature of beginning that something new is started which cannot be expected from whatever may have happened before."[19] Each essentially new experience negates previous experience, since otherwise, it would not be new. A rebirth (a new beginning) is possible by surpassing (ending) the old experience. The old has to die to allow the new to occur, or to put it differently, this is the view of "death as an act of creation," which brings us back to *The Fountain*.

The consideration of philosophical writings of Heidegger and Arendt on the issue of death and rebirth puts *The Fountain* in a new light, as a truly philosophical film. We can look at it as a possible adaptation of Heidegger's *Being and Time*, one of the most important philosophical works of the twentieth century, and a notoriously difficult matter for interpretation. Of course, in such philosophical work there is no narrative to be adapted, but Heidegger's view of primordial temporality with simultaneous ecstasies of future, present, and having-been, and his view of anticipatory resoluteness toward death for an authentic mode of existence, are illustrated in *The Fountain*.

Take Heidegger's temporality as a "future that makes present, in the process of having-been." Tom, the space traveler from the future, with the body wound from the past, reappears in the past as the enlightened being, prompting the

---

[17] Heidegger, *Being and Time*, 143.
[18] Hannah Arendt, *The Human Condition* (Garden City, NY: Doubleday Anchor Books, 1959), 10.
[19] Ibid., 157.

Mayan priest to sacrifice himself. Hence, past and future do not happen sequentially, but simultaneously. Tom from the future and Tomas the conquistador (having-been from the past) "live" simultaneously in Tommy the scientist from the present: Tomas' love for Queen Isabella translates to Tommy's love for his wife Izzi, and Tom's determination to achieve victory over death translates to Tommy's determination to find a cure for cancer. Identifying the character of Tomas/Tommy/Tom with *Da-sein*, the being of human being whose essence is existence, the film visualizes his transformation from inauthentic toward authentic existence. The narrative provides visual equivalents to *Da-sein*'s existentialism (falling, discourse, understanding, and attunement). Tommy is a human character, hence thrown into existence by falling prey to the commonality of others. He engages in discourse with others and displays affects and moodiness. His understanding is initially, and for the most part, restricted by the scientific frame of mind based on factual evidence. Different aspects of his existence are united in the phenomenon of *care*, incorporating his emotional state and love for Izzi, his scientific efforts to find the cure for an incurable disease facing humanity, and the concern for his own being. The struggle to achieve authenticity (as Izzi achieved prior to her death) is visualized in nonlinear time, presenting the development of Tommy's anticipatory resoluteness toward death: at the end, he accepts death as a necessary part of life.[20]

It takes courage to create a film such as *The Fountain*, with so many possible interpretations and philosophical implications. On the micro level of searching for consistency and meaning of details, various elements disrupt the formal logical reasoning. Looking at the film narrative on a macro level, with regard to a general sense of meaning, we become aware that not everything can—or should—be explained.

Visual correspondences and symmetry versus asymmetry in *The Fountain*

The three stories apparently separated by centuries are connected visually, not only by the characters and by the nonlinear time that superimposes one story

---

[20] Heidegger writes, "Temporality is experienced as a primordial phenomenon in the authentic being-a-whole of *Da-sein*, in the phenomenon of anticipatory resoluteness." Heidegger, *Being and Time*, 281.

over another, but also by numerous visual correspondences. Superimposition of visual correspondences is an element of Aronofsky's tactic already present in both π and *Requiem for a Dream*.[21] For example, when Tommy ascends the staircase to the museum, it is an analogy of Tomas ascending the stairs on the Mayan pyramid. Or, the extreme close-up shot of Tommy caressing Izzi's skin repeats the shot of Tom caressing the tree's trunk. The night lights in sixteenth-century Spain resemble the stars in the future story. The cinematography of Libatique and the use of color contribute to the mood of each story: the past is darker, as the search is further removed from our individuality, becoming lighter in the present, and even lighter in the future. The task facing each character in the three stories is the same: the search for immortality. However, in the past, Tomas not only carries out the search for the Queen, but also for Spain in opposition to the Church, so that his search has a political connotation, and not just a personal one. In the present, Tommy searches for the cure for cancer for his wife Izzi, but also as a career scientist, for the benefit of humanity. In the future, Tom tries to revitalize the Tree of Life for his own life, but also to protect the Tree of Life, the continuity of life in general. The Queen in the past, then the wife in the present, and finally, the self only in the future indicate the *narrowing* of the subjective space, leading toward emotional "egoism," as eventually the main issue behind the fear of death is our *own* death (sounds like Heidegger). The country of Spain in the past, humanity in the present, and life in general in the future indicate *augmentation* of the objective space, of objective reasons for surpassing death. When the possibility of our own death approaches, it seems that this possibility overrides all other allegiances and is positioned in the widest possible terms, cosmic terms.

As previously in π, in *The Fountain*, Aronofsky stays clear of technological references, so that the film does not become outdated. This works well since specific technology does not contribute to the theme of the film. Looking through a microscope to augment human vision to see something very small is similar to looking through the telescope to see something very big. In each case, the desire is to go *beyond* naked-eye vision. The special effects were done without CGI, with star sequences generated organically with images created by the macro-photographer Peter Parks by using Petri dishes and a microscope. The

---

[21]   As already mentioned, early in the development of film, Dziga Vertov was a strong advocate for montage based on correspondences with consecutive unrelated images connected by visual similarity, or by conceptual similarity, or by some other association.

organic approach to special effects in a story about the human concern with
biological (or organic) death and its role in biological re-birth adds to the poetic
strength of the narrative.

A prominent visual element in the film is the use of geometry to distinguish
and to connect the stories at the same time. Aronofsky has said that he used
different geometric shapes in the film to indicate evolution over time: the past is
represented with triangles (e.g., pyramids); the present, with rectangles (TV sets,
buildings); and the future, with spheres (bubble, celestial bodies). However, it
seems that geometry is important in another aspect as it carries the impact of
symmetry versus asymmetry.

The interplay and the aesthetic import of symmetry versus asymmetry is
discussed in many writings, including those of philosophers like Kant and
Adorno. Symmetry exhibits the mathematical properties of proportion, balance,
and order, but its "rigidity" could have a counter-positive effect when judging
aesthetically. Indeed, regarding symmetry, Kant writes:

> Everything that shows stiff regularity (close to mathematical regularity) runs
> counter to taste because it does not allow us to be entertained for long by our
> contemplation of it; instead it bores us, unless it is expressly intended either for
> cognition or for a determinate practical purpose. On the other hand, whatever
> lends itself to unstudied and purposive play by the imagination is always new to
> us and we never tire of looking at it.[22]

Kant sees aesthetic value in freedom of imagination, unrestricted by rigid rules.
However, complete freedom or exaggeration in an artistic expression would
undermine its value. What is needed is a skillful combination of symmetry
and asymmetry, of freedom of expression, but subject to some underlying
rules. Adorno states that, "In terms of its artistic value, asymmetry is only to
be comprehended in its relation to symmetry."[23] This symmetry–asymmetry
interplay is evidenced when employed in musical and theatrical improvisations,
and it connects with Deleuze's philosophy of becoming.

Artistic expressions often use the tension between symmetry and asymmetry
to underline the difference between order and chaos.[24] The artistic use of

---

[22] Immanuel Kant, *Critique of Judgment*, trans. Werner S. Pluhar (Indianapolis, IN: Hackett Publishing
      Company, Inc., 1987), Ak. 242.
[23] Adorno, *Aesthetic Theory*, 158.
[24] Examples of symmetry–asymmetry relation important in paintings from the Italian Renaissance is
      presented in I.C. McManus, "Symmetry and Asymmetry in Aesthetics and the Arts," *European
      Review* 13, no. 2 (2005).

Figure 3.6 The contrast between external symmetry and internal turbulence: the Grand Inquisitor in his room, flagellating himself (*The Fountain*, 2006)

symmetry versus asymmetry is particularly interesting in film because visual depictions of contradictory order and chaos can describe characters and their positions vis-à-vis the environment. If there is imbalance and chaos (i.e., asymmetry) inside a character, it can be brought forward more forcefully when contrasted with the symmetry of the outside scene.[25] The duality of order and chaos asks for the duality of symmetry and asymmetry.

In *The Fountain*, the symmetry is strikingly present in the story from the past. The Mayan temple with its altar and lighting is symmetric, contradicting the chaos inside the jungle and the emotional unrest of the Mayans and especially of their priest. However, even more striking is the symmetry of scenes with the Moorish architecture in sixteenth-century Spain. The perfect symmetries of the court and the Church (the Grand Inquisitor's room) stand as symbols of their grandeur and power, based on order and rules. In contrast, we see the Grand Inquisitor flagellating himself, sensing his inner turbulence and religious fervor.

The scene with the court of inquisition and hanging bodies, projecting human tragedy and insignificance before the might of the Church, is intensified visually by the contrast between symmetry and asymmetry, that is, between the symmetry

25 The property of symmetry is also important in physics because it designates parts of systems that remain unchanged under some transformations, leading to the "conservation laws" characterizing such systems (e.g., the law of conservation of energy). Hence, the symmetry of outside environment might suggest indifference toward the inner turbulence of a character.

of environment (the Church institution) and the suffering of individuals, suggesting the imposition of outside order on the experience of individuals. The ornamental dress of Queen Isabella suggests the additional layer of order and restraint due to her role as Queen, constraining her womanhood. Queen Isabella is depicted in much lighter colors than the rest of her environment, adding a sense of transcendence to her, as if she is an apparition, related to the future. Looking in retrospect, we might ponder whether she has already lived her future as Izzi and as the integral part of the reborn Tree of Life, as a "future that makes present, in the process of having-been" (to quote Heidegger again).

The scenes from the Mayan jungle and Tomas's obsession with reaching the Mayan temple at all costs, lead to an association with another film dealing with Spanish conquistadors (albeit within the Inca territory), *Aguirre, the Wrath of God* (Werner Herzog, 1972), an early Herzog film about obsession in searching for something that is unreachable.[26] In Herzog's film, the tension between subjectivity and objectivity—between Aguirre's obsession and madness, and the indifference of the jungle—is presented mostly aurally: the men floating on a raft experience the silence of the jungle as a merciless threat, creating anxiety regarding the unknown. As already mentioned, unlike fear directed at something or someone objectively present, anxiety is not connected with an objective presence; it is a sense of a possible future doom. There is no place for symmetry since there is no visible order, neither man-made nor natural. The visual impression is of an immense chaos: on the one side there is humanity trapped in its obsession for gold (as a symbol for whatever happiness it might bring), moving along on the confined space of a raft; and on the other side, there is nature with silence and indifference, intruding only with poisonous arrows by invisible natives guarding their habitat. The men on the raft destroy the possibility of salvation offered by the two arriving natives after killing them for the silly reason of blasphemy.

In *Aguirre, the Wrath of God*, the jungle plays the role of a character as the mysterious, distanced, omnipotent entity beyond the comprehension of the men on the raft. In *The Fountain*, the equivalent character role is played by the Mayan

---

[26] The issue of death and how people cope with it is prominent in Werner Herzog's cinematography. He talked about death in an interview, and when asked about the possibility of death and how he would cope with it, Herzog replied, "Martin Luther was asked, what would you do if tomorrow the world would come to an end, and he said, 'I would plant an apple tree today.' This is a real good answer. I would start shooting a movie." Steve Rose, "Werner Herzog on Death, Danger and the End of the World," *The Guardian* (2012), http://www.theguardian.com/film/2012/apr/14/werner-herzog-into-the-abyss.

culture expressed through its myth of creation, and visualized by the pyramid as the place of worship and the ceremony of the sacrifice. However, the ritual of sacrifice is a social creation complying with rules, and the presence of symmetry in scenes of ritual sacrifice supports the underlying order of the ritual. In *Violence and the Sacred*, René Girard explores the nature of the sacrificial act in ritualistic practice and argues for a sacrifice as a form of violence.[27] Girard argues that sacrifice is based on *the principle of substitution*: in a cultural group that has tensions and impulses toward violence, but that cannot act as one against another, the ritualistic act of sacrifice provides a vent, or a way out, bringing a kind of closure. Hence, the presence of order in ritualistic violence serves to pacify the chaotic everyday violence. What is common to all sacrifices is that a victim bears some resemblance to the object for which it is substituted (e.g., animals with some human characteristics), otherwise the sacrifice would lose its power to pacify an underlying impulse for violence. In the Mayan myth of creation referenced in *The Fountain*, the First Father provides a semblance of a God. In general, the spectrum of sacrificed *human* victims is very wide: from prisoners of war to children to kings. These all share an uncommon position in society: either outcasts or marginalized subjects, or outsiders due to their specific position (a king). The subject of human sacrifice is never a common man, that is, somebody who represents an average member of society. Such a member is connected to society, while sacrificial subjects always are in tension with society and are missing a social link, so that when they die, there is no need for vengeance.

The Fountain's story from the present visualizes Tommy's and Izzi's private spaces in their apartment, some institutionalized spaces (lab, museum, hospital), and the outside place for Izzi's graveyard. The apartment captures contemporary reality, with cramped spaces and a possibility for stargazing from the balcony. The scene in which Tommy leaves the apartment to go to the lab, with the two sets of lights stretching along the street in the night, creates the feeling of a growing distance between Tommy and Izzi, and of the indifference of the outside environment. The camera angle from above when filming the scenes in the laboratory creates a sense of an omnipotent position, so that a spectator distances him- or herself from the main protagonists. The museum space is symmetric, projecting neutrality toward the wealth of historical artifacts housed there. Many scenes from the present include blinds, horizontal dividers suggesting capture,

[27] René Girard, *Violence and the Sacred* (London: Bloomsbury Academic, Series Continuum Impacts, 2005).

confinement, and the inability to experience freedom. The constraints are self-imposed; we could get rid of the blinds and get the natural light in, but that might interfere with the planned work. The long shots presenting Izzi's grave and the surrounding snow-covered field insinuate transcendence, and work well for the theme of death and rebirth.

In the future, the immensity and mystery of the cosmos is visualized by chaotic patterns in constant movement, suggesting the impossibility of any humanly imposed order, unlike in sixteenth-century Spain. The biosphere bubble, Tom's "personal" space, is represented only by the dying Tree and a few artifacts (an old knife for cutting pieces from the tree, the old pen for making a tattoo, and an old utensil for heating the pieces from the Tree). The continuation of life is restricted to a bare minimum, a hallucinatory hope for a solution to the insoluble problem of death viewed as a disease.

The music score by Mansell, its rhythm and tonality, connects the past and the future stories by provoking a feeling of moving forward and retreating at the same time, projecting again a convoluted sense of time. Mansell's music score works by creating a sound that suggests a future mystery enriched by past "heroism," and vice versa. The music accompanying the present story adds to the sense of urgency (e.g., with scenes in the lab). Tommy's moment of scientific inspiration is related to the future story in visual and aural terms, so we hear a theme from the future. The correspondences among the three intertwining stories are presented in aural as much as in visual terms, creating a stylistic unity despite a narrative gap of a thousand years.

It is suggested that *The Fountain* addresses tough philosophical questions and that it is a film with a lasting impact. I have proposed to view it as a possible adaptation of Heidegger's *Being and Time*. The question is how well the film works for a spectator unfamiliar with philosophical writings connecting the issue of death and temporality. We can get a feeling that the film tries to say more than it shows, and too much narrative detail could provide distraction from a meditative mood fit for contemplating the mystery of the life-death-life cycle. While *Requiem for a Dream* presents a *visual* poem about addiction, and works with little dialogue to provide explanation, *The Fountain* relies strongly on dialogues, on explanations (from Izzi, Tommy, the Franciscan priest, Queen Isabella, Tom). Thinking about an audio-visual poem about the mystery of human existence leads to Kubrick's *2001: A Space Odyssey* (1968), and how sparse the dialogue is there. It seems that in *The Fountain*, Aronofsky displays a mixture of two diverse cinematic sensibilities: Spielberg's and Kubrick's.

Aronofsky's style: Between Spielberg's narrative and Kubrick's duality

We can ask if Aronofsky's artistic sensibility can be placed in the gap between Kubrick's exploration of humanity and Spielberg's emotionality, that is, between Kubrick's concern for the state of humanity and Spielberg's narrative, triggering a sense of awe. *The Fountain* seems to provide an answer in the affirmative.

Indeed, all three directors are storytellers with stories they feel strongly about, and not storytellers "for hire." Spielberg said that, for him, "the fountain of youth" is an idea or a story, and that the wish to tell a story keeps him going. Kubrick said that he could never attempt to film a story that he was not "finally in love with." Aronofsky said that he has to tell a story that will be cool to him and his friends, something unique, and that only he can tell, hoping that the others will connect.

The Lucas–Spielberg era of 1980s blockbusters influenced many filmgoers and filmmakers. The sense of adventure, the hero's journey influenced by Campbell's writing on mythology, and its development for screenplay writers in Vogler's *The Writer's Journey* (first edition in 1998),[28] was best exemplified in the highly successful franchises *Star Wars* and *Indiana Jones*. Spielberg's prolific filmography is diverse in genre, ranging from adventure blockbusters to historic and sci-fi films. His Indiana Jones movies project a sense of adventure and childlike wonder, enjoying comic strip exaggerations and inviting the spectator to identify with the cool character of Indiana Jones. At the end, the hero finishes the task, gets the girl, and the bad guys are punished, so the audience feels uplifted with a sense of optimism. However difficult the task might look, with various obstacles, and even with personal drawbacks (Indy's fear of snakes), the ending is fulfilling and optimistic.

The story from the past in *The Fountain* is to some extent reminiscent of the adventures of Spielberg's Indiana Jones, our favorite archeologist in search of something endowed with powers that surpass humanity. In the first film, *Raiders of the Lost Ark* (1981), he searches for the Ark of the Covenant, which allegedly confers invisibility. In its prequel, *Indiana Jones and the Temple of Doom* (1984), he fights for the Shiva Linga stone, a symbol of the Hindu God Shiva, representing the energy and limitlessness of Shiva and bringing prosperity. In *Indiana Jones*

---

[28] Christopher Vogler, *The Writer's Journey: Mythic Structure for Writers* (Michael Wiese Productions, 2007).

and the Last Crusade (1989), he is searching for the Holy Grail, providing eternal life to whoever drinks from it. Lastly, in *Indiana Jones and the Kingdom of the Crystal Skull* (2008), he is after a crystal skull with mythical powers. The Indiana Jones film that conveys the darkest tones is *The Temple of Doom*, with scenes of religious cult ritual involving human sacrifice and child slavery. The three Sankara Stones glow when put in a proper position; a pit of swirling flame for engulfing sacrificial victims resembles a cosmic nebular scene. There is a fight scene between Indiana and the Kali priest Mola Ram on the cut rope bridge. Such scenes and the theme of the search for something magical are reminiscent of some scenes in *The Fountain* with the natives in the jungle, Tomas fighting against them in search of the immortality-securing Tree of Life, and his encounter with the Mayan priest ready for the ritual of human sacrifice for sustaining the myth of creation.

On the other hand, the future story with Tom, the space traveler, references Kubrick's epic about humanity's evolution, *2001: A Space Odyssey* (1968). It has already been stated that Tom in his bubble brings associations with David Bowie's Major Tom from his *Space Oddity* album (1969), which was, in turn, influenced by Kubrick's film. The scenes of space and the final explosion of Xibalba are reminiscent of the Star Gate scene in Kubrick's film, leading to the transformation that transcends human powers.

With its narrative combining the Indiana-Jones-style adventure from the past, the odyssey-in-space-style meditation about death and rebirth from the future, and illustrating Heidegger's existential phenomenology of being and time (*Da-sein* and temporality) in the process, *The Fountain* points to the possible unity of a blockbuster with an original auteur's voice. Aronofsky unites elements of the 1980s blockbuster adventure stories with the 1970s auteur's subjective voice and concern with existential problems facing humanity. This line of work led him afterward to the Biblical epic *Noah* (2014), which will be discussed in a subsequent chapter.

In addition to *The Fountain*, and looking at Aronofsky's six feature films from 1998 with π to 2014 with *Noah*, his sensibility indeed seems to fall in-between Spielberg's and Kubrick's sensibilities. All three directors are passionate storytellers, with narratives that have a sense of adventure and that put a spectator under their spell. Aronofsky's plots contain elements of horror (π, *Requiem for a Dream*, *Black Swan*), melodrama (*Black Swan*, *The Wrestler*), and spectacle (*The Fountain*, *Noah*), and his movies are very emotional with ambiguous endings. But, even in the face of death, his characters achieve human dignity (*The*

Wrestler); and even when succumbing to weaknesses (madness, obsession, addiction), they project strength in their vulnerability (Max from π, Randy from *The Wrestler*, Nina from *Black Swan*). Aronofsky's emotion and wonder regarding the human condition in its weaknesses and strengths brings him close to Spielberg. However, there are scenes in Aronofsky's oeuvre that one cannot imagine Spielberg doing (e.g., the "ass to ass'" scene from *Requiem for a Dream*). Aronofsky's dedication to subjecting his characters to battles between contradictory forces shaping their lives and their stubbornness not to let go (Max in π, Randy in *The Wrestler*, Tommy in *The Fountain*, Nina in *Black Swan*) brings his sensibility close to Kubrick's. In general, Kubrick's style presents excess and contrasts in human behavior, influenced by Jungian "duality of man." Kubrick's titles point to contradictions between the mechanical and the organic: *A Clockwork Orange, Full Metal Jacket, Eyes Wide Shut*. However, we do not see Kubrick's characters crying, while Aronofsky's characters (especially male characters) do cry: their emotion is not restrained. Kubrick and Spielberg project completely different sensibilities, and we might characterize Kubrick as too cold and pessimistic regarding the humanity of his characters, and Spielberg as too emotional and optimistic. Yet it seems that they understood each other, confirmed by Kubrick's asking Spielberg to take on his screenplay for a sci-fi film, which was completed by Spielberg after Kubrick's death, resulting in *A.I. Artificial Intelligence* (2001).[29] In an interview with the film critic Joe Leydon in 2002, Spielberg said, "All the parts of *A.I.* that people assume were Stanley's were mine. And all the parts of *A.I.* that people accuse me of sweetening and softening and sentimentalizing were all Stanley's. . . . This was Stanley's vision."[30] In fact, we can argue neither that Kubrick is cold, nor that Spielberg is overly emotional, and there are books written about both of them. In *The Stanley Kubrick Companion*, Kubrick states in an interview with the *Sunday Times*, "Emotionally, I am optimistic. Intellectually, I'm not. I do things in spite of all the things I'm intellectually aware of, such as the burden of my own mortality."[31] Indeed, all Kubrick's films show concern for humanity, albeit without sugar-coating

---

[29] *A.I. Artificial Intelligence* propagates a view that a computer can be programmed to love, that is, that emotional states originating in the brain can be programmed when viewing the brain as a big computer based on neuronal circuitry; however, the bodily mechanism cannot be programmed. Harlan and Struthers depict the making of *A.I.* and the efforts of both Kubrick and Spielberg in Jane M. Struthers and Jan Harlan, eds., *A.I. Artificial Intelligence: From Stanley Kubrick to Steven Spielberg: The Vision Behind the Film* (London: Thames & Hudson, 2009).

[30] Brian Eggert, "Deep Focus Review: *A.I. (Artificial Intelligence)* (2001)," 2011.

[31] James Howard, *Stanley Kubrick Companion* (London: B. T. Batsford Ltd., 1999), 109.

humanity, pointing to problems, and in turn, asking us to reconsider some of our actions and entrenched beliefs, and possibly to change for the better. Spielberg talks about his characters in an interview with Siskel and Ebert, in *The Future of Movies* (1991), stating, "The child is still alive inside of you even if you dwarf it just by sheer neglect....And we should take a step toward what we don't understand and what we don't know about and what scares us."[32] Leaving aside Spielberg's films with racial and war thematic such as *The Color Purple* (1985) and *Schindler's List* (1993), there are some dark thoughts lurking behind his films often considered overly optimistic and behind his lovable characters, as presented by Friedman in *Citizen Spielberg*.[33] Regarding Spielberg's male characters, Friedman writes, "At the center of any of his films you will find a man who is never quite sure how to interact with his parents, his children, his wife, or his lover. Only when faced with physical challenges or forced by uncontrollable events to alter his life radically does he move forward with any degree of assurance or authority."[34] Spielberg's films do not have memorable female roles, and only in *The Color Purple*, do we see a complex female character. Referring to Spielberg's female roles, Friedman writes, "His mothers usually appear oblivious to their surroundings and to the suffering of their children.... His romantic partners seem more like fun-loving pals than sexual lovers, tomboys instead of mature women."[35] Similarly, Kubrick's films do not have memorable female roles (except maybe *Lolita*).

Aronofsky combines elements of Kubrick's excess visible in the human condition and leading us toward the limit of existence in obsession or madness, and of Spielberg's emotion and the wish to leave a ray of hope, regardless of how hopeless the situation might be. In this, he creates his own recognizable mark and the spectator has certain expectations when talking about an Aronofsky film. In contrast to both Kubrick and Spielberg, Aronofsky finds a place for strong female roles. In *Requiem for a Dream*, Sara Goldfarb is probably the most memorable character; *Black Swan* is predominantly a female film with Nina Sayers and her transformation, her mother, and her nemesis Lily.

After this digression of comparing Kubrick's intellectual and Spielberg's emotional cinematic sensibilities, and of placing Aronofsky's sensibility

---

[32] Ebert and Siskel, *The Future of the Movies: Interviews with Martin Scorsese, Steven Spielberg, and George Lucas*, 53–72.
[33] D. Lester Friedman, *Citizen Spielberg* (Champaign, IL: University of Illinois Press, 2006).
[34] Ibid., 7.
[35] Ibid., 8.

in–between Kubrick's and Spielberg's, it remains to see how Aronofsky's sensibility works in *The Fountain*. As mentioned already, the making of *The Fountain* went through a difficult period, and Aronofsky had to modify the initially envisioned script, with a much smaller budget. In the film as well as in the original script as available in the graphic novel, Aronofsky presents the complex narrative dealing with the philosophically challenging themes of love, death, and rebirth. It might be the case that too much narration and verbal expression slants the film more toward an adventure, making the spectator busy figuring out how the stories are connected, as if solving a puzzle, and making it more difficult for the spectator to enter a meditative state. On the other hand, after multiple viewings, the film strikes us as a visual piece of existential philosophy, multidimensional, and changing our intuitive senses of time and space. But, how many viewers will engage in this film in such a way with multiple viewings?

Aronofsky mentions Truffaut's *Hitchcock* among his favorite books. Talking about *Marnie*, Truffaut calls it "a fascinating film, but a box-office flop," belonging to the category known as the "*great flawed films*."[36] He goes on to say that such a category denotes a masterpiece that for some reasons projects a "gap between the original intention and the final execution" and that such a film can "apply only to the works of a great director." But, continues Truffaut, a spectator ("a true cinephile") can sometimes prefer such a film over an acknowledged masterpiece of the same director because it works on a different level of sincerity, a higher level, showing its director in a state of perfection when he or she "lets it go" (to quote Aronofsky's choreographer from *Black Swan*).

In his first novel, *A Portrait of the Artist as a Young Man* (1916), Joyce talks about three consecutive artistic forms: starting with the *lyric form* as "the form wherein the artist presents his image in immediate relation to himself," progressing to the *epical form* as the form of "a mediate relation to himself and to others," finally resulting in the *dramatic form* in which "he presents his image in immediate relation to others."[37] When the dramatic form is achieved, the work begins a life of its own, surpassing the artist and his intentions and inviting the spectator to experience it by finding a source of inspiration in it, losing herself in the allure of the work. *The Fountain* presents an interesting case, making it difficult to decide on its artistic form the way Joyce writes. The first

---

[36]   Francois Truffaut, *Hitchcock: The Definitive Study of Alfred Hitchcock, Revised Edition* (New York: Simon & Shuster Paperbacks, 1983), 327.

[37]   James Joyce, *A Portrait of the Artist as a Young Man* (New York: Penguin Books, 1976), 214.

viewing can find the spectator unprepared for the depth of the film, as he or she struggles to connect the narratives and senses a lyrical form in trying to decipher its artistic meaning. With subsequent viewings, after knowing the narrative, the spectator has time for meditation about death and rebirth in general (epical form), and finally, meditates on his or her own death (dramatic form). Hence, the *immediacy* of the relation between the film's artistic "image" and its spectator is not easily attained. Given the scope of themes presented in *The Fountain*, maybe a less involved narrative would have worked better for the film's general accessibility. On the other hand, its treatment of plot in nonlinear time and its visual complexity in its presentation of correspondences from different epics qualify it to be a film about primordial temporality as a grounding structure for our existence, a daunting task indeed. Acceptance of death seems to invoke Aronofsky's questioning elaborated in *The Fountain*, implying that it could serve as the underlying support for the fulfilling experience of being alive.

The Wrestler: Melodrama and the Gift of Death

You know in this life you can lose everything that you love, everything that loves you. . . . You people here are the ones worth bringing it for because you're my family. I love all of you.

Randy "the Ram" Robinson in *The Wrestler*

In 2008, Aronofsky directed *The Wrestler*, a story written by Robert D. Siegel about an aging wrestler. Despite visual tools different from his previous movies dealing with obsession, addiction, and coming to grips with death, *The Wrestler*, in some aspects, continues Aronofsky's thematic preoccupations. The main character is completely subsumed in his public persona, obsessively insisting on carrying on the role, addicted to the allure of performing for the cheering crowd, and at the end, ready to sacrifice his life for the role. However, in *The Wrestler*, there are no dream or hallucination sequences, and the narrative is mostly linear with some photographs telling about the past. The main character is the 56-year-old wrestler Robin Ramzinski, who goes by his wrestling name Randy "the Ram" Robinson. Some twenty years earlier, in the 1980s, Randy was in his prime as a professional wrestler, but currently does some weekend local performances while living alone in a trailer park in New Jersey. He frequents a local strip bar and communicates semi-amicably with an aging stripper, Cassidy, whose real name is Pam and is a single mother planning to withdraw from the stripping job and start a different life. Following a suggestion by his manager, Randy agrees to the twentieth anniversary rematch with his former opponent Bob "the Ayatollah." However, before it happens, Randy suffers a heart attack and has to reexamine his future. At the doctor's order, he retires from wrestling, takes an ordinary job in a supermarket's deli department, tries to reconcile with his estranged daughter Stephanie, and attempts to get romantically involved with Pam. Unfortunately, things do not go smoothly: Pam rejects his advances, and Randy goes out drinking and engaging in casual sex, and misses the possible reconciliation with his daughter the next day. At work, he gets annoyed and

Figure 4.1 An old stripper and an old wrestler: Cassidy (Pam) and Randy (Robin) (*The Wrestler*, 2008)

agitated, cuts his thumb on a slicer machine, quits the job, and goes back to his manager insisting on the rematch with "the Ayatollah." He leaves for the match, and Pam follows him, seeking reconciliation and asking him to let go of the match, reminding him of his heart condition. However, Randy has made his decision, realizing that he belongs to the wrestling arena, anticipating how it will end. The last scene, when Randy climbs on top of the ropes to perform his final "Ram Jam" dive, his eyes full of sadness and determination, is very emotional. Ram throws a last brief look toward the place in the arena where Pam was standing, but she has already left. It is implicit that he knows he is jumping into the abyss of death, and the spectator is left to ponder such a decision: Is it worth it or not? Is there any other way out?

Visualization of artificial reality: persona versus ego and the sacrifice

The Wrestler is the only Aronofsky film (of the six films from 1998 to 2014) for which Libatique was not the cinematographer. The cinematographer is Maryse Alberti, who provides a visual depiction of a real world saturated with artificiality, appropriate for the subject of the film.

The Wrestler starts with Randy's muscular torso filmed from the back, so at first, a viewer does not see his worn and old face, creating a surprise. As the story unfolds, we learn of his past celebrity status, and later when he starts the deli job, we learn his real name and that he has an estranged daughter. Hence, the spectator is asked to imagine Randy at the beginning of his career. Obviously, in the past, he abandoned his real name, inverting and appropriately modifying the last and the first name to sound more entertaining, and adding a nickname as is customary in the wrestling world. He had a family, but abandoned it because it was not compatible with his wrestling career. If he made some money, it is obviously gone since he lives in a trailer park and does not have enough for the rent, so has to spend a night in his car. The car is filled with memorabilia and photos of Randy's celebrity days, and it feels like a parody of a shrine, except it is not a worship of God, but of "the Ram," the persona that consumed Robin Ramzinski's ego. Aronofsky's films prior to *The Wrestler* all include scenes of hallucination and daydream, providing insight into the characters' minds: Max Cohen in *π*; Sara, Harry, and Tyrone in *Requiem*; and Tommy in *The Fountain*. However, there is no way to get inside the Robin/Randy interior: Robin is nonexistent, subsumed into his persona, his alter ego Randy, who is a public persona, a mask. The only nonlinear digression occurs when, during Randy's heart problem, the presentation goes back fourteen minutes in time to show the fight. But, the presentation is objective, informing the spectators of what went on without being allowed into Randy's interior. In Latin, *persona* means "a theatrical mask," a role played for spectators. As such, persona stays on the surface, and it would be counterproductive to "peek" below the mask since it would undermine the illusion of the role. Hence, when presenting Robin/Randy, it is very appropriate to stay away from the presentation of inner thoughts, daydreams, or hallucinations. There are a number of scenes in which the camera follows Randy, whom we see from the back, indicating his point of view; but, we never get inside his mind. However, even if the mask shows a happy face (e.g., a clown), the eyes through the mask's openings can reveal sadness, despondence, and despair. Randy's eyes show his humanity and his heart, inviting compassion from the spectator. He should not be a sympathetic character, but he is. From the point of a commonly perceived ordinary life, he appears selfish (abandoning his daughter) and reckless (do not we each have to provide our own security for old age?). However, the film stays away from putting explicit blame on society or on unhappy childhood or on some other customarily used reason for such behavior. No, it is Robin's decision to get transformed into

Figure 4.2 Camaraderie between Randy and his cofighters (*The Wrestler*, 2008)

Randy, to get the allure of performing in the wrestling arena, to get recognition from the cheering crowd, and he feels comfortable in such a role. Even in his older age, he never appears bitter or cheated by life, and we get the sense that he would do it all over again. There are no loser-type accusations of could have, would have, should have—Randy is almost stoic about his life, accepting it as it is. He is aware of old-age decay and sees his comrades with deteriorating and crippling bodies (as when signing a few autographs), but there is no bitterness. He is very comfortable with children, appearing almost as one of them in his lack of planning for the future. He has good relations with his cofighters from the arena and with his managers. Of course, managers make money, but unlike in a number of boxing movies, we do not see a greedy, corrupt manager making use of the fighter.

The social critique in *The Wrestler* is more subtle: the main culprit appears to be the bloodthirsty audience, asking for modern gladiators, rewarding them with celebrity status (including recognition, a sense of being somebody) when they perform well, and discarding them when their prime runs out and they become "broken pieces of meat." The character of the crowd is sketched by its chants, such as "You sick fuck" or "Use his leg" (when asking Randy to use a prosthetic leg as a weapon) or "You're so dead." We can contemplate how far we have progressed from Roman times and the gladiator fights between men and beasts for the enjoyment of the masses. Despite being perceived as a fake fight, wrestling matches can be very painful, and the more bloody they are, the more enjoyable they are for the audience.

Italian neorealism of the postwar period presents society coming to grips with the consequences of the war, showing poverty and oppression, and ways of coping with it. In some sense, *The Wrestler* presents contemporary American realism, the age of spectacle and the commodification of individuality, or of putting ourselves up for sale. The cinematography and the use of colors add to the spectator's perception of life's artificiality, especially in the bar environment, but also in the facades of Randy's trailer and the ACME supermarket. The tonality of the film changes when Randy awakens in a hospital following his heart attack, indicating the protrusion of reality, with darker tones and non-intensive colors. The exclusive use of hand-held cameras gives the feel of a documentary. In Aronofsky's words, the film can be described as a proactive documentary because the action follows the script, unlike in a real documentary that is reactive, following action as it happens unplanned. Yet, due to the style of filming, including the use of real audiences for the wrestling matches and the use of real shoppers in a supermarket scene, the filmed action is prone to improvisation, further underlying the implied realism. However, there is a difference between the reality of representation and the reality of life itself: documentary style can be used to present the artificiality of life. The theme of fake fights in wrestling runs parallel to the theme of the fake (artificial, constructed) reality that the characters embrace as their lifestyle. Real-life wrestlers, like actors in real-life matches, naturally assume their roles as actors in the cinematic fiction, blurring the line between life and art. A subsequent section will discuss this issue in more detail. The visual style of *The Wrestler* captures this poignant character of contemporary reality, when individuality is buried beneath a mask for public display, a mask that eventually takes over and that makes life become saturated with artificial elements, emphasizing exterior surface presentation and erasing interiority. Regarding the audio elements in *The Wrestler*, the use of popular music in addition to Mansell's score further points to the blurring of the lines between virtual cinematic reality and actual objective reality. The title song "The Wrestler" playing over the closing credits, written and performed by Bruce Springsteen, captures the defiance, self-destruction, charm, nostalgia, and humanity embodied in Rourke's acting and reality.

The investment in a body (done by both Randy and Cassidy) seems more lucrative and easier than investing in, say, an education or a career based on the use of knowledge. The problem is that the body is prone to decay, and the

Figure 4.3 Randy and Stephanie on the boardwalk (*The Wrestler*, 2008)

consequences will depend on our consideration of the future. Randy did not make any provisions for the future, while Cassidy seems to be more realistic and is planning to leave the stripper's job, and with her savings, continue her life as Pam. Hence, she has a plan, and it could be realized. Randy does not have any plans, so when he has a heart attack after one of his matches, he is lost, unprepared for the events that follow. Still, he is a fighter and tries to get back his life in multiple dimensions: getting a job, repairing relations with his daughter, and becoming romantically involved. However, his attempts are never sincere enough: he does his moves since that would be the general wisdom and Robin Ramzinski should do it—but Robin does not exist anymore, overtaken by Randy "the Ram." In terms of Jungian archetypes, Randy "the Ram" Robinson is at the same time Robin Ramzinski's conscious persona and his unconscious shadow, creating disorientation.[1] After an emotional get-together on a deserted boardwalk reminiscent of a happier past, Randy blows a possible reconciliation with his daughter by spending a night using drugs and engaging in casual sex.

At a deli-counter job, he is annoyed by being called by his real name, gets agitated when a customer recognizes him as "the Ram," and leaves the job theatrically, cutting his thumb and rampaging through the store.

---

[1] Randy's character is analyzed in light of Jung's *Mysterium Coniunctionis* as compared to Fisher King, with the consequences of identifying the ego with the persona, in Lydia Lennihan, "The Dark Feminine in Aronofsky's the Wrestler," in *Jung and Film II: The Return* (East Sussex, UK: Routledge, Taylor & Francis Group, 2011).

Figure 4.4 Randy speaking to Stephanie, an attempt at reconciliation (*The Wrestler*, 2008)

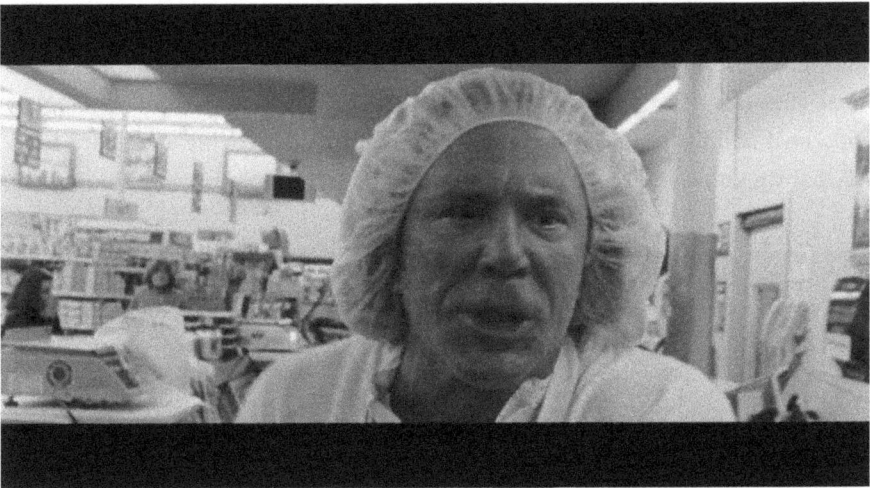

Figure 4.5 Randy's breakdown at the supermarket (*The Wrestler*, 2008)

At the promise of a possible romantic relation with Cassidy, just prior to his rematch with "the Ayatollah," Randy finally realizes the futility of life outside the wrestling ring. Cassidy could represent Randy's anima, his female side, but he himself also exhibits some female characteristics as necessitated by his performance (dying his hair, tanning, and shaving). With respect to the male/female dichotomy in Randy's psyche, there is no problem: they are reconciled in

Randy's psyche, which is a step toward achieving unity of unconscious and conscious material, leading toward Randy's identity. However, Randy's individuation, a process of his personal development, cannot be completed since his ego (Robin) and his persona (Randy) cannot be reconciled. Hence, it seems that death presents the best of the worst outcomes for Randy. In fact, if Randy were to perform a straightforward suicide (e.g., a bullet in his head), it would undermine his character. He is not a depressed individual without a way out and without any wish. He wants to perform, to sacrifice his life for the crowd, to satisfy the crowd, giving them even more than what they expect. And there is a possibility of fate: that all goes well and he survives. The film ends while Randy is in the air, leaving a ray of hope, although the logic tells it is hopeless. But, hope is not entirely tied up with logic—otherwise it would not be hope.

Now, suppose the ending were different: Cassidy/Pam arrives at the last moment and saves Randy, who decides not to wrestle (knowing that it is suicide), and they leave together, two imperfect souls who nonetheless found each other and are able to start anew. And afterward, maybe Pam could help Randy/Robin to mend his relationship with his daughter. Such a scenario would be a happy ending, loved by the audience, and there are many films that end along similar lines. However, it would be a fake happy ending, supporting some ideological ends, as if adding a sugar coating to a picante meal, destroying a culinary feast. All that we know and can see about Randy is that he is an imperfect individual,

Figure 4.6 Randy's final performance in preparation for the final jump (*The Wrestler*, 2008)

good-natured but selfish, who chose his way of life and likes it: the only way for him to attain selfhood in the Jungian sense, or the unity of the conscious and unconscious elements of the psyche, is to end his life's adventure consistently with the choices he made previously. His death is and is not heroic at the same time: it is not heroic as if dying for somebody else, or for a country, or for a political conviction. On the other hand, it is heroic since he sacrifices his life for his self, attaining unity at last, and maybe he senses that he will end his life this way, showing not too much concern for the future. His sacrifice and the nickname "the Ram" refer to the biblical story of Abraham ready to sacrifice his only son Isaak after following God without questioning, with God changing the sacrifice in the last moment to a ram, and thereby, saving Isaak. After his heart attack, Randy hesitantly tries to restart his life away from wrestling, to sacrifice his world of wrestling, unable to continue it. Sacrifice would amount to a life not chosen freely, and we might wonder how long it would go on before he became utterly unhappy with his job, his inability to keep a relationship with his daughter, or his relationship with Pam. Life is the most precious thing, but some would agree that living at all costs might be worse than death. This issue is highly controversial. Take, for example, the issue of euthanasia, which follows from the Greek word denoting "good death" and is defined as the practice "of intentionally ending a life in order to relieve pain and suffering." Voluntary euthanasia is legal in some countries. Although Randy's case is different and does not qualify for euthanasia due to the absence of a terminal, crippling, and painful illness, nonetheless his euthanasia-type way out seems to be the final wrestling performance, with his signature Ram Jam, assuming the fate of the sacrificial ram.

The Wrestler brings to mind two movies that feature characters with changed identities, having some relevant elements for comparison. *Resurrecting the Champ* (Rod Lurie, 2007) presents a homeless man who calls himself "the Champ," a former boxer who takes the identity of a former heavyweight boxing contender. Other aspects of the movie, such as the integrity of journalism and the father–son relationship, are presented didactically and the film ends with the (standard) happy ending of redemption and reconciliation. However, the character of the homeless man presents an interesting case of the need to switch identity. Tommy Kincaid, the real person and a lesser boxer, assumes the identity of Bob Satterfield, a successful heavyweight boxer who once defeated him in the ring. "The Champ" is homeless, so he does not need "the persona cover" to perform in public. In fact, the persona works against him since the young hooligans attack the elderly man, provoked by his claim that he is "the Champ." He does not get anything in return for his mistaken identity, except possibly a fantasy to soften his harsh everyday reality of being homeless. He is not crazy and seems to be conscious of his real identity, but needs the fake identity to soften his existence. When a reporter does a story on him, "the Champ" does not see it as an opportunity for himself, but as a way to help the reporter who states his need for a good story for career advancement. The story of "the Champ" illustrates the need for the past to sustain the present. Even a *fabricated* past can be a support if needed to endure the current present. The array of psychical protective mechanisms is indeed wide: from reinforcements of looking up to a hero to madness as creating a different reality and all the shades in between. Indeed, the psyche of "the Champ" seems to be in between fascination and madness, and it works for him—he does not seem bitter or angry, or a loser. As he says, "I am no bum, I am just homeless."

Another film that has some common elements with *The Wrestler* is *Kagemusha* (Akira Kurosawa, 1980). Despite different times and cultures, the final scene of death as a sacrifice resonates very strongly in both films. In *Kagemusha*, based on his physical appearance, a thief is selected to serve as a political decoy for the warlord of a Takeda clan in sixteenth-century Japan. When the warlord is killed, after some hesitation, Kagemusha takes over as the warlord, his persona gradually takes over his ego, and he becomes what he is supposed to personify. Kagemusha's role is played sincerely, making everybody believe that he is the real warlord, including the warlord's concubines and his grandson. However, Kagemusha gets carried away and is thrown from the warlord's horse, revealing his false identity. He is sent away from the palace, and the warlord's son takes over, leading the clan's army into total defeat. Kagemusha observes the battle from a bush, agitated by what he sees and by his inability to do anything. Finally, when the clan is defeated, after the long sequence in a leveled battlefield with corpses and dying, agonized horses, Kagemusha rises up and goes toward the enemy, single, knowing well how it will end. The last scene shows him mortally wounded falling into a river, close to the falling clan's flag. Kurosawa's film illustrates the allure of inhabiting another identity and the consequences of such identification. Kagemusha does not die for fame or entertainment, since nobody witnesses his death; rather, he dies an anonymous death, but such a death allows him to reach unity in his selfhood: given that his ego was overridden by his persona, in order to be true to himself, he needed to end his life in the way the warlord would do it; he needed to end his life with the end of his clan. Life after it would be a life of regrets, misery, and doubts—there is no way back since he took his role too sincerely; he was not playing it—he *became* the warlord, and in the process "killed" the original thief. This story raises the question of what is real and how reality changes in relation to physical appearances and psychic constructions.

The stories of Kagemusha and Randy "the Ram" are similar in their approaches to death as personal heroism, although there are cultural and historical differences. In historic Japan, Kagemusha dies anonymously for his clan, as is symbolically presented in the last scene by his dying body and the clan's flag in the river. In contemporary America, Randy dies in a spectacular way, in the midst of a full arena and a cheering crowd. If he would have killed himself in his trailer home, nobody would have reported it or cared about an old "broken piece of meat" killing himself. His death during the performance would get attention, and so at least, it would be worth something. In both cases, however, the death is not a suicide in the sense of killing a real person. Both the thief in *Kagemusha* and Robin Ramzinski in *The Wrestler* have already "died" a voluntary death, viewing death as rebirth (to quote Aronofsky from *The Fountain*): death of the ego to allow the fully-fledged birth of a persona overtaking the ego. The issue of voluntary death, which is not suicide, brings into consideration some philosophical writings about the gift of death.

Death as a gift?

The issue of *gift-giving* appears frequently in Aronofsky's movies: Marcy Dawson gives a gift (the Ming Mecca chip) to Max, Harry gives a TV set to his mom, Izzy gives a pen and ink to Tommy, Ram gives a shirt and a jacket to his daughter, and Nina's mother gives a cake to Nina. But, gift-giving is always with some motive: to get something back or to clear a conscience.

The question arising from *The Wrestler* is about death and gift-giving: can we offer our own death as the ultimate gift? The ending, when "the Ram" does his final Ram Jam, knowing well that it might be the end, but does it consciously, finding wholeness in death, triggers a question: Are there things worth dying for? Do we need to live at all costs? Is "the Ram" a hero or a coward when he performs the final jump?

A suicide can be perceived as a cowardly act, a flight from the challenges of life. What makes "the Ram" different from a person who ends his or her life because there is no way out is the last-moment chance with Pam, but he lets it go, finding wholeness instead in his death, producing a final gift to his audience, maybe to his daughter, and maybe to Pam as well. A heroic death, as a sacrifice for something perfect or for somebody else, can be seen as the ultimate present, a gift to someone else. This leads us to the consideration of philosophical writings about the impossibility of giving gifts. Specifically, Jacques Derrida in *Given Time: I. Counterfeit Money* (1994) argues for the impossibility of giving a gift, because it is related to an economy of giving and receiving. He considers the limit of the notion *gift*, as giving without receiving anything in return (which would relate to an economy), arguing for its impossibility. Derrida writes, "For there to be a gift, *it is necessary* that the donee not give back, amortize, reimburse, acquit himself, enter into a contract, and that he never have contracted a debt. . . . It is thus necessary, at the limit, that he not *recognize* the gift as gift."[2] This necessity characterizes a gift as impossibility, "The very figure of the impossible."[3] Derrida argues that recognition of a gift annuls its nature since recognition leads to its appearance and the consequences of that, for example, gratitude. Derrida connects the true gift with time and writes, "The difference between a gift and every other operation of pure and simple exchange is that the gift gives time."[4] The event of the gift has to be unforeseeable, unnecessary, and unexpected, that is, disinterested. However, it cannot be an effect of pure chance since that would undermine the meaning of gift. Hence, there is a paradox of unexpectedness and intention, at the same instance. As Derrida writes, "There must be chance, encounter, involuntary, even unconsciousness or disorder, and there must be intentional freedom, and these two conditions must—miraculously, graciously— agree with each other."[5]

Even if we give anonymously, but are conscious about it, the gift is related to an interest: the giver feels good about being generous or altruistic. The only possible gift, the gift of time that cannot repay the giver, is the gift of death. It connects two impossibilities: Heidegger's death as the "ownmost possibility of impossibility" and Derrida's gift as "the very figure of the impossible."

We are all mortal; hence, our death is a natural event, and natural or involuntary death has no connections to gift-giving. Voluntary death can be related to various levels of responsibility. A suicide is often considered irresponsible, but who is to

---

[2]   Jacques Derrida, *Given Time: I. Counterfeit Money*, trans. Peggy Kamuf (Chicago: University of Chicago Press, 1992), 13.

[3]   Ibid., 7.

[4]   Ibid., 41.

[5]   Ibid., 123.

judge a person taking his or her own life? Who can judge his or her sense of responsibility in such a case? A voluntary death perceived as heroic when dying to save somebody else, or for some cause, is related to responsibility and ethics. In *The Gift of Death* (1996), Derrida considers the notion of responsibility and asks:

> How does one give *oneself* death? How does one give it to oneself in the sense that putting oneself to death means dying while assuming responsibility for one's own death, committing suicide but also sacrificing oneself for another, *dying for the other*, thus perhaps giving one's life by giving oneself death, accepting the gift of death, such as Socrates, Christ, and others did in so many different ways.... What are the relations among sacrifice, suicide, and the economy of this gift?[6]

Derrida's answer starts with the reevaluation of the concept of responsibility: responsibility based on knowledge undermines its ethical structure since it becomes rule-based decision-making. In the contemporary technological world, individuals are identified with the roles they play in society, with a persona and not a person. Modern individualism is tied up with the objectivity of a given role. Returning to *The Wrestler*, the individualities of wrestlers, of Randy and all the others, are overridden by their roles of being wrestlers. In that sense, Randy's responsibilities become responsibilities reduced toward his wrestling appearance, neglecting everything else. The reevaluation of responsibility as ultimately detached from a specific objective presence and understood in the most general sense, this "awakening to responsibility," occurs with the readiness to death, "when the soul is not only gathering itself in the preparation for death but when it is ready to receive death.... By means of the passage to death the soul attains its own freedom."[7] Randy's conscious decision to do the final Ram Jam presents a double gift: a gift to the crowd thirsty to see violence and blood, and a gift to himself to attain authenticity and wholeness of his personality.

Viewing death as a sacrifice in front of a violence-hungry crowd brings into consideration Girard's *Violence and the Sacred*, which was mentioned earlier in the chapter about *The Fountain*, dealing with Mayan ritual practice.[8] Girard's hypothesis is "a theory of sacrificial substitution" since he claims that with the ritual of sacrifice a person vents a desire for violence that could otherwise come out in a problematic way, jeopardizing the well-being of a society. Hence, sacrifice

---

[6] *The Gift of Death*, trans. David Wills (Chicago: University of Chicago Press, 1996), 10.
[7] Ibid., 40.
[8] Girard, *Violence and the Sacred*.

is a form of violence.[9] In describing violence, Girard argues that if violence cannot be addressed to its main trigger, then it will find a surrogate, something else to deal with, such as when we kick a cat when we are angry at our boss. This behavior seems to have a root in human psychology. In "primitive" societies such a surrogate or a substitute for violence constituted a sacrificial act. In our modern world, it seems that the substitute for violence is violent entertainment, and wrestling as "sport entertainment," with all its picturesque individuals, unregulated blows and ever-surprising moves, fits well with the contemporary need for an outlet for violence. Similar to desire, which (in Girard's view) is mimetic, violence is also mimetic. Namely, desire is generated by the desires of others; similarly, violence feeds on other violence, and the more humanity tries to curb violent desires, the more they appear to be uncontrollable. The violent crowd induces violent behavior in an individual. It seems that "fake" violence (e.g., as entertainment) is needed to keep in check the real violence. Girard's anthropological argumentation for the development of common mechanisms for dealing with violence—from preventive mechanisms in sacrificial rituals to corrective mechanisms in judicial systems—could be augmented by considering violent forms of contemporary entertainment. Sport can be violent, but there are rules and calls for fair play, so that it is a true competition. Boxing is often referred to as the "Noble Art," as opposed to entertaining wrestling. Violence coming from a sports competition includes the element of fairness that neutralizes its irrationality. However, violence presented for pure entertainment signals the need to vent irrational violent impulses.

Art imitating life or life imitating art: Rourke and von Stroheim

Mickey Rourke's career path brings poignancy to his role of Randy "the Ram," adding to the emotional suture with the spectator. In "Why Does Mickey Rourke Give Pleasure," K. Walsh depicts Rourke's career, from his movies in the 1980s as a sex symbol in *9 1/2 Weeks* to the abandonment of his acting career in 1991 to do boxing to his subsequent return to acting. Rourke's off-screen behavior, his

---

[9]   Religion, according to Girard, carries a role of preventive mechanism, connecting violence and the sacred. Religious calls for nonviolence are often carried out through violence, performing acts of violence in the form of *pietas*; hence, religious sacrificial rituals connect moral and religious issues in a society.

career choices, and his face showing traces of his lifestyle, all contribute to the charisma of a unique individual: talented, resourceful, yet self-destructive. It seems that Mickey Rourke embodied a wide spectrum of contradictory human characteristics: between dominance and submission, egoism and altruism, masculinity and femininity, hope and despair, strengths and weaknesses, ultimately giving rise to a human complexity that cannot be classified under a certain type. The tension between the character of Robin Ramzinski and his alter ego Randy "the Ram" Robinson attains additional complexity by adding the real-life character of Mickey Rourke. His autobiographical elements intrude upon Randy's exterior (appearance) and interior (utterance) domains. When, in the final match, Randy enters the arena, the song playing is "Sweet Child O'Mine" by Guns and Roses, which was Rourke's entrance song when he was boxing professionally. His appearance follows his real lifestyle. Walsh writes:

> Bursting into the ring with heavy-metal hair, wristbands, and green sequin spandex tights, Rourke hits all the themes of his career: the rock'n'roll theatricality, the embrace of victimization, the celebration of excess, the willingness to pay the price, the attempt to create an alternative family, the offering of pleasure to others through endurance of pain, and the most literal instance yet of Rourke's throwing himself out.[10]

The monologue Randy delivers before the match coincides to some extent with Rourke's life choices, living hard and playing hard, and burning the candle at both ends. It also points to a confusion between reality and fiction due to a conflict between ego and persona. Randy says to the crowd, "You know in this life you can lose everything that you love, everything that loves you," adding after a few sentences: "You people here are the ones worth bringing it for because you're my family. I love all of you." The two statements put together give a low credence to the utterance "I love you." However, the case with Mickey Rourke is that despite objectively appearing disingenuous, he makes the utterance sincerely believable. His life choices bring credence to his role. An example of ambiguity between sincerity and fakeness is when Randy talks to his daughter, with tears in his eyes, telling her, "I used to try to forget about you. I used to try to pretend that you didn't exist. But, I can't. You're my little girl." However, we know that it was Cassidy/Pam who reminded him that he has a daughter, and when he looks for her photo, it is in a junk-filled shoebox. In an overly sentimental film, he would

---

[10]   Kerry Walsh, "Why Does Mickey Rourke Give Pleasure?," *Critical Inquiry* 37, no. 1 (2010): 159.

probably carry Stephanie's photo in his wallet, and without anybody's suggestion, take it out to look at it with teary eyes prior to calling her. But Siegel and Aronofsky do not fall into such a sentimental cliché trap. Hence, when Randy speaks to Stephanie, at first glance we are moved by his words and his appearance, but on second thought, he appears insincere, as though he is giving just another performance. On third thought: maybe it is sincere after all since Randy seems that he genuinely believes what he is saying. The scene is poignant in its ambiguity, as a tightrope walk on the sincerity/fakeness line. This is Rourke's charisma: we are never sure how much is performance and how much is reality, blurring the concepts of performance and reality, of surface and interior. His surface goes deep inside at the same time as his personality comes to the surface.

A good actor could deliver a role without actually living it, but it seems that the role of Randy was perfect for Mickey Rourke, and his real-life associations contributed to the semi-documentary style of the film. In addition to Rourke's reality being compatible with the role of Randy, the film features a number of real-life wrestlers, augmenting the realistic feel. The appearance of Randy "the Ram" with long blond hair is similar to the real-life wrestler Steve Austin when he started wrestling in 1989 under his real name, Steve Williams, before changing his appearance and taking a number of stage names—such as "Stone Cold" Steve Austin, "Stunning" Steve Austin, "Superstar" Steve Austin, "the Ringmaster," "the Texas Rattlesnake," and "the Bionic Redneck"—ultimately retiring from wrestling in 2003. He took up an acting career, starring in *Knockout* (Anne Wheeler, 2011) in the role of a retired boxer turned school janitor.[11] On April 7, 2014, the famous real-life wrestler "the Ultimate Warrior" (real name James Brian Hellwig) appeared on *Monday Night Raw*, a professional wrestling TV program, and delivered a touching speech by putting on a mask with his trademark face paint and performing his signature "rope shake" move. He was visibly struggling with his breathing, but was giving his last performance with a speech indicating that "every man's heart one day beats its final beat" and addressing the audience with "You, you, you, you are the legend-makers of Ultimate Warrior!"[12] He died one day later; his ending combining tragedy and performance similar to the ending of Randy in *The Wrestler*.

---

[11] Interestingly, both Mickey Rourke and Steve Austin starred in *The Expendables* (Sylvester Stallone, 2010).

[12] Kyle Newport, "The Ultimate Warrior's Final Speech to Fans on 'Monday Night Raw,'" *Bleacher report* (2014), http://bleacherreport.com/articles/2022961-the-ultimate-warriors-final-speech-to-fans-on-monday-night-raw.

The interplay between cinematic fiction and reality brings into consideration the classic question about the interdependence of art and reality. Following *The Wrestler*, one association comes to mind: Erich von Stroheim.

Eric von Stroheim, "The Man You Love to Hate," was an Austrian immigrant who came to America in 1909 and started his movie career playing Prussian officers during the war. He capitalized on his European background, inventing his persona as an aristocrat with military background and acting in movies (others' and his own) always as a negative character: a decadent, cynic, rotten European. Von Stroheim films often presented the clash of cultures of Europe and America, being critical of both and exaggerating both in stereotypes, creating a sophisticated parody. The penultimate film von Stroheim directed (and from which he was expelled before completion) was *Queen Kelly* (1929) starring Gloria Swanson. When years later Wilder was set to make *Sunset Boulevard* (Billy Wilder, 1950)—a film critical of the Hollywood environment with all its incessant drive for success, characters that could be bought, and career fadeouts and the psychological problems resulting from them—he offered the role of butler Max von Mayerling to von Stroheim, and the role of a fading silent star Norma Desmond to Gloria Swanson. Max conveys to Joe Gillis, a young screenwriter who becomes Norma's love and professional interest, that he is her former husband and the one who made her a star, adding "I was one of the three greatest directors of the silent era: D.W. Griffith, Cecil B. DeMille, and Max von Mayerling." Max explains that he did let go of his directorial career and became Norma's butler because of love. His statement, "I could have continued my career, only I found everything unendurable after she had left me," can be paraphrased as "I could have continued my career, only I found everything unendurable after I had to sacrifice my artistic impulse." This dialogue creates a strong intertwining between filmic illusion and life's reality with von Stroheim playing basically himself, and pairs with a scene from von Stroheim's *Queen Kelly* with Gloria Swanson. Von Stroheim's self-destructive career behavior was driven by his artistic credo, and he is recognized as one of the most authentic auteurs of the silent era, being much ahead of his time and providing a sharp critique of human vices, such as greed, sleaziness, conformity, such that we could argue that he was a romantic and emotional humanist.

Sunset Boulevard ends with Norma's complete delusion and the words, "You see, this is my life. It always will be. There's nothing else, just us and the cameras, and those wonderful people out there in the dark." This statement resonates similarly to the confession of Randy "the Ram" when he addresses the crowd in his final wrestling match, stating, "... you're my family. I love all of you." Similar to that of Randy, Norma's ego is annulled by her persona. Aronofsky's casting of Mickey Rourke, the former movie star turned boxer, in the role of Randy "the Ram," seems equally as poignant as Wilder's casting of von Stroheim in the role of a former director. The intrusion of real life into filmic illusion makes the perception of the two films more complex for the spectator, blurring the line between fantasy and realism.

Social connotations in *The Wrestler*

The old Roman motto of pleasing the masses with bread and games, *panem et circenses*, can be sensed in the 1930s during the Great Depression due to the proliferation of various games and sporting events, and the glorification of sports heroes. The games can be viewed as a metaphor for reinforcing rules and for the evaluation of the notion of fairness; furthermore, "Even the New Deal borrowed its name from the language of the poker game."[13] The 1930s witnessed the increased popularity of boxing in real life and as represented in films of that era. Unlike team sports, boxing is one-on-one, without social cooperation, fitting as a metaphor for capitalism, with the alienated labor of the boxer, profit taken by a manager, and the individual fighting to succeed in the social jungle. A number of boxing movies present the reality of the working class, creating an outlet for the disenchantment of alienated labor, while at the same time promoting elements of the dominant ideology. B. Balthaser writes:

> Films like *Kid Galahad*, *The Champ*, *The Killers*, *They Made Me a Criminal*, *Body and Soul* and *Golden Boy* ... portrayed the boxer as often ethnically marked and working-class, exploited by a world of gangsters, consumerism, greedy promoters, and literally cut-throat competition that threaten his morality and, often, his life. ... Ultimately, the boxing narratives of the 1930s portray the sport as a kind of unregulated, brutal competition that preys on the dreams of second-generation immigrants to improve their lot and enter the mainstream of society.[14]

More than half a century later, the crisis of capitalism and technological changes creating rifts in available jobs became a strongly-felt reality. In addition to the mainstream media, the film industry responded with its own visual discourse

---

[13]   Benjamin Balthaser, "Re-Staging the Great Depression: Genre as Social Memory in Darren Aronofsky's *The Wrestler*," *Cultural Logic* (2010): 5.
[14]   Ibid., 6–7.

on the contemporary social terrain. *Cinderella Man* (Ron Howard, 2005) presents the story of a real-life boxer from the 1930s Depression era, directly referencing the social and economic situation of the Great Depression. However, *Cinderella Man* differs from a typical 1930s boxing movie: instead of a social critique, it presents self-reliance and family values without questioning other factors like racial inequalities.

The Wrestler was released in 2008 as a fictional story and it presents a social critique of the contemporary fascination with public appearance, the role of the body as a predominant marker of our identity, and the consequences of bodily decay affecting the psyche. In analogy to boxing films of the 1930s, which present the realities of the Great Depression, *The Wrestler* presents the reality of contemporary American society. It depicts elements of consumerism, commodification of our individuality, and class differences, but also social connection based on class, regardless of racial difference. In this respect, a film about wrestling seems more appropriate than a film about boxing since professional wrestling implies staged fighting for mass entertainment. The impact of TV and the possibility this presented for wrestlers to attain celebrity status drew bigger numbers of wrestlers, and bigger requests for performance tactics. In the 1980s, the World Wrestling Federation (WWF) promoted "sports entertainment," and in 2001, changed its name into World Wrestling Entertainment (WWE). The social impact of *The Wrestler* consists in getting behind the scene and showing that there are real wounds obtained in fake fights, and there is real support between cofighters behind fake bursts of aggression or nationalism (e.g., between Randy and "the Ayatollah"). The film does not insinuate any social unrest based on class inequality; its protagonists (Randy and all the wrestlers, Cassidy) are not motivated to change the economic rules. Cassidy intends to quit her stripping job eventually, but does not see any problem with her current job and is willing to endure whatever degradation is necessary in order to make money (as when customers harass her and Randy interferes, making her lose the tip). The wrestlers communicate and it is obvious that they feel comradeship, and call each other "brother" or "sir," indicating intimacy or politeness and respect with dignity. But, they are all arrested at the status quo of their positions, without a wish or a will to change it. Instead of a way out based on some social consciousness of a marginalized class and a struggle to improve the working conditions, the way out for Randy is the retreat into his persona, "the Ram," under the spell of fame, reinforced by the fictitious love from his audience. As is sometimes the case, the victim of abuse finds a rationale for the abuser, creating a split identity; thus, it seems that the sense of success that comes from being in front of a cheering crowd entertained by a fake yet painful match provides the excuse for dismissing a dull life of everyday existence.

This discussion leads to two similar films, *Requiem for a Heavyweight* (Ralph Nelson, 1962) and *Fat City* (John Houston, 1972). *Requiem for a Heavyweight* was written by Rod Serling and based on his teleplay from 1956. The story follows a 37-year-old boxer Mountain Rivera (real name Luis Rivera) who, after 17 years of boxing, is ordered by a doctor to stop fighting because of a severely injured eye. In his prime days, Rivera was "almost the heavyweight champion of the world." He is lost in the real world, tries to get any job, and encounters Grace Miller, a woman who is attracted to him and wants to help him by organizing an interview for a job at an athletic summer camp for kids. Rivera's manager Maish, short for money, wants Rivera to compete in fake wrestling matches by assuming the persona of an Indian chief. Rivera cannot do it, feeling humiliation at the prospect of performing in a fake fight, while the wrestling manager explains, "Only two things to learn in my business: how to fake it, make it look real, and how to land so you don't hurt yourself." Maish leads Rivera in getting drunk, ruining his chances of getting a job and the girl. At the end, even after learning that Maish made a bet against him, but feeling the obligation toward him, Rivera enters the wrestling ring in the costume of the Big Chief Mountain Rivera, full of shame, and the film ends there. The scene in the bar between Rivera and Grace, both drinking beer and listening to music, has some similarities with the scene in *The Wrestler* when Randy and Pam have a beer and listen to music. However, while in the *Requiem for a Heavyweight*, it was Grace who initiated the encounter; in *The Wrestler*, it is Randy who takes the initiative and asks Pam to have a beer together. In contrast to Randy who cannot stand hearing his real name, Mountain Rivera accepts his real name Luis and holds on to his background, displaying family photos. There are real boxers in the film (Cassius Clay, Jack Dempsey) similarly to the real wrestlers in Aronofsky's film. Randy and Rivera are both good-natured guys, both have to stop what they do because of bodily problems, both miss a chance for a new start by getting under the influence in a bar, and both lose the prospect of a romantic relationship. However, Rivera has the possibility of one step down: leaving the "Noble Art" of boxing, he accepts the humiliation of fake wrestling entertainment and he continues his life. Half a century later, *The Wrestler* can be seen as the sequel to the *Requiem for a Heavyweight* with a new look at wrestling, resulting with real wounds and the more gripping allure of fighting entertainment. Randy as persona has completely taken over his real ego Robin, and when he is unable to perform, he does not have a step down he can take, only one last chance to perform, to end it in style.

Fat City (John Houston, 1972) is the story of an "older" boxer (in fact, he is only thirty years old), a younger one (eighteen years old), an alcoholic woman, and her black boyfriend. The older boxer left fighting, drinks a lot, is divorced, and works on a farm with migrant workers. Upon meeting the younger guy, he encourages him to consider fighting, deciding himself to return to the ring. He meets an alcoholic woman in a bar and moves in with her when her boyfriend is sent to jail. His fight with another aging boxer is won after mutual knockouts and he earns only $100. The younger boxer is not successful and has to get married because of a baby on the way, but continues some fighting. At the end, the two boxers meet by chance and end up in a bar, observing the aging server and contemplating life's choices. "How would you like to wake up in the morning and be him?" asks the older boxer. "Maybe he is happy," says the younger one. "Maybe we're all happy," says the older boxer with an ironic smile. "You think he was ever young?" "No." This philosophical meditation serves as an excuse for fights lost with life and for the inability to secure an existence despite trying in our own way. All the characters in *Fat City* appear as good-hearted, and the spectator is led to feel compassion toward them. They are good people, but unable, without reasonable opportunities, to face life's challenges; hence, they end up living marginalized lives. These characters invite comparison with characters from Aronofsky's *Requiem for a Dream* who are also likable but unable to realize their American Dream. While in *Fat City* the lives of characters are not as drastic as in *Requiem*, in both films their driving force is hope, regardless of how dim it is.

We could say that *The Wrestler* is *Fat City*'s coming of age. The young, ethnically diverse boxers from *Fat City* become the aging wrestlers in *The Wrestler*. Similar camaraderie exists between cofighters in both movies, and the movies project the similar inabilities of the protagonists to be sewn into the fabric of everyday life. We could ask which ending is more pessimistic, that of *The Wrestler* or *Fat City*. On one hand, the older boxer in *Fat City* has his life, but the prospect of his future does not look at all promising: he is an alcoholic, and without any willingness or a possibility to get a job, he is alone. We can anticipate his bleak future: maybe homelessness, maybe suicide, or maybe something can happen that will turn his life in a positive direction. The way the two boxers sit at the bar, mute, without the energy to fight life itself, insinuates that the younger one could follow in the footsteps of the older boxer, creating uneasy continuity, although there is some hope for the younger boxer. Houston's film resonates realistically and is quite depressing. *The Wrestler* is nominally more pessimistic since in all likelihood Randy dies following his Ram Jam, and this loss of life is irreparable. It is not the case that every wrestler has to follow Randy's path, for example Bob "the Ayatollah" retires successfully from wrestling and works at a car dealership, even doing some business prior to the rematch with Randy. So, he will be okay. But, the character of Randy is specific, as much as it is a clichéd old wrestler. He acts as a clichéd character when preparing for a fight, communicating with his group and going to a bar. But, from a clichéd environment with its established rules and ways of communication, he comes out as a memorable individual, and the spectator is aware that not many people will act as Randy does, so drastically, at the end. The way he delivers his performance seems fulfilling for himself—he will follow his persona to death, will give himself the gift of death as discussed previously. While *Fat City* ends more or less realistically, *The Wrestler* ends melodramatically. In a discussion of his 2007 film *Before the Devil Knows You're Dead* with Charlie Rose, Sidney Lumet said, "In a well-written drama, the story comes out of the characters. The characters in a well-written melodrama come out of the story." This definition seems well-suited to *The Wrestler* since Randy's character develops as a consequence of his wrestling career: the demands of the job (bodily appearance and performance) contradict the natural aging process, leading to a twisted reality and Randy's inability to cope with it, except by ending it in the style dictated by the wrestling performance. A drama would follow if a strong character decides to take upon himself a reevaluation of the wrestling culture, and starts social unrest leading wrestlers into an organized body against their exploitation, and so on. But, it seems that the contemporary situation is not a revolutionary one, and people struggle to make it in any way possible, where all is for sale. As the necessary bodily decay approaches, we are willing to accept lower and lower rewards, desperately clinging to the illusion of our successful appearance. As long as there is a struggle between imperfect human nature and the incomprehensibility of existence, there will always be a story involving melodrama.

Since he is motivated by a social component in a contemporary melodrama, Aronofsky is worth comparing with Fassbinder, a director who is often credited with reinventing the melodrama genre and whose endings are often perceived as pessimistic at first glance, but after subsequent analysis, are deciphered as the best of the worst outcomes.

Aronofsky, Fassbinder, and the redefinition of *melodrama*

Initially, the division of cinema into genres followed upon the division of literature into genres, which stems from the characterization of some common elements in the depiction of a story. Due to the more complex cinematic structure incorporating narrative, visual, and sound effects, film genres are differentiated along various dimensions. We often think of a film belonging to a certain genre based on its narrative details (gangster, western, war, melodrama, sci-fi). However, a genre can be perceived as any set of common characteristics, for example, whether the film is a literary adaptation, whether it has a big budget as do blockbusters, or whether its content deals with racial or sexual identity (Black cinema, Queer cinema). Many films transgress genres (e.g., a war melodrama) and can project different moods inside a genre (pro-war or anti-war). Today, even the division between animated and nonanimated fiction is invalid: the new technology creates quasi-human characters (synthespians) based on the animation technique of performance capture (or motion capture), for example the character of Gollum in *The Lord of the Rings* trilogy.

Maybe the most general genre is *melodrama*, since elements of heightened emotionality can arise in any historical and geographical environment. *Melodrama* can be seen as "the modern mode for constructing moral identity."[15] It can be present in many other genres, as enhanced emotionality in response to the challenges of the pressures generated by modern society. While during the nineteenth century melodramatic theatrical plays were valorized as an equivalent of classic drama, by the end of the nineteenth century realistic presentations (e.g., Ibsen, G.B. Shaw, Chekhov) attained a higher social status, denigrating melodrama to a lower, uneducated class. Harsh realism became identified with masculine orientation, with melodrama reduced to female emotionalism. The emergence of cinema further emphasized the difference between realism as a set of explainable facts and objective proofs, and the irrational emotional forces existing in the midst of realistic depictions. The power of cinema to direct and condition an audience's emotional response was demonstrated early on by the Kuleshov effect (1929), underscoring the importance of editing and montage.

The highly stylized melodramas of the 1950s by Douglas Sirk were rediscovered in the early 1970s, bringing the melodrama genre to the artistic

15 Jackie Byars, *All That Hollywood Allows: Re-Reading Gender in 1950s Melodrama* (Chapel Hill, NC: University of North Carolina Press 1991), 11.

level and analyzing it more carefully to find insinuations, symbols, and meanings beneath the surface representations of the standard narrative template of the unfortunate heroine, good guy, villain, and the happy ending restoring order. (Happy not necessarily for the protagonists, but happy in the sense of restoring the order by preserving the dominant ideology of class, gender, family.)

Kovacs, in *Screening Modernism* (2007), reminds us that "Melodrama had foremost importance in the development of the art-film practice."[16] Melodrama survived inside modernism because of its emphasis on *individuality*, albeit modernist melodrama replaced the traditional over-emotionality with modernist over-*non*emotionality, so to speak. The modernist nothingness, where all the senses are dulled and the individual is ready to give up on life, speaks forcefully about the changed human condition, for example Jean-Paul Belmondo's role in *Breathless* (Jean-Luc Godard, 1960). While a romantic hero is ready to die for love, a modernist hero is ready to die—period. This seems equally melodramatic, regardless of its nominally opposing nature. Hence, as long as there is a human entity equally endowed with reason and irrationality—melodramatic expression will continue to attract creative filmmakers and viewers.

Due to intensive characters and emotions, Aronofsky's films contain elements of a melodrama genre, for example, in *The Wrestler* (the character of Randy "the Ram") and *Black Swan* (the mother–daughter relations and the power of ambition), but Aronofsky's innovative visual style and ambiguous endings defy genre classification. In this respect, Aronofsky appears similar to Fassbinder. What Truffaut and the French New Wave did for Hitchcock, Fassbinder did for Douglas Sirk, bringing forward the artistic merit of his melodramas, and in the process, reinventing the melodrama genre. He was situated in a certain time period, his *BRD Trilogy* speaking most eloquently about moral issues during the great economic boom of postwar Germany. In regard to Sirk's melodramas, Fassbinder commented that "love seems to be the best, most sneaky and effective instrument of social oppression."[17] Love as a commodity for manipulation was explored in his films as well. Fassbinder's melodrama, on the surface, proceeds with simultaneous social-political-national drama in the background as a frame that incarcerates the characters and provides deviations from initially positive

---

[16]   Andras Balint Kovacs, *Screening Modernism: European Art Cinema, 1950–1980* (Chicago: University of Chicago Press, 2007), 84.

[17]   Rainer Werner Fassbinder, *The Anarchy of the Imagination: Interviews, Essays, Notes*, ed. Michael Totenberg and Leo A. Lensing, trans. Krishna Winston (Baltimore, MD: The Johns Hopkins University Press, 1992), 84.

human feelings such as love and social consciousness. In his stories, Fassbinder wanted to combine the glamour and melodrama of Hollywood, and the harsh reality of post-war Germany with the economic boom leading to all kinds of changed identities in the world where all is for sale. But, in addition to a social critique of contemporary Germany, Fassbinder's films provide a more universal depiction of human character and its strengths and weaknesses, a story about consumerism and identity change.

The presentation of some universal traits of human character as sewn into the current social fabric resonates well with Aronofsky's films. His characters show obsession (Max in π, Nina in *Black Swan*, Tommy in *The Fountain*) and different types of addiction (the four protagonists from *Requiem*, Randy in *The Wrestler*) as they stumble along the bumpy contemporary social terrain. The allure of the American Dream, in the form of recognition by others at all costs, disorients the otherwise good-natured personalities.

In artistic terms, *modernism* as the period from the late-nineteenth century until the mid-twentieth century was characterized by fascination with authenticity, sincerity, spirituality, and the structure of a work of art. Fed up with the two wars, with industrial proliferation, and with the hypocrisy of life perfect on the surface, starting around the late 1950s, *postmodernist* artistic efforts were focused on the negation of modernity. Postmodernist artists sought to dismantle modernist "myths" as utterly missing the reality of a nervous, neurotic, narcissistic, and disillusioned individual lost in the broken political promises following World War II, and broken personal ideals in a big meltdown of individuality in the age of consumerism and mass production. The end of the 1990s started to show signs of saturation with postmodernist artistic experiments and a sarcastic stance toward life and society. Various strands of what could be called *post-postmodernism* appeared, for example *new sincerity*. Postmodern visual art questioned many concepts, provided a brisk and often justifiable critique of life devoted to consumerism, its lack of identity, and overall inequalities of race and gender. Yet, at the end of the day, we get weary of sarcasm, cynicism, and irony, asking for emotional outlets. One of the current directions in philosophy and aesthetics is in-between modernism and postmodernism, called *Metamodernism*, emphasizing the human condition between life and death, rationality and irrationality, empathy and selfishness, dominance and submission, and all other human characteristics. Human existence is described with Plato's *metaxy*, the "in-between" of opposing poles of humanity. This type of sensibility provides a way to describe the tension between a character and the environment, with elements of modernist authenticity and sincerity embodied in a character, and the postmodern environment of consumerism and its lack of individuality. Such a clash between a modern character and the postmodern world can generate stories with heightened emotionality, invigorating the melodrama genre. Aronofsky's films, with memorable characters caught in the pressures of the contemporary environment, often end ambiguously and tragically, but with some hope or with a presumed satisfaction in the encounter with death.

The melodramatic elements and the ambiguity of endings in Aronofsky's films invite comparison with Fassbinder's oeuvre. Indeed, Fassbinder's films often have ambiguous endings and contain melodramatic elements. In the Preface of *Fassbinder: The Life and Work of a Provocative Genius*, Thomsen quotes Fassbinder from a 1975 interview:

> My films are often being criticized for being pessimistic. In my opinion there are enough reasons to be pessimistic, but, in fact, I don't see my films like that. They developed out of the position that the revolution should take place not on the screen, but in life itself, and when I show things going wrong, I do it to make people aware that this is what happens unless they change their lives.[18]

While Fassbinder's predominant themes include exploitation and repression, and the ambiguity between submission and dominance, Aronofsky is predominantly a philosopher's filmmaker whose films consider the themes of life and death, obsession and sacrifice, and provoke thinking on the meaning of life and the process of individuation and selfhood. Yet, both directors project a sense of the fragility of hope. Aronofsky's subsequent film, *Black Swan* (2010), discussed in the next chapter, is a visual poem on the struggle and sacrifices undergone to achieve artistic perfection.

---

[18] Christian Braad Thomsen, *Fassbinder: The Life and Work of a Provocative Genius*, trans. Martin Chalmers (Minneapolis: University of Minnesota Press, 1991), ix.

Black Swan: Limit Experience and Artistic Perfection

Perfection is not just about control. It's also about letting go. Surprise yourself, so you can surprise the audience. Transcendence.

Thomas Leroy in *Black Swan*

Following *The Wrestler* (2008), Aronofsky's next film is *Black Swan* (2010), which to some extent relates to *The Wrestler* as it deals with bodily changes and psychological turmoil. *Black Swan* is the story of Nina Sayers, a ballerina trying to land a leading role in the new production of *Swan Lake*. In the scheme of "life imitating art," Nina's story follows some elements of the story depicted in *Swan Lake*. The main problem is that Nina has to perform both roles, the innocent White Swan and the seductive Black Swan, but she is initially unable to embody the dark sensuality of the Black Swan. Usually described as a psychological thriller, *Black Swan* can be also interpreted as a metaphor for achieving artistic perfection, with all the psychological and physical challenges we might encounter. The screenplay by Mark Heyman, Andres Heinz, and John McLaughlin provides a rich and complex psychological study of a "limit experience," while Aronofsky's direction and Libatique's cinematography visualize the story in which reality and hallucinations coexist and the psychic transformation is projected upon the body, presented through bodily changes.

Nina experiences the full trajectory spectrum of an emotionally and professionally insecure person moving toward an artistically liberated performer, albeit her story ends ambiguously. Erica, Nina's mother, is a neurotic and domineering person who orchestrates Nina's arrested emotional development, keeping her incarcerated in a childish environment. The name *Nina* means "little girl" in Spanish, providing an additional character identifier. Thomas is a choreographer who tries to awaken Nina's artistic potential, with sometimes quite unorthodox measures. Lily is Nina's opposite, a technically imperfect dancer, but sensual and imaginative. There is also Beth, the older ballerina whose role Nina takes and who cannot accept her career coming to an end.

The characters' roles in *Black Swan*

The complexity of *Black Swan* allows for multiple interpretations, for example, as a psychological study of repressions, as a melodramatic thriller, as a body horror film. In addition to all the literal interpretations of the narrative, the film can be perceived as a poetic metaphor for the birth of an artist, that is, as a visual representation of Nina's psychic odyssey toward achieving artistic perfection and of the price to be paid for it. Due to the task of embodying both the Black and White Swans, Nina's road to artistic maturity requires an examination of the contradictory forces brewing inside her psyche. To achieve this examination, she needs to liberate herself from her mother's influence, one that forcefully suppresses any sexual or darker impulses she might have. She also needs help, a mentor, to guide her toward the darker side she needs to exhibit. Finally, in the attempt to reconcile the two poles inside her, she needs to endure a fight with her own self, visually presented in the form of the rival/helper figure. Hence, the main characters interacting with Nina are her mother Erica, her choreographer Thomas, and Lily, another ballerina. Each of those characters performs a decisive role in Nina's transformation.

Figure 5.1 Nina waking up at the beginning of the film (*Black Swan*, 2010)

Erica, Nina's mother, is the cliché of a mother who did not have a successful career and blames it on her motherhood, saying to Nina that she had to give up her career in order to give birth to her. To this, Nina responds, *sotto voce*, "You were twenty-eight," clearly implying that Erica was too old for a ballet career. Erica projects her anxieties regarding her unrealized career upon her daughter, assuming responsibility and the power to be in charge of Nina's life. Nina, with her room full of toys and artificial colors, is too sensitive, insecure, inexperienced, and unable to break Erica's dominance. Her environment as well as the relation with her mother is saturated with artificiality.

From the first scene when we see Erica, her eyes send chills combined with frustration and power: a deadly combination, indeed. Her overprotective stance toward Nina projects a coldness comparable to the chilliness of the housekeeper in *Rebecca* (Alfred Hitchcock, 1940). Her maddening insistence for arresting the sexual development of her daughter is reminiscent of Carrie's mother in *Carrie* (Brian De Palma, 1976). Erica is not a religious fanatic, but is a fanatic considering her daughter's ballet career. At the end, however, after Nina's stunning performance in the role of the Black Swan, the two of them share a look, and Erica is very emotional, with tears, appearing for the first time sincerely in touch with her daughter, finally letting go of her frustrations and accepting Nina for the artist she became, and expressing motherly emotion. This is a point at which the psychological thriller gets a melodramatic element in mother–daughter reconciliation: maybe too late, maybe not.

Figure 5.2 Artificiality of Nina's bedroom full of toys (*Black Swan*, 2010)

Thomas Leroy is an ambitious and talented choreographer, knowing what he wants from his lead dancer in the role of the Swan Queen. He sees potential in Nina, but also her lack of sensual passion and freedom of expression. He needs the same dancer to embody the innocence and wickedness. Nina's style of technically perfect movements convey restraint and order, but that is only half of perfection. The other half is the ability to let go, to let restraint and the rules be overruled by unrestrained passion. Thomas is aware of the artistic challenge in presenting the dual nature of humanity, and his name is perfectly chosen by the screenwriters. It denotes a "twin," and *Black Swan* is the story of a double all over: the white and the black swan, Nina and Lily, and Thomas who unites both poles and emphasizes the need for uniting the perfect form and an imperfect content to create the special brand of human perfection that is *perfection in imperfection*. In most scenes, especially at the beginning of the film, Thomas is always dressed in a white shirt and a black pullover, insinuating the coexistence of white and black, good and bad. A dialogue he shares with Nina trying to explain to her what she does wrong is characteristic of his artistic credo: "In four years, every time you dance I see you obsessed on getting each and every move perfectly right but I never see you lose yourself. All that discipline for what?" "I want to be perfect," replies Nina. "Perfection is not just about control. It's also about letting go. Surprise yourself, so you can surprise the audience. Transcendence. And very few have it in them," explains Thomas. Following this dialogue, Thomas kisses Nina, and she bites him. The scene is accompanied with a brief unarticulated sound, a growling sound announcing the Black Swan hidden in Nina. This bite convinces Thomas that the Black Swan waits inside Nina and that he can help her get it out. His style is unconventional as when he calls her to his apartment and assigns her homework: to go home and touch herself. Or when, during a rehearsal, he apparently seduces her, and it is subsequently revealed that his intention was to make a point and not to seduce her. Sometimes he needs to act cruelly, such as when he lets Beth go, albeit following his professional requirements. Beth is the older former star, and he calls her "my little princess." She might have been his lover, but that is left ambiguous in the film; he might have treated her as his muse. He is a choreographer first of all, a professional who lives for his career. His apartment looks very sophisticated but somewhat sterile, indicating that he does not have a life outside his ballet troupe. The only indication of his self-serving way of treating his lead dancer is when, at the end, he calls Nina "my little princess," the same nickname he used for his former star dancer Beth. This adds reality to his character, obsessed with his art, and it indicates the continuity and inevitability of Nina's future (assuming she survives).

Lily, a ballet dancer arriving from San Francisco, embodies Nina's shadow in terms of a Jungian archetype, presenting all that is hidden in Nina's unconsciousness. As with the names of Nina and Thomas supporting their character roles, the name Lily symbolizes the purity of the flower, but it can also be associated with the biblical name of the first wife of Adam, Lilith, symbolizing dark seduction and uninhibited sexuality. Her arrival from San Francisco possibly insinuates perceived cultural and emotional differences between culturally and intellectually sophisticated East (New York) and instinctively and emotionally emancipated West (San Francisco). In various scenes the person that Nina looks at is herself, suddenly transformed into Lily, for example, the first time Nina sees her/Lily in the subway. Lily manages to get Nina to a club, where they meet a couple of random guys, and Nina tries drugs and gets into the rhythm of a techno dance. The cuts are very fast, conveying the frenzied feel of the music and the movement. Black Swan comes out of Nina for the first time, in a flash. When watched on a DVD in slow motion, the dance scene reveals appearances of the evil sorcerer from Swan Lake, and the interchanging faces of Nina and Lily suggest that Nina's interiority spills into exteriority, creating hallucinations.

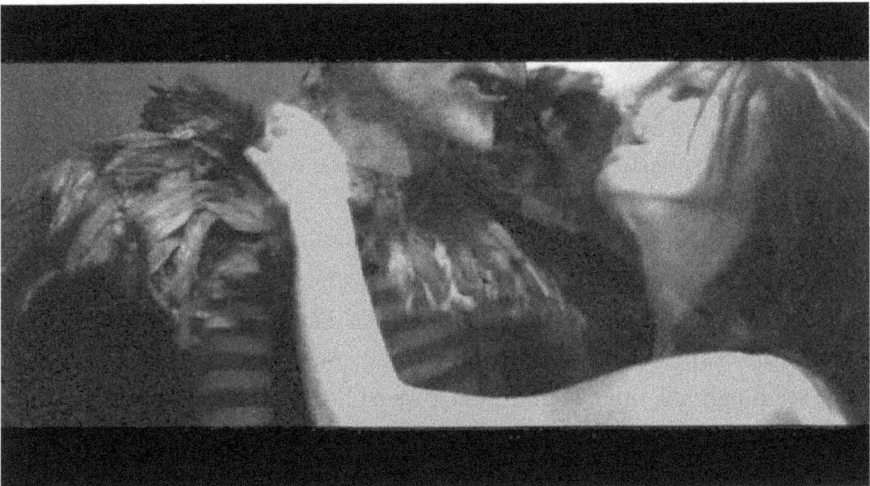

Figure 5.3 The appearance of the Evil Sorcerer in a fast cut from the club scene (*Black Swan*, 2010)

Indeed, the most intriguing relation in the film is between Nina and Lily, who is psychically her repressed shadow and visually her rival and her alter ego. The strong visual imagery depicts the beginning of Nina's transformation, and the emergence of Nina's shadow from the darkness of the unconscious. In Nina's bedroom afterward, she and Lily engage in a sexual encounter, later to be revealed as Nina's hallucination only, to Lily's amusement and Nina's horror. The protrusion of Nina's darker sensual part into consciousness is accompanied by her physical changes, scratches and a rash, anticipating Black Swan's feathers. Aronofsky's direction of Nina's final identification with her shadow is presented as a poetic thriller when Nina/Black Swan attacks and seemingly murders Lily/Nina (represented by their interchanged faces) to be able to finally set free the Black Swan inside her and deliver a masterful performance. She gets rid of the physical (literal) personification of her dark side to be able to express it through her own body. However, afterward she needs to embody the White Swan, and to do it on the same masterful level, she needs to get rid of her good-girl persona Nina, which is poetically presented in the realization that her wound is personal and that she herself, like the White Swan in the ballet story, is wounded. While having a frightened look in a dressing room, expressing the fear of death; when on stage, Nina delivers the role as directed by Thomas, being "not fearful but filled with acceptance," realizing at the end that she achieved perfection. Nina's character can be perceived as undergoing a descent into madness due to an obsession, due to the dominance of an overbearing mother, due to the stress of professional rivalry, and due to sexual repression. However, such an interpretation will miss the poetry present in the film, the thin line between madness and brilliance, and the limit experience of an artist perishing in his or her art. As already stated, I propose to interpret *Black Swan* as a visual poetry presenting artistic metamorphosis. The white screen at the end suggests transcendence, the achievement of perfection.

The problem with performance art, or any performance requiring a young, strong, and healthy body (as in Aronofsky's *The Wrestler*), is its inevitable collision with the natural process of aging. In *Black Swan*, this is presented through the character of Beth, the former star, now getting too old for the role, while seemingly still quite young. Beth once had it, as Thomas explains to Nina, "Everything Beth does comes from some dark impulse. I guess that's what makes her so thrilling to watch. So dangerous. Even perfect at times. But also so damn destructive." He contrasts Beth's performance to Nina's, trying to free Nina from her restraints, saying, "You are stiff like a dead corpse. Let it go! Let it go!

Let it go!. . . The only person standing in your way is you. It's time to let her go. Lose yourself." Nina recognizes Thomas's brilliance as a choreographer and artistic mentor, and tries to deliver what he asks of her.

Thomas here speaks as C.G. Jung would speak. In the *Commentary to "The Secret of the Golden Flower,"* the "Chinese Book of Life," Jung writes, "The key is this: we must be able to let things happen in the psyche. For us, this becomes a real art of which few people know anything. Consciousness is forever interfering, helping, correcting, and negating, and never leaving the simple growth of the psychic processes in peace."[1] Jung articulates the need to invoke active imagination, to be involved without too much thinking or calculating, constrained by the rules. The psyche needs freedom to evolve toward the unification of conscious and unconscious material, necessary for the processes of individuation and self-development. This seems to be the lecture that Thomas gives to Nina, sensing that she has the potential for the dual role of the Swan Queen. Interpreting *Black Swan* as the confrontation with our shadow to achieve artistic perfection leads to viewing the characters in the film in relation to Jungian archetypes and Campbell's hero's journey. Nina's ordinary world is presented as an artificial environment with her overprotective mother and the call to adventure comes as the challenge to secure the role of the Swan Queen. She gets guidance from Thomas who encourages her and helps her to tap into her unconscious darker side. Lily is both a helper and a detractor in Nina's journey, basically her double. However, *Black Swan* departs from the usual hero's journey: Nina's supreme ordeal is mixed with her supreme reward. Prior to the performance of Black Swan, she hallucinates about wounding Lily, delivers a masterful performance, realizes her own wound, and finally, performs the role of White Swan with a very ambiguous final reward: satisfaction with the perfect performance and its implied death.

Death of the main character as a climax is implied in both *The Wrestler* and *Black Swan*. However, although in *The Wrestler*, we do not see it exactly, it is clear that death is taken in the literal sense, as a physical death: all other possible avenues are closed. If Randy does not die, then he will die next time; his end is inevitable. In *Black Swan*, there is the possible interpretation that what we see is either Nina's hallucination again, as a preparation for the upcoming performance, or a self-inflicted but not life-threatening wound, as

[1]   C.G. Jung, *Commentary to the "Secret of the Golden Flower,"* trans. Richard Wilhelm and Cary F. Baynes (London: Kegan Paul, Trench, Trubner & Co., Ltd., 1947), 89.

part of the ambiguous creative/destructive process that enhances her performance. Hence, an optimistic interpretation of the ending of *Black Swan* could assert the birth of a true artist with a promising future ahead, at least for the time being, until she reaches Beth's stage, the stage of an old ballerina. Beth's ending is, in some sense, analogous to Randy's ending in *The Wrestler*. She cannot accept the end of her career; her ego is completely subsumed by the persona of a star ballet dancer; and her accident might not be random, but done on purpose to achieve a theatrical end. Whether her accident is random or not remains ambiguous in the film, leaving the spectator to interpret it in his or her own way.

Visual elements presenting Nina's psychic and bodily transformation

Black Swan corresponds with other Aronofsky films. For example, Nina's breakfast (boiled egg and half a grapefruit) resembles Sara Goldfarb's meal in *Requiem for a Dream*. Despite the differences between Nina's "noble" wish to maintain her figure for performance in a ballet and Sara's deranged hope of appearing in a reality TV show, both are driven by obsession and have to undergo a similar struggle. Nina's preparation of her dancing shoes and her feet resemble Randy's preparation for the wrestling match in *The Wrestler*. Nina's walk through corridors insinuates personal imprisonment due to her fixation with her performance and her inability to function normally in life's other spheres, similar to Randy whose fixation on his wrestling career leads to his drama. However, while Randy abandons his family due to pressures from the job, he finds camaraderie with his fellow wrestlers. They approach each other with "Sir," and show mutual respect and a sense of understanding each other's pain and challenges. Such noble behavior is in contrast to the perception of their performances as a low type of entertainment, based on the audience profile, the audience that asks for blood and brutality, just for entertainment, knowing well that the match is a fake competition. In contrast to wrestling, ballet presents a sophisticated entertainment for a knowledgeable audience, the pure embodiment of performance art. Below the surface, though, are the immensely ambitious ballerinas, working extremely hard and seeing each other as competitors only, with no camaraderie or friendly interaction. The competition in this case is real, and the stakes are high because only one woman can get the leading role. Hence, in the social department, Nina is completely alone, regardless of the fact that she lives with her mother. The two personalities helping her to achieve a breakthrough in her artistic side are Thomas, the choreographer, and Lily, her competitor and double, each in his and her own way.

The use of color is prominent in the film and supports the duality of white and black, innocence and dark sensuality. Nina's light-colored clothes, Lily's dark clothes, and the black and white combinations that Thomas wears support their characters. Nina's mother is always dressed in dark colors, projecting restraint, rigor, and negative influence. The light artificial colors in Nina's room, with giant pink fluffy rabbits obstructing her windows, convey her arrested development, purposely enforced by her mother.

Similar to Aronofsky's earlier film *The Fountain*, the interplay between symmetry and asymmetry underlines the conflict between a character's exteriority and interiority. Interior passion and turbulence are underlined by the perfect order and symmetry of the outside environment projecting either indifference to movement or providing a perfect backdrop for artistic expression. For example, the perfect symmetry of the entrance to the reception hall, with the statue of the evil Rothbart, increases the intensity of the encounter among Beth, Nina, and Thomas. Similarly, the outdoor scene following the news of Beth's accident, is perfectly symmetrical, with the fountain in the middle, invoking the symbolism of

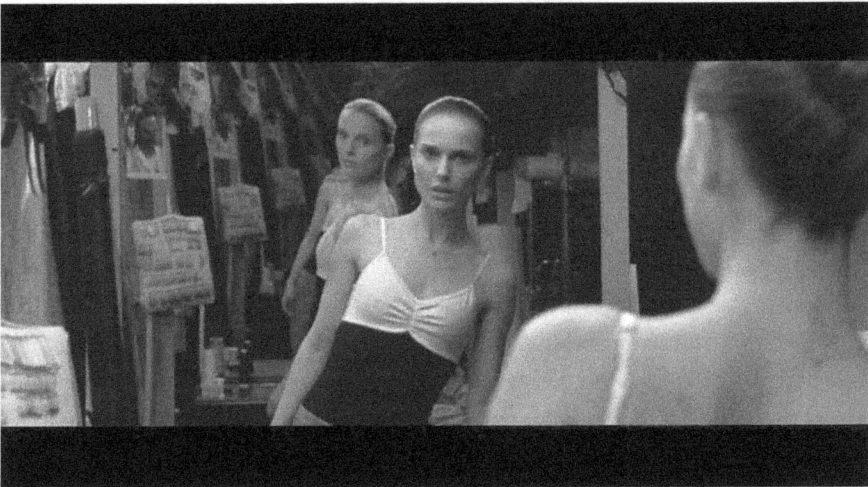

Figure 5.4 Nina's hallucinations: mirror image as an originary image (*Black Swan*, 2010)

the fountain in the death-rebirth cycle. Finally, the symmetry of the stage when Nina performs Black Swan, as well as at the end prior to her jump as White Swan, provides a fitting backdrop for her performance, forcing the spectator's gaze to Nina's masterful movements.

The use of mirrors and reflections adds to the theme of doubling and multiple layering of Nina's personality. Mirrors are used in various films, often suggesting a deficient personality or artificiality of the character's persona. For example, Fassbinder (greatly inspired by Douglas Sirk) used mirrors as a symbol of narcissism, of doubling, and of illusion in many of his films. The role of images is important for the development of subjectivity, as Lacan asserts in "The Mirror Stage as Formative of the *I* Function, as Revealed in Psychoanalytic Experience."[2] The mirror is often described as a dream symbol, relating unconscious and conscious psychic spheres. In *Black Swan*, with regard to ballet, it is obvious that there has to be lots of mirrors. When Nina practises, she looks at herself in the mirror in order to see and improve her movements. Hence, mirrors serve to strengthen her dancing persona. However, when her image in the mirror becomes an originary image, detached from her real presence, it is a hallucination in which Nina's unconscious comes to the forefront, and the mirror visualizes the interaction between consciousness and unconsciousness. The conflict culminates in Nina's hallucination when she struggles with Lily/Nina and hits her, breaking the mirror. The broken mirror insinuates the disappearance of her old self, and Nina is now free to express her Black Swan. The broken piece of mirror she later pulls from her chest suggests the inability to completely let go of the White Swan inside her, allowing for her final performance.

In *Black Swan*, CGI is used to present interiority coming out in bodily transformation. This transformation is most effectively shown on Nina's face and body, and in the interchanges between Nina's and Lily's faces, as befits Nina's oscillation between reality and hallucination. The hallucinatory club scene with the appearance of the evil sorcerer and the interchanged Nina/Lily faces creates a dizzying effect on the viewers' capacity to process the images, resulting in disorientation and strong bodily involvement since the senses and accompanying reflection are disconnected: reflection cannot follow upon perceptual experience. As in the previous films *π* and *Requiem*, the fast cutting provokes viewers' neuronal activity to act unconsciously, resulting in an understanding that defies

---

[2] Jacques Lacan, *Ecrits*, trans. Bruce Fink (New York: W.W. Norton & Company, 2002), 3.

Figure 5.5 Extreme close-up of Nina's face during the transformation (*Black Swan*, 2010)

Figure 5.6 Nina's bodily transformation on stage (*Black Swan*, 2010)

reflection, that is, a bodily simulation that pulls the viewer into the virtual reality presented on the screen.

The combination of real movements and CGI enhancement in Nina's final performance as Black Swan is mesmerizing and captivating for the audience watching the movie, and for the ballet audience within the movie. Nina's stunning transformation is poetry in motion and testifies to the creative use of computer technology. Natalie Portman delivers an award-winning performance in a leading role.

The search for artistic perfection, limit experiences and the disintegration of reality

Black Swan illustrates the disintegration of reality that can occur when an artist seeks perfection, overstepping the thin line between reality and imagination, between reason and madness, and perishing in that threshold. Nina acknowledges the acceptance of death, with a content look saying, "I felt it. Perfect. It was perfect." Now, this is too extreme and seems utterly pessimistic. For the performance of the final act of *Swan Lake*, Thomas directs Nina with strong words:

> The final act! Your final dance! You tasted your dream, touched it, only to have it crushed. Your heart is broken! Wounded! Your life force fading. The blood drips. The black swan stole your love! There's only one way to end the pain! You're not fearful but filled with acceptance! And you look down at Rothbart and then at the prince, and then, yes, at the audience. And then you jump![3]

Nina delivers a truly masterful performance, perishing in the role, finally giving all that she has in an experience that brings an artist into the limit of consciousness, transgressing into madness. This type of experience ties *Black Swan* to philosophical writings about *limit experiences*. As in his other movies, Aronofsky's visual style serves as an artistic illustration adding to relevant philosophical positions.

Various artists go "overboard" in the search for a novel expression (verbal or visual), succumbing to their passions, leaving their spectators in awe. Philosophers such as Nietzsche, Jaspers, Blanchot, Bataille, and Foucault emphasized the importance of limit experiences as an untamed facet of humanity, trespassing intellect and analytic order. Karl Jaspers, a psychiatrist and existential philosopher, devoted a study to two artists who succumbed to madness, Strindberg and van Gogh. (Jaspers was referenced in the discussion of the character of Max Cohen from π.) Jaspers argues that conscious reasoning is bounded by rules and

---

[3]   Darren Aronofsky, *Black Swan* (2010).

Figure 5.7 Nina's expression at the end, achievement of perfection (*Black Swan*, 2010)

observable facts, and that in order to achieve true authenticity, we have to transcend the limited world of facts and appearances, searching for the limitlessness that comes from inside. Achieving transcendence is necessary for creating something essentially new, be it in science or art. Unfortunately, sometimes the mental strain is too powerful and a person cannot recover from it, ending in psychosis or in a full-blown madness. A discussion about Aronofsky's π references some notable mathematicians who pushed the boundaries of mathematics and who succumbed to madness. In a study about Strindberg and van Gogh, Jaspers cites their schizophrenia as originating in limit experiences with the unification of opposing drives of creation and destruction. Jaspers writes:

> One is tempted to explain the productivity which becomes evident during the state of insanity with the liberation of forces which, up to then, had been retarded; that the illness removes the inhibition; that the unconscious, so to say, comes to the fore; the obstruction, imposed by civilization, is broken up; that this gives cause to the similarity between dream and myth, and a childlike mentality.[4]

[4]   Karl Jaspers, *Strindberg and Van Gogh: An Attempt at a Pathographical Analysis with Reference to Parallel Cases of Swedenborg and Holderlin*, trans. Oscar Grunow and David Woloshin (Tucson, AZ: University of Arizona Press, 1977), 197.

However, continues Jaspers, in some cases, a mental illness does not only serve to free the repressed forces, but to generate new forces, "forces which, within themselves mental, are neither healthy nor sick but thrive on the soil of the illness."[5] He argues for evidence of such developments in the works of van Gogh and Hölderlin.

Nina's character, with her psychotic behavior, her recurring hallucinations, and her effort to bring Black Swan to life, has all the characteristics leading to the transgression of stepping into a new realm of experience. The visual mastery of the film, enhanced with the creative use of CGI, illustrates the excess beyond the world of appearances. The film's narrative, the preparation of the ballet *Swan Lake*, and the request for a single dancer to perform both roles serves as the perfect topic by which to visualize the process of going toward a limit experience through attempts to unite contradictory forces in our character.

Georges Bataille's writings are predominantly concerned with excess and transgression, characterizing a human being beyond the ordered world of rules and the utilitarian character of possessions. According to Bataille, as conscious beings we are separated, and death brings us to the continuity of being, a theme akin to the subject of the story presented in Aronofsky's *The Fountain*. The wish to step outside our separate lives relates to the desire for transgression, for excess, for violence winning over reason. Without excess, something new cannot be created. As Bataille writes, "The fact is that creation is inextricable, and cannot be reduced to any other impulse of the mind than to the certitude, being exceeded, of exceeding."[6] Maurice Blanchot provides homage to the writing of Bataille and defines the *limit experience* as "the response that man encounters when he has decided to put himself radically in question."[7] He names "Goya, Sade, Hölderlin, Nietzsche, Nerval, van Gogh, Artaud" as examples, and questions if it is possible to achieve a kind of perfection without passing through madness or falling into it. In *The Infinite Conversation*, Blanchot credits these artists and writers with the capacity to relate unreason and madness; unreason being the obscure and ambiguous concept defying knowledge, while madness is a well-defined scientific concept.[8] Michel Foucault addresses Bataille's work on excess, eroticism, and

---

[5]   Ibid.
[6]   Bataille, *Eroticism*, 269.
[7]   Maurice Blanchot, *The Infinite Conversation*, trans. Susan Hanson, vol. 82 (Minneapolis: University of Minnesota Press, 1993), 203.
[8]   Blanchot credits those artists and authors with "the relation that each of them seems to have maintained between the obscure knowledge of Unreason and what the clear knowledge of science calls madness." Ibid., 199.

transgression in his essay titled "A Preface to Transgression" (1963).[9] Transgression is overcoming limits, that is, reaching limitlessness, and is only possible in our interiority, as limitlessness is inside a human being. The outside world is objective, hence limited.

When Thomas tells Nina that she is the only person standing in her way and that she needs to lose herself, it is clear that Thomas understands the nature of externally posed inhibitions and the internal potential to override them. Nina's character resides on the boundary of reason, where humanity is most vulnerable. Or would that vulnerability be a sign of strength? Personal tragedy, combined with the rapture of creative achievement, defies a simple answer.

Thriller, melodrama, and the issue of gender in Black Swan

Black Swan is a film with predominantly female characters, featuring conflicts and rivalries among Nina, her mother Erica, her double/rival Lily, the older ballerina Beth, and the company dancers. The only male character is Thomas, the choreographer. Depiction of the gender relationships in Black Swan generated disagreement among some commentators. For example, Film Quarterly published a debate about Black Swan in which "Mark Fisher asserts that the film is a subversive 'Irigarayan horror film,' while Amber Jacobs claims that on the contrary it is a masturbatory patriarchal fantasy."[10] According to Fisher, while the film presents "a female horror film," it is not misogynistic, and "If Leroy embodies patriarchy, then Nina's relationship with other women show the damage that patriarchy has done." Later on, he adds, "Black Swan is a film that is in large part about autoeroticism and fantasy. . . . Nina's madness is a howl against the power structures that gave rise to it; it doesn't simply confirm those structures."[11] Jacobs' view differs, and she writes, "Under the patriarchal conditions Black Swan replicates, women's attempts to achieve subjectivity result in madness, breakdown, self-destructivity, and premature death."[12]

It seems too restricted to relate the psychological and visual richness of Black Swan to the politics of gender. The film's purpose is not didactic or moralizing

---

[9]   Foucault, *Language, Counter-Memory, Practice*, 29–53.
[10] Mark Fisher and Amber Jacobs, "Debating *Black Swan*: Gender and Horror," *Film Quarterly* 65, no. 1 (2011): 62.
[11] Ibid., 61, 62.
[12] Ibid., 59.

in the sense that it alerts the audience to the patriarchal conditions between choreographers and ballet dancers. The fact is that many successful choreographers are male, and Thomas's gender seems appropriate. The stereotype of the overly ambitious, narcissistic, and womanizing choreographer is to a certain degree due to the legacy of George Balanchine or to Bob Fosse's autobiographically-derived character in *All That Jazz* (Bob Fosse, 1979), although Thomas Leroy is no Joe Gideon. Thomas is ambitious and involved in his art, but we do not know much more about him. In addressing the comment about patriarchy and its destructive impact on female subjectivity, that is, the argument that patriarchy is responsible for Nina's rivalry with other women is misleading, as if patriarchy is not responsible for male relations as well. Nina's gender seems irrelevant, and her transformation can equally apply to a young man. In the patriarchal society presented in *Dead Poets Society* (Peter Weir, 1989), young men feel the need to liberate and express themselves, which is facilitated by the unorthodox measures of their teacher. Against his father's wishes, a young man wants to pursue an acting career, and when his father forces him to let it go, he commits suicide. We could list many films presenting the complexity of father–son relations as there are many films depicting troubled mother–daughter relations (e.g., *Mildred Pierce* (Michael Curtiz, 1945) and *Imitation of Life* (Douglas Sirk, 1959), and the more contemporary *The Piano Teacher* (Michael Haneke, 2001)). How many movies deal with male competition? Nina is not forced to pursue her ballet career and she could have stopped if she wanted. It is her ambition and persistence— as an emerging artist, irrelevant of her gender—to perform in the role of the Swan Queen. Of course, the story in *Black Swan* is exaggerated, but the mixture of reality and hallucination invites a metaphorical interpretation beyond the literal rendering of narrative facts. It is even possible to interpret the whole story as the hallucinatory dream of a young, insecure ballerina, troubled by the standard questions of whether she has what it takes and whether the effort is worthwhile. (Nina's content face when she wakes up at the beginning of the film is similar to her content face at the end, as seen in Images 5.1 and 5.7.) This interpretation could merge the characters of Nina and Erica: Nina senses her future as coinciding with her mother's life story, and is scared of the inability to obtain a successful career. In any case, the allure of *Black Swan* is that it offers a wide range of possible interpretations, inviting the spectator to provide his or her own interpretation.

Black Swan has elements of the horror and melodrama genres combined in visually compelling scenes dealing with bodily changes. However, it does not completely fit into those genres as they are presented in "Film Bodies: Gender, Genre, and Excess" (1991).[13] Williams discusses three genres dealing with bodily functions: pornography (defined by its excess of sex), horror (defined by its excess of violence and terror), and melodrama (defined by its excess of emotion). She observes that in each of the three genres, the female body is used to represent the emotions of pleasure, fear, or pain despite being directed toward different audiences (porn to active males, horror to adolescents, and melodrama to passive females). While pornography and horror attain a low-cultural esteem, melodrama is much broader and all three genres can be put under the "extended melodrama" genre as a stylistic and/or emotional excess over the realistic narrative. However, Williams's article restricts the term *melodrama* to "weepies," films with excessive emotional representation.

During the early 1970s, feminist film critics focused their critique on explicating Hollywood films as oppressive toward women. The feminists during the 1980s also maintained a stance that all traces of the feminine in the film industry serve to maintain the patriarchal order; their research being predominantly concentrated on analyzing examples of manipulation and power, but not involved with the theoretical explication of concepts such as gender, class, and race.[14] Byars concentrates on the Hollywood melodramas of the 1950s in order to analyze "representations of the American mainstream for the American mainstream (read: predominantly white and middle-class)."[15] The 1950s was a period of considerable social changes: women entered the workforce; and with the promise of financial independence, there came the possibility to make marriage decisions based on love and not on calculated economic opportunities. The basic tenets of patriarchal society were changing, such as breadwinning roles, family, and motherhood; hence, a number of melodramas with lead female figures surfaced in that period. Regarding gender (without considering other pressing societal categories of class and race), a classical feminist critic could find clear signs of patriarchal ideology striving to preserve traditional roles and traditional family. However, argues Byars, on a closer and a more open look, we can find elements that clearly articulate female voices and point to changes in gender ideology. She argues that feminist analysis should be broader and should inquire into

[13] Linda Williams, "Film Bodies: Gender, Genre, and Excess," *Film Quarterly* 44, no. 4 (1991).
[14] Byars, *All That Hollywood Allows: Re-Reading Gender in 1950s Melodrama*. (Chapel Hill, NC: University of North Carolina Press, 1991).
[15] Ibid., 7.

what remains unresolved or repressed in such cinema, or in other words, that it should extract female voices hidden beneath the phallocentric and paternal surface. The last section of her book explores themes in Sirk's *Imitation of Life*, ending with an Epilogue that poses a number of questions, including: To what extents is a film critic influenced by his or her own ideological conditioning?

Reflecting different ideologies throughout history, from the late 1950s to the mid-1990s, Sirk's films have been addressed as "subversive, adult, trash, classic, camp, and vehicles of gender definition."[16] Sirk's characters as well as his endings are open, leaving it to the spectator to make inferences about them. In an interview with Peter Lehman in 1980, Sirk stressed the importance of the heart, of feelings, without putting all the emphasis on the intellect. He said, "There's a thinking of the heart, too. At the same time as you can be an intellectual, you can be very sophisticated. I think the great artists, especially in literature, have always thought with the heart."[17]

Melodrama presents a way to vent frustrations arising in societal and personal contradictions. According to Aristotle's theory of tragedy, in antiquity, tragedy had a cathartic function by involving emotions of pity and fear. Melodrama might be a modern equivalent of classic Greek drama: it provides an outlet for strong emotions brewing in an individual caught up in the unfortunate net of psychic and physical repressions, without Olympian gods messing with human fate. Aronofsky's *Black Swan* as well as his other films are emotional and present thinking with heart, often ending in obsession. Duality of human nature and the inability to reconcile its contradictory forces, coupled with pressures from the environment, naturally lead to heightened emotionality.

Black Swan and some relevant films

The influences Aronofsky mentions in relation to *Black Swan* are very diverse: the ballet *Swan Lake*, the novel *Double* by Dostoevsky, and the movies *All About Eve* (Leo Mankiewicz, 1950) and *The Tenant* (Roman Polanski, 1976). *All About Eve* is a story of rivalry, ruthless ambition, and the destructive power of the desire to be in the spotlight. To some extent, it resembles the apparent relation between

---

[16]   Barbara Klinger, *Melodrama and Meaning* (Bloomington, IN: Indiana University Press, 1994), xv.
[17]   A quote taken from Tom Ryan, "Great Directors in Senses of Cinema, Issue 30" (2010).

Lily and Nina. *The Tenant* is a psychological thriller exploring the notion of the disintegration of identity due to outside pressures, leading to the obsession and paranoia of Trelkovsky, the main protagonist. While Trelkovsky assumes a different identity, Nina's obsession works toward freeing her own identity. The issue of the double can be explored in terms of escaping imprisonment and suffocation in a meaningless existence or a way to escape psychic imprisonment, which provokes a confrontation with the unconscious. With the theme of the double, *Black Swan* invites some comparisons with *The Double Life of Véronique* (Krzysztof Kieslowski, 1991), a philosophical film about intuitions, apprehensions, and fate. A filmic illustration of reality higher than factual reality, with an emphasis on the intuition of connectivity of events and lives surpassing common everyday knowledge, *Double Life* attests to the power of cinematic art to raise questions about life's mysteries as if slightly lifting a veil in order to see nature more clearly. Separated by language and geography, the two main protagonists (Véronique and Weronika) complete each other, being unconsciously emotionally connected. The film works on many levels, exploring the notions of subjectivity and art, and with possible social connotations relating France and Poland. Another European film exploring the theme of identity crisis and the double, with artistic and social connotations, is *Despair* (Rainer Werner Fassbinder, 1978), an adaptation of a novel by Vladimir Nabokov. At the end, the main character Hermann Hermann (with a fitting double name) is caught by the police and falls into madness stating, "I am a film actor, I am coming out." This scene is reminiscent of *Sunset Boulevard* and Gloria Swanson's exit, and the fall into madness in which a person assumes him- or herself to be a performer. Fassbinder dedicated the movie to three artists who succumbed to madness: Antonin Artaud, Vincent van Gogh, and Unica Zürn (a German author and painter who suffered from depression and killed herself). The issue of the double nature of a person's desire is presented in *That Obscure Object of Desire* (Luis Buñuel, 1977). The same person, a flamenco dancer, is played by two actresses portraying women with significant physical and emotional differences. In this film, the same person is "split" in two as she is viewed and experienced by her lover. Buñuel's visual mastery creates ambiguity in narrative meaning, emphasizing the multitude of feelings brewing in a person's sexual desire and the way in which it eludes satisfaction.

In addition to films dealing with the issue of the double, other prominent elements in *Black Swan* invite comparison with some notable movies. For example, my interpretation of *Black Swan* as a metaphor for the birth of an artist has similarities with themes prevalent in *Blue* (Krzysztof Kieslowski, 1993). The narrative story, with many rehearsal scenes and the dancers' story following the story being performed as life imitating art imitating art relates to *Carmen* (Carlos Saura, 1983). The troubled mother–daughter relation, sexual fantasies, and the use of glass to inflict pain resonates with *The Piano Teacher* (Michael Haneke, 2001).

Kieslowski's *Blue* is part of his *Three Colors Trilogy*, with colors from the French flag each symbolizing an ideal: blue stands for liberty; white, for equality; and red, for fraternity. In commentaries, it is stated that *Blue* represents the development of individual emotional liberty. In addition, I wish to argue that *Blue* could be interpreted as the birth of an artist, as emotional liberation allowing artistic maturity. In *Blue*, given the tragic event, further events result in rebirth and continuation in a positive direction. Following a car tragedy in which Julie loses both her husband, a famous composer, and her daughter, and after contemplating suicide, she starts a new life, leaving everything behind except a chandelier made of lots of small blue glass pieces. The chandelier can represent her inner life, made of past impressions and inspirations that have time to "settle down" (i.e., to take on solid form), unlike her daughter's impressions broken by the accident (the blue candy paper). Blue color stands for immensity, inspiration, and unboundedness. The woman gradually liberates her inner strengths and accepts her creativity that had previously been hidden under the shadow of her husband's fame. She starts to compose under her own name. She also deals with her inner fears and childhood traumas (the mice scene), and with reborn strength returns to the context of her previous life (the house, the unfinished music). Acting freely, even when it goes against socially accepted norms, she invites her husband's pregnant mistress to live in her house. Visually compelling scenes represent her creation: a combination of visual perceptions of events and faces, and music that is born during her laps in the swimming pool. *Blue* radiates optimism, despite the tragic events of the car accident and the discovery of infidelity. Moreover, the tragic events serve as a sharp contrast to the inherent optimism of the liberation of her creativity.

Black Swan does not radiate optimism, and the tragic event at the end when Nina realizes her final wound but delivers a perfect performance to her own satisfaction, leaves the spectator confused, wishing that all ends well and that Nina recovers. After experiencing Nina's hallucinations, a spectator becomes an accomplice to Nina's journey, feeling for her and wishing for her triumph.

A film dealing with the blurred line between art and life is Saura's *Carmen*, the second film in his *Flamenco* trilogy. The narrative follows a flamenco troupe preparing a dance using music from Bizet's opera *Carmen*, in turn, based on the novel *Carmen* by Prosper Mérimée. The plot of the novel—in which an officer falls for a gypsy girl Carmen, follows her, and finally, in a rage of jealousy, kills her—is mirrored by the plot of the movie. The choreographer Antonio searches for a lead dancer to play Carmen. He finds a dancer (her name is Carmen) at a flamenco school, sensing her passion as perfect for the role. Carmen comes late to the class with a cigarette and sips a drink before starting the audition, projecting unrestrained sensuality prone to transgression, similar to Lily in *Black Swan*. Antonio falls for Carmen, but she does not accept his possessive love, and wants her independence and freedom to have affairs, and Antonio kills her in a rage of jealousy, repeating the story of *Carmen*. The fuzzy line between art and life is also indicated by the selection of actors playing basically their life roles, for example, the choreographer Antonio is the real-life choreographer Antonio Gades, Carmen's rival Cristina is the real-life dancer and choreographer Cristina Hoyos, and the flamenco guitarist Paco is the legendary Paco de Lucía. The passion of the protagonists, echoed by the passionate flamenco dance and the accompanying music captivates the gaze of the spectator, and creates a thrilling experience regardless of the known outcome. As in *Black Swan*, there are many rehearsal scenes inviting a spectator into the dance world of the protagonists and their relations. In contrast to the insecure Nina, Carmen is a seductive, independent woman, perfectly equipped for the role of Carmen. She can emotionally identify with the role of Carmen, with her passion, desire, and seduction. Just as Carmen's life supports her performing role, Nina's life prepares her for the role of the Swan Queen, the dual role of Black and White Swan. Similarly to the plots of their performances, both Carmen/Carmen and Nina/White Swan end tragically. Another poetic film about passion and independence, with the independent and sensual young gypsy Radda (similar to Carmen), is *Gypsies Are Found Near Heaven* or *Queen of the Gypsies* (Emil Loteanu, 1975). It is a melodrama with a fascinating music score, which presents the tragic love story of the two gypsy lovers. We are left to wonder whether ultimate freedom is possible only in death.

A troubled mother–daughter relation, combining career rivalry and the repression of Nina's sexual drive, presents the defining obstacle to Nina's psychic development. Similar themes are explored in Haneke's *The Piano Teacher*. It presents the story of Erika, a piano teacher in her late thirties who lives with her mother. Erika projects a cold and unapproachable person, who is reserved and interested only in her teaching job. Her favorite composers are Schubert and Schumann. Schubert (1797–1828) died very young and left a significant opus in the early Romantic style. Schumann (1810–56) was Schubert's successor in Romanticism, with a poignant life story involving parental meddling and mental disorder. After a hand injury stopped his piano player's career, he started composing and became one of the most important Romantic composers, but suffered from the mental disorder of melancholia and died in a mental hospital. In a recital at a private house, Erika meets Walter, a much younger student interested in music. Their conversation preceding the playing turns to acknowledging "the benefit of illness," meaning mental illness, which the ordinary people in the room do not understand. Erika mentions Adorno's writing about Schumann's *Fantasia in C Major*, produced at the outset of Schumann's mental illness, during his twilight. Erika explains, "It's not Schumann bereft of reason, but just before. A fraction before. He knows he's losing his mind. It torments him but he clings on one last time. It's being aware of what it means to lose oneself before being completely abandoned."[18] Here, Erika performs the role of a good teacher, talking about her favorite composers. However, Erika's fascination with Schumann's illness possibly insinuates her troubled mental state. In contrast to her reserved and distanced public persona, she is sexually active, albeit in her own way. We see her engage in voyeurism in a sex shop and in observing a couple having sex in a car, and we see her engage in sexual self-mutilation. She seems very confident and determined when entering a sex shop with male customers only and when heading for a viewing booth to watch porno scenes. Her masochistic sexual drive carries over in her relationship with Walter, ending with obsession, jealousy, and self-inflicted wounds. Seeing a rival in Anna, an insecure female student with a likewise overambitious mother, Erika puts broken pieces of glass in Anna's pocket, causing the girl's wounds and rendering her unable to perform at a concert. Erika does it in a calculating manner, able to foresee the outcome. Although she is scheduled to replace Anna, seeing from a distance Walter arriving at the concert, Erika stabs herself in the shoulder and exits the theater. The exterior of the concert hall is perfectly symmetric, in contrast with the turbulent relations inside the building, similar to the reserved exterior of Erika, and in contrast to her turbulent eroticism and sexual drive.[19] Erika's mother is overprotective, but unable to control Erika. We

---

[18]   Michael Haneke, *The Piano Teacher* (2001).
[19]   The perfectly symmetric exterior in contrast to turbulent relations among protagonists or inside a character is often presented in Haneke's films, for example in *Funny Games* (Michael Haneke, 1997, 2007).

can imagine that in *Black Swan*, Nina's relationship to her mother could evolve along the lines of Erika and her mother from *The Piano Teacher*. Suppose that Nina never achieves a breakthrough in her career and ends up being a spinster in her late thirties, but with an already awakened sexual drive that finds a perverse outlet, albeit below the radar of her overprotective mother who becomes too old to enforce any significant domination. Interestingly, the name of Nina's mother is Erica, maybe chosen at random, but maybe relating the two films and alluding to the possibility of alternative endings for a character such as Nina or Erica. Despite some similarities, *Black Swan* and *The Piano Teacher* differ in many aspects: Nina's apparent collapse indicates her greatest achievement and a possible reconciliation with all her influences (her mother, Lily, Thomas). Erika in *The Piano Teacher* incurs in all likelihood a minor wound, continuing on her path of self-mutilation, her sexual habits, and the relationship with her mother. While *The Piano Teacher* stays clear of melodramatic elements, attesting to a certain emotional detachment present in Haneke's films, Aronofsky's *Black Swan* is a heightened emotional drama, testifying to the alluring value of a good melodrama.[20] As quoted in the writing about *The Wrestler*, Lumet states, "In a well-written drama, the story comes out of the characters. The characters in a well-written melodrama come out of the story." This quote seems particularly fitting for distinguishing the two films. The events in *The Piano Teacher* are orchestrated by Erika, an unyielding character determined to get her way, creating drama in the process. In *Black Swan*, the insecure Nina is led by the flow of events that she did not start, but has to fight, and is transformed in the process. Aronofsky's inclination toward heightened emotional situations brings him closer to Fassbinder. Both Haneke and Fassbinder present human behavior, asking spectators to make their own judgment. While Haneke's films present narratives without much emotion, asking spectators not to identify with the characters, but to judge them according to their own sense of morality, Fassbinder's films are very emotional, inviting character identification and asking spectators to finish the story in their own way. Both directors stated that their films are meant to provoke spectators. Likewise, Aronofsky's films provoke

---

[20] The filmic oeuvre of Michael Haneke is addressed in Catherine Wheatley, *Michael Haneke's Cinema: The Ethic of the Image (Film Europa)* (New York: Berghahn Books, 2009). She argues that Haneke's films are not moralizing in the sense of prescribing a certain view, but have a pedagogical function, "for the intention of his work is to place spectators in a position whereby they can lucidly assess the content of the film, and ... from which they can assess their own relationship to that content." Ibid., 189.

spectators to participate in making their own ending, after an emotional ride and identification with the characters. The climax in *Black Swan* ends on a similar note as that in the ending of *The Wrestler*.

In relating the three European auteurs (Kieslowski, Saura, and Haneke) to Aronofsky, and in adding to the list Polanski, Fassbinder, and Buñuel, it becomes clear that the theme, the directing style, the *mise-en-scène*, and the cinematography in *Black Swan* result in an intriguing, challenging, and artistically rewarding film. Aronofsky succeeds in connecting the existential ambiguity so valued in European art movies, with the classic feel of a Hollywood melodrama, creating a work with his own recognizable sensibility. In an interview after the release of *Black Swan*, Vincent Cassel, the French actor who plays Thomas Leroy and who also acted in *Eastern Promises* (David Cronenberg, 2007) and *A Dangerous Method* (David Cronenberg, 2011), was asked to compare Cronenberg and Aronofsky, to which he answered that both are fascinated with body horror material and have an inclination toward similar subject matter. Cassel adds, "And David is not actually American at all, he's Canadian. And Darren is not really American, he's from Brooklyn! And they both have a European quality to what they do. A dark European quality."[21] Regarding Brooklyn, in Aronofsky's π, there is a striking ethnic diversity of female characters: Asian little Jenna, Indian neighbor Devi, black Marcy Dawson, and white landlady. This ethnic diversity underlines the perceived (and real) view of ethnic diversity in that neighborhood. It rings true that many of Aronofsky's influences are non-American directors, including many European directors. Moreover, the "dark European quality" that Cassel refers to, protrudes from Aronofsky's film, but it is combined with elements of Hollywood genres, creating an auteur's melodrama, personal, controversial, and unsettling. Aronofsky's next film, *Noah* (2014), results in the merger of his auteur's signature and the American blockbuster production.

---

[21]   Robert Beames, "Interview: Vincent Cassel on *Black Swan*, Darren Aronofsky, Eastern Promises 2!," in *Whatculture.com* (2011).

Noah: Responsibility, Love, and the Moment of Choice

The choice was put in your hands because He put it there. He asked you to decide if we were worth saving. And you chose mercy. You chose love.

Ila in *Noah*

In March 2014, a TV advertisement for Aronofsky's *Noah* quoted the *Rolling Stone Magazine* proclaiming *Noah* as "the first must-see blockbuster of the year." There is a problem right there: Can a blockbuster, as we know it, be related to a distinctive directorial approach as we expect from Aronofsky based on his previous movies? In some reviews, *Noah* has been compared to movies such as *Gladiator*, or *The Lord of the Rings* and *Indiana Jones* trilogies.[1] In writing about *The Fountain*, I have proposed to position Aronofsky's filmic sensibility between the opposing sensibilities of Kubrick and Spielberg, and will argue that *Noah* gives more evidence to such a claim.

Due to the biblical thematic, many reviews compare Aronofsky to Cecil B. DeMille. For example, one review in the *Los Angeles Times* from March 27, 2014, states, "With its determination to tell this traditional story in its own way, it begins to oddly echo the very different but equally individualistic Old Testament epics put out by the old master himself, Cecil B. DeMille."[2] To the comparison of Aronofsky with DeMille, I wish to add a comparison with two other former directors, von Stroheim and Curtiz: von Stroheim for his insistence on his own artistic expression, and Curtiz for his film *Noah's Ark* (1928) relating

---

[1] Kathleen Parker, "*Noah's* Arc of Triumph," *The Washington Post Opinions* (2014), http://www.washingtonpost.com/opinions/kathleen-parker-noahs-arc-of-triumph/2014/03/14/3678b092-abaa-11e3-98f6-8e3c562f9996_story.html.

[2] Keneth Turan, "Review: Energetic 'Noah' Goes Overboard—to Riveting Effect," *LA Times: Art and Entertainment* (2014), http://www.latimes.com/entertainment/movies/moviesnow/la-et-mn-noah-review-20140328-story.html#ixzz2xHBqitkQ&page=1.

the biblical story to a more contemporary situation, in this case the ravages of
World War I.

The term *New Hollywood* applies to films starting to come out in the mid-1960s
and especially in the 1970s, showing a burst of filmmaking auteurs whose
creativity was allowed by the momentary pause in the studios' power due to a
changing audience and the threat to profits from television. Then, the 1980s
saw the birth of blockbusters and the big studio was again in the game. The
independents from the 1990s continued into the new millennium, facilitated by
the development of technology, for filming and for dissemination. The second
decade of the new millennium seems to be ripe for a marriage between a
subjective approach and a blockbuster. Aronofsky's *Noah* presents a poetic
hybrid between a spectacle and an intimate vision, between general questions
facing humanity, and intimate and artistic answers to those questions.

The story of Noah, as written by Aronofsky and Handel, follows the Bible, but
with artistic freedom, giving a contemporary significance to one of the best-
known biblical stories. To accuse Aronofsky that he did not follow the standard
depiction of the white-bearded Noah leaving in his ark is ludicrous and would
be a waste of talent and of spectators' time, regardless of possible budgetary
considerations. In today's world, when a person is concerned with climate
changes, environmental pollution, the global financial crisis, political upheavals,
fear and awe regarding technology, and the general sense of possible impending
doom, the story of Noah, presented in an original and poetic way as Aronofsky
and Handel propose, begging for questions and not serving the old answers on a
platter, is timely and worthwhile. It is always a challenge to make a film about a
known character, either religious or mythological, or about a historical character:
How to connect historical narration and contemporary impact, adding layers of
meaning? The film created controversial receptions from religious communities,
evidenced by a number of articles and opinions published on the Internet. Even
before the final cut, a tension between Aronofsky and Paramount was evident in
test screenings of alternate cuts to get responses from religious audiences. Some
audiences "questioned the film's adherence to the Bible story and reacted
negatively to the intensity and darkness of the lead character,"[3] but the final cut
supported Aronofsky vision. However, Paramount Pictures stated a disclaimer

---

[3]   Kim Masters, "Rough Seas on 'Noah': Darren Aronofsky Opens up on the Biblical Battle to Woo
      Christians (and Everyone Else)," *The Hollywood Reporter* (2014), http://www.hollywoodreporter.
      com/news/rough-seas-noah-darren-aronofsky-679315.

Figure 6.1 Noah's dream of a flood (*Noah*, 2014)

referring to artistic license taken in the film. Furthermore, because of Islamic prohibition to show images of prophets, *Noah* was forbidden from a number of Muslim countries.

Aronofsky's *Noah* uses the biblical source to remind us of the first disaster upon humanity. Because of human irresponsibility toward life on earth, the Creator decides to punish humanity by preserving only the innocent and starting life anew. Hence, the punishment is to be delivered by a great flood in order to preserve the innocent from the guilty. The water has the ability to preserve as well as to destroy, unlike all-consuming fire. Noah, the righteous man (in Aronofsky's film, a vegetarian) lives peacefully with his wife and three sons, but has dream visions about the flood disaster to happen and what he should do, the significance of which is confirmed by his grandfather Methuselah. He has a great responsibility: to decide who is innocent and who is not, who lives and who dies. It seems unfair to place such a burden on one man's shoulder, but Noah takes it as a request from the Creator, to be obeyed and not to be questioned.

The movie presents the separation of good from evil along two different lines. First, there is Noah's version, the strict separation between humanity and the rest of life, the world of animals and plants. Second, there is the implied inseparability of good and evil in humanity, something that characterizes Noah's psychological adventure and his transformation. In Noah's interpretation, animals are all shown as innocent and as victims of human greed, intolerance, and brutality. The same goes for plants, with scenes showing barren land and the dry stumps of trees, with only a few bushes. The small, delicate white flower that Noah's son Ham picks up is just one of a few such flowers, indicating the plant's innocence and vulnerability. He gets a lesson from Noah: "They have a purpose. They sprout and they bloom, the wind takes the seeds and more flowers grow. We only collect what we can use. And nothing more. You understand?"[4] The barren area is miraculously replanted from the seed from the Garden of Eden given to Noah by his grandfather Methuselah, so that Noah and his helpers can build the ark, providing an example of "collecting what needs to be used." Despite usability, the cutting of trees results in deforestation as in the clearing around the ark as it is being built. The animals in the film are shown only as innocent victims, which raises an issue. We can argue that the animal world shows brutality as well and not only for satisfying bare needs. A stronger animal kills a weaker one to eat, to survive, but sometimes that does not appear to be the only reason. When a cat kills a mouse, or gets its paws on a bird's hatchling, and delivers it in front of its owner's door to show its hunter's expertise, it seems that it is not done out of hunger necessity, but out of some instinct to show force. A number of natural disasters can be attributed to some animal species going out of control, destroying plant life or another animal species. We can argue that when a beautiful deer eats shrubs and new trees down to the bark, destroying vegetation, it does it out of hunger, and it is unconscious of the future consequences. Plants can also show aggressiveness, as when a plant with stronger roots arrests the growth of a less aggressive plant. There are even carnivorous plants that find nutrients from insects, that is, animals. Maybe in the wish to underline humanity, the film does not question the survival impulse—the mixture of innocence and brutality—in *all* life forms, including animals and plants. Man is a different creature, endowed with consciousness about possible consequences, and with the power to interfere in various ways with the environment: with the knowledge of irrigation to make the dry land fertile and with the power to destroy the naturally fertile land.

Hence, the line between good and evil negotiated by humanity is a very porous line. And this is where the movie *Noah* attains its biggest strength and its poetic import. Noah is a vegetarian, convinced of the innocence of animals. (We wonder if his tent was ever attacked by a wild animal or how he perceives the serpent that tempted Eve to take the forbidden fruit. The innocent snakeskin that a serpent sheds in its transformation becomes a talisman for prosperity and fortune.) But, Noah sees the arrogance and brutality of man and is eventually

---

[4]   Darren Aronofsky and Ari Handel, *Noah* (New York: Rizzoli, 2014), 12.

convinced that humanity needs to be extinguished in the new world after the flood, and he is ready to sacrifice his two newborn granddaughters. Despite his conviction that only the innocent will come on board of the ark, his family shows cracks in their relations, unable to dispense with human desires. His determination is based on his dream visions and miraculous signs (a suddenly sprouting flower and bursting vegetation to provide wood for the ark), showing how a truly religious person does not question God's will, but is ready to carry it out at all costs. In this respect, he prefigures his successor Abraham ready to sacrifice his son Isaak. The heavy moral dilemma facing Noah is the decision of who will survive and who will not. Noah goes through a transformation, and the film depicts his agony and the pain of making decisions that go against his emotions. He first decides to save his family, including the adopted daughter Ila, a survivor of a massacre. So, he assumes that she is innocent and worthy of joining his family. When his son Ham laments that he is alone and will need a wife to start a life after the flood, Noah goes to the tent city and observes a trade between starving refugees and Tubal-Cain's soldiers, trading boys to become soldiers and girls to provide sex, in order to get meat. Noah is horrified by the sight. The screenplay written by Aronofsky and Handel reads, "... Noah takes the step forward, he has to stop it. And then he sees someone stronger than the others fight his way out of the crowd. This STRONG MAN smashes others away. He carries a large chunk of meat in his hands. He takes a big bite and turns to look at Noah. The STRONG MAN is Noah himself."[5] This convinces Noah that wickedness exists in *all* humanity and that humanity should be extinguished. His wife Naameh tries to convince him otherwise by mentioning their three sons' goodness (Shem's loyalty, Ham's integrity, and Japheth's kindness), but Noah sees it differently and responds that, "Shem is blinded by desire. Ham is covetous. Japheth lives only to please." He is determined to organize the eradication of the human race, giving instruction to his children as to who will bury whom. When by a miracle Ila gets pregnant and gives birth to twin daughters, Noah is determined to kill them, but in the last moment he cannot do it, dropping the knife. Afterward, he confesses to Ila that he was not able to kill the babies since all he had in his heart was love. Hence, humanity is not guided only by brutal impulses or by destructive impulses for survival based on physical needs, but also by love and by sacrifice. Human desire might be irrational, but it is part of our nature. A nice touch in the film is Methuselah's craving for berries in the

[5]   Ibid., 57–58.

scene when he searches for a berry, in the last moment of his over 900-years-long life, the flooding apocalypse approaching, and he smiles, happy to find a berry, and ready to die.[6]

The unusual and surprising characters in the film are the Watchers, the fallen angels punished because of their helping humans by providing them with knowledge that the humans, in turn, used to destroy their own habitat. The Watchers are depicted as a kind of prehistoric transformers, in an artistic vision connecting the longing for the natural world of the past and the apprehension of the technological world of the future, enhanced with powers that surpass humanity. The Watchers contain a divine light trapped into their irregular shapes made of rock and mud, suggesting life's entrapment in hostile environment. They are giants with six "arms" who decide to help Noah build his ark and to fight against Tubal-Cain and his followers. The way they move resembles the movements of a transformer, and it reflects the contemporary fascination with nonhuman creatures that can either help or harm humanity. The Watchers add to the mythological fantasy world of preflood life. On the one hand, they convey a sense of apprehension related to the dry and destroyed land we see; but on the other hand, they project a sense of adventure and curiosity that enlivens the barren land.

The story of Noah and Campbell's view of mythology

The story of Noah leads us to "the hero with a thousand faces," as presented in Campbell's writing and elaborated in Vogler's "A practical guide...," for moviemakers. According to Campbell, the patterns in all myths coincide, showing similarities in the main elements of a hero's journey, despite differences in details. The common players in an adventure lead to Jungian archetypes and testify to the common unconscious. In an interview with Bill Moyers for PBS in 1988, Campbell talks about the power of myth.[7] For Campbell, God is the ultimate word for transcendence. He states:

"Transcendent" is a technical, philosophical word, translated in two different ways. In Christian theology, it refers to God as being beyond or outside the field of nature. That is a materialistic way of talking about the transcendent, because

---

[6] The scene in the film adds some humor and acceptance of death with dignity. In the comic book version, this scene is missing, and it is Ila who gives berries to Methuselah. Darren Aronofsky, Ari Handel, and Nico Henrichon, *Noah* (Berkeley, CA: Image Comics, Inc., 2014), Book 2, 41.

[7] Campbell and Moyers, *The Power of Myth*.

God is thought of as a kind of spiritual fact existing somewhere out there. . . . But "transcendent" properly means that which is beyond all concepts. Kant tells us that all of our experiences are bounded by time and space. . . . Being and nonbeing—those are categories. The word "God" properly refers to what transcends all thinking, but the word "God" itself is something thought about.[8]

In the movie *Noah*, the word *God* is not used; instead, the reference is to *The Creator*. This name seems more philosophically appropriate since it leaves out the whole iconography associated with representations of God, heavens, angels, and so on. But, it retains the essence of our world and the life on it as a creation, so that there has to be a Creator. Actually, God is mentioned only once in the movie when Ham talks to Tubal-Cain, "My father says there can be no king. The Creator is God."[9] The stories from Genesis could be understood as metaphors for human nature and not as historical facts, that is, not as happening according to our concepts of time and space. The duality of man is metaphorically presented in the fall from the timeless Garden of Eden, when Adam and Eve eat from the Tree of Knowledge of Good and Evil, that is, of opposites. Then they first realize they are different, male and female, and cover themselves in shame. Then they realize they are different from God, and hence, enter the difference between humanity and divinity. Then they start to differentiate between good and evil, and human nature is stuck in its duality. So, humanity begins from one forbidden thing. The snake is a symbol of leaving the innocence of past and continuing life: it sheds its skin, which is positive, but it can also have a negative meaning, temptation. Because it was Eve who took the forbidden fruit, it is the woman who brings in the world of polarities: she is the more dangerous one, plus she is the one who can deliver a new life. Hence, Noah's decision to kill a granddaughter while preserving a grandson is a pragmatic one.

Nowadays, the pace of life seems too fast for myth creation. Hence, it is not surprising that there is a proliferation of films with biblical themes (*Son of God* [Christopher Spencer, 2014], *Exodus* [Ridley Scott, 2014]). On the other hand, there are a number of films about technology and the end of world as we know it, for example, *Her* (Spike Jonze, 2013), *Transcendence* (Wally Pfister, 2014), and *Interstellar* (Christopher Nolan, 2014). Obviously, a contemporary person is on the threshold of great changes, needing the spiritual support from the past, to see what can be learned from the past. Also, our apprehension of the future finds an

[8] Ibid., 75–76.
[9] In the published screenplay, Ham says, "My father says there can be no king in The Creator's garden." Aronofsky and Handel, *Noah*, 48.

Figure 6.2 Extreme closeup of Noah and Tubal-Cain (*Noah*, 2014)

outlet in presentations of human–technology interaction. As Campbell writes, a myth can awaken awe, gratitude, and rapture with themes that have supported man's life over millennia. However, he reminds us that myths (including the stories from Genesis) should not be taken as literal historical events. Hence, without engaging in religious argumentation, it seems that biblical stories have the power to retain their relevance throughout changing times over millennia. In that sense, instead of being taken literally, they are more effective when taken as the template of a story around which a contemporary situation can be wrapped, telling us something about our current situation. Aronofsky could have made a standard Bible film such as the *Son of God*, and used the magic star power of Russell Crowe and other actors without taking risks. But, he took risks and created some controversy. His predecessors in biblical depictions with an auteur's mark include *The Last Temptation of Christ* (Martin Scorsese, 1988) and *The Passion of the Christ* (Mel Gibson, 2004).

Noah's character shows human imperfection, and goes through the hero's journey as underlined in Vogler's influential memo.[10] Noah carries the burden of

---

[10] Vogler summarizes the hero's journey, "The hero is introduced in his ordinary world, where he receives the call to adventure. He is reluctant at first but is encouraged by the wise old man or woman to cross the first threshold, where he encounters tests and helpers. He reaches the innermost cave, where he endures the supreme ordeal. He seizes the sword or the treasure and is pursued on the road back to his world. He is resurrected and transformed by his experience. He returns to his ordinary world with a treasure, boon, or elixir to benefit his world." Christopher Vogler, "A Practical Guide to Joseph Campbell's the Hero with a Thousand Faces" (1985).

seeing his father die, and when he is a grownup, his ordinary world is shattered, environmentally barely alive. He gets a call to adventure in dreams and visions. Uncertain of what it means, he needs the assurance from his mentor, the wise old man (who happens to be his grandfather). In the next act, he decides to build the ark, to "cross the threshold," going through battles with Tubal-Cain and his warriors, through a dilemma on whether to find wives for his sons or not. In addition to the enemies, he has unusual helpers, the Watchers. His faith in the mission to save life on earth is tested by his emotional allegiances as when he leaves Na'el, the girl Ham wanted to take to the ark. As the ark is completed and apocalypse hits the earth, Noah presents the story of creation, and the animals are peacefully asleep. But, there is an ordeal ahead, the consequence of Ham's tragic loss, the survival of Tubal-Cain on the ark, and the miraculous event of Ila's pregnancy. The ordeal ends with Tubal-Cain's death and with Noah's inability to kill his granddaughters, feeling remorse toward his assumed role. The reward of saving babies is put against his sense of being defeated, unable to deliver his chosen role. The road back from the adventure is not the return to the land, the resurrected land on earth, but to his family, and it is bumpy. In the new world, Noah is alone, drunk, full of remorse. He is resurrected in the moment when asked by Ila why he spared the babies, and he responds, "I looked down at those girls and all I had in my heart was love." Ila helps him to understand that his act is not a failure, but an act of love:

> He chose you for a reason, Noah. He showed you the wickedness of man and knew you would not look away. But when you looked you saw goodness, too. The choice was put in your hands because He put it there. He asked you to decide if we were worth saving. And you chose mercy. You chose love.[11]

Hence, Noah's resurrection occurs upon his understanding that innocence and sin, love, and hate, are inseparable in humanity, and he is ready to live with it. He returns to his wife Naameh, who accepts him, and they find peace together, a new beginning.

In Aronofsky's movie, the hero's journey ends cautiously happily, posing recurring questions about the human condition. The situation is not that peaceful, and the future in this new world carries uncertain elements. The set of survivors does not include wives for Noah's three sons, hence the futures of Ham and Japheth are left ambiguous, and the new world is not free of sin, leading to

---

[11] Aronofsky and Handel, *Noah*, 123–24.

subsequent disaster stories as told by the Bible and by various myths in other cultures. As in all Aronofsky's films, the ending is ambiguous: something is won; something is lost, and maybe it is the best of the worst possible endings. There is a ray of hope, but cautious hope.

Exteriority versus interiority in *Noah*: audio/visual elements

Unlike *The Fountain*, *Noah* uses computer-generated special effects extensively. The collaboration with the Industrial Light & Magic (ILM) Company (a division of Lucasfilm) resulted in many innovative solutions, from creating the whole animal kingdom, flood scenes, and the poetical story of evolution. An article by Ian Failes describes the technical aspects of the effects, and the collaborative nature between the various filmmakers who contributed ideas. When discussing the evolution scene, Failes writes, "On the ark, Noah describes to his family the history of creation on Earth. The accompanying imagery is a two-minute long exploration of 14 billion years of evolution, told in a timelapse 'staccato' form. ILM handled the unique sequence, which took a year to do...."[12] As a viewer lacking technical knowledge of computer-generated imagery and effects, I can only restrict my comments to the impact the effects produce.

Noah opens with the black screen, insinuating nothingness, and then the story starts in inter-titles cross-cut with the images of a serpent, an apple, and a murderous hand, accentuated by strong sound. The close-ups of those images are separated by images of the immensity of sky in a fast-moving rhythm. This beginning of the film (the use of symbols associated with the first sin, the fast cross-cutting) conditions the viewer to expect a poetic audio/visual description of a known biblical story. The unexpected creatures (Watchers) come into focus first in a close-up, then the focus moves away (in a CGI scene resembling a tracking shot) to introduce the environment split horizontally into a darkened barren land and a light sky, prefiguring the thematic issue of light versus darkness, or good versus evil. The fast editing pace to depict changes over thousands of years, with one shape changing into another, creates a sense of awe, and the viewer is caught by the allure of the audio/visual narrative, oscillating between intimacy and distance. The close-ups provoke the viewer's sensibility and preconscious bodily movement,

---

[12] Ian Failes, "Character Ark: The Visual Effects of *Noah*," *Fxguide* (2014), http://www.fxguide.com/featured/character-ark-the-visual-effects-of-noah/.

creating a virtual environment in which he or she inhabits the scene, resulting in empathy and a sense of adventure. The scenes with wide perspectives, with changing environments and the contraction of time provoke the viewer's sense of being an objective observer with mixed feelings of significance (omnipotent observer) and insignificance (with respect to the immensity of space and time). The effect on viewers mimics the story to be told about the contradictory nature of humanity. This rather detailed description of the beginning of the film serves to underline the approach of Aronofsky and his collaborators toward the importance of the initial effect. In this way, a viewer is instantly transported into the virtual reality of the moving images, when the mind suddenly summarizes all the consequences and the symbolism of the first sin, and the neuronal activity leads to embodied simulation. The viewer is ready for the story to unfold. The narrative starts as an action movie, with a sweeping panoramic view and suggestive music. Mansell's recognizable music tonality and performance by the Kronos Quartet create a composite mood of importance mixed with vulnerability, of nostalgia mixed with fear, nodding to life's ups and downs and the unstoppable passage of time. A cut that shows a child develop into a grownup introduces Noah as the main character. A close-up shot counter-shot between Noah and his wife Naameh, with seductive voices and with only their faces illuminated in the darkness by soft light, creates a dream-like feeling. Indeed, it serves as a precursor to Noah's initial dream of the flood, and the subsequent poetic image of the silhouettes of Noah and Naameh against the crimson redness of the awakening day.

Numerous special effects work to distort time and space (e.g., suddenly sprouting trees, protruding rivers changing the environment, suddenly changed shapes of the man-made environment), and present exaggerated movement (e.g., a horde of animals moving toward the ark, a commotion of people in the tent city, battle scenes). The most stunning and the most poetical use of special effects is in the two-minute sequence of the evolution story narrated by Noah to his offspring. A viewer is lead into a trip following fast-moving images of the speculated birth of our world, the evolution of living creatures, the miraculous arrival of Adam and Eve, the first sin and expulsion from the Garden of Eden, and the subsequent centuries of various combatants, but with unchanged urge to kill each other and to destroy the habitat. Regardless of different subjective views of evolution versus creationism, a viewer can enjoy the artistic imagination and cinematic expertise able to make the sequence and to trigger his or her consciousness of the body prior to making judgments of agreement or disagreement with the message of the scene.

Figure 6.3 Arrival of Adam and Eve in Noah's story of creation (*Noah*, 2014)

Figure 6.4 An image from the sequence of fast cuts presenting the history of combatants (*Noah*, 2014)

From a viewer's perspective, *Noah* provokes the feeling of a dream-like experience, as if a contemporary man reads the story of Noah in Genesis, and afterward, dreams about it. The dream combines elements of the story, but adjusted to contemporary apprehensions and fears.

As a man hardened by the harsh realities of everyday life, without experiencing the beauty and joy of life, and with the sheer struggle for survival, Noah from the beginning shows his hardened soul. When Noah's young son Ham picks up the small white flower, in all the innocence of a child who sees beauty and follows the instinct to hold on to it, Noah delivers a lecture that "we only collect what we can use," forgetting that we need beauty as well as bare necessities for sustaining physical bodily needs. This incident helps to position the character of Noah, and the subsequent tension and final parting with Ham. The encounters with Tubal-Cain and his warriors, the view of hungry people in the tent city, and the stubbornness with the irrational task to separate innocence from guilt plays out in cinematographically stunning dream sequences as well as in close-ups of characters' faces, following all three generations (old Methuselah; middle-aged Noah, Tubal-Cain, and Naameh; and young Ham and Ila).

Methuselah's face shows wisdom, a trace of playfulness, as confirming that in old age (here: very old), we resume a childish sense of wonder and desire. Methuselah's desire presented in the search for a berry amid the approaching apocalypse parallels Ham's desire when picking a flower to hold on to beauty. Both desires are an irrational but integral part of complex human nature, cherished and irreplaceable. Noah's face shows determination to fulfill the role for which he was chosen, followed by the pain of sacrifice, be it of the intimacy of his family, as a parent unable to follow the wishes of all his children, or be it on a larger scale when he is determined to let innumerable people die by forbidding their entrance to the ark. Are all those people really guilty? In the tent city, they were shown as motivated by starvation and not by bacchanalias such as in Roman times, that is, motivated by the lack of the basic means to support life and not by an unrestrained waste of resources. They were "hungry, frightened, desperate."[13] Tubal-Cain's face shows aggression, but also the conviction that he is doing the right thing, as when he shouts toward the skies, "I am a man made in your image. Why do you not converse with me?" He is Noah's shadow, equally convinced of the rightness of what he is doing.[14] The face of Noah's wife, Naameh, shows the transformation from accepting his lead and convictions to finally realizing his hardened soul, unable to follow him upon his decision to kill the babies, and making a clear moral and emotional line that cannot be overstepped. The younger protagonists, Ham and Ila, project innocence mixed with desire,

---

[13] Aronofsky, Handel, and Henrichon, *Noah*, 45, Book 2.

[14] In the graphic novel, Noah negotiates with Tubal-Cain to accept twenty-five of his men with women on the ark, leaving it to Tubal-Cain to make a choice. But, Noah does not intend to keep the promise, afterward mimicking God's rage because man was warned, but did nothing. Ibid., 24, 64, Book 2.

adding sadness to the mix, Ham because of his lost girlfriend, Ila because of the fear of losing babies. The ending shows Ham leaving for the unpopulated world, alone and saddened, carrying within himself the curse and the promise of humanity: innocence, desire, setbacks, loneliness, determination, courage, and never-ending hope. Over the end credits, Patti Smith and the Kronos Quartet perform Smith's original song written for the film, "Mercy Is," which was also a lullaby song between Noah and Ila in the film. Smith's performance over the end credits leads a spectator to a meditative state, pondering the themes explored in the film, adding a ray of hope, and finally, adding to the overall poetry of Noah's biblical story and the film.

Aronofsky's direction and Libatique's cinematography skillfully oscillate between the panoramic views of the external environment and close-ups of the protagonists' faces, the complex terrain of internal environment. Hence, despite extensive use of CGI, of aerial and panoramic images to present the environment, of mass fighting scenes, and of hordes of animals entering the ark, the film retains the strength of an intimate character study. The camera moves capture actors presenting humanity in its full complexity, in all the shades between innocence and brutality, fear and hope, responsibility and desire. Artistic sensibility uncovers some hidden relations, as if slightly lifting the veil, and forces us to see some aspects of reality more clearly. In an artistic drama, nature comes into conflict with society, creating tension and the need to question

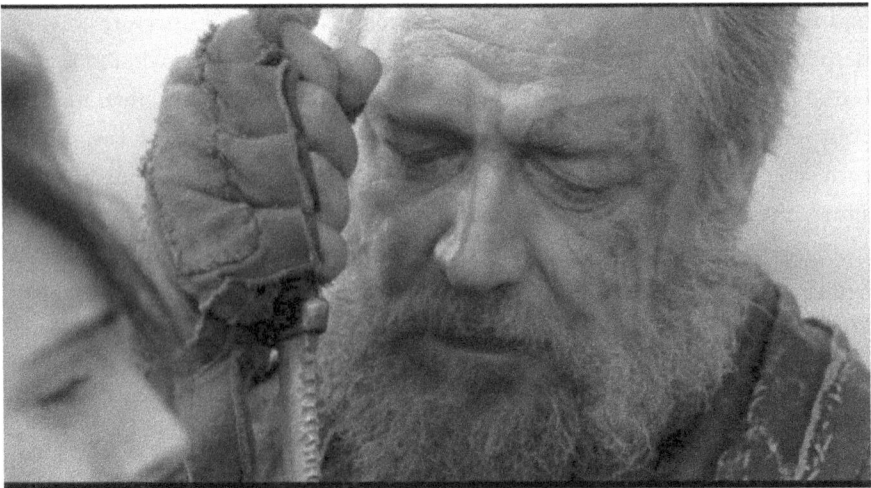

Figure 6.5 Noah's moment of decision (*Noah*, 2014)

ourselves; it speaks to an individual. In *Noah*, the close-ups are used frequently, as if searching for the reality on the characters' faces.

At the end, the film presents Aronofsky's recurring theme of death and rebirth. Noah and his family start a new life in the New World, but that life is not completely new, and the seeds of that life carry all the previous seeds, starting with the seed from the Garden of Eden with all its innocence and goodness residing in man, to the subsequent seeds transformed by life on earth, by the necessity to fight for survival, combining beauty with usefulness to carry on the double-sword of human progress. And, as we know, the apocalypse of Noah was subsequently repeated in other doomsday stories, for example, the story of the Tower of Babel. As told in Genesis, when God realized the futility of the Great Flood, the inability of water to separate the innocent from the guilty, he decided to change his tactic and let people carry their own punishment: the misunderstanding among them.

In many aspects, *Noah* can be seen as a kind of prequel to Aronofsky's *The Fountain*, also written jointly with Handel. Life continues after the great flood and Noah's ordeal, and humanity is forever trapped in its duality of opposites, unable to reconcile them in its finite lifetime. The way out is the search for immortality, but immorality is again misunderstood in the literal sense as the everlasting long life, instead of its being understood as a metaphor for the continuous cycle of death and rebirth. There is the lifespan of an individual, and of a civilization ... so, could we not expand upon this notion to say that there is also the lifespan of a planet, a galaxy ...? The mystery of life will exist as long as there *is* life, and the apprehension of, or anxiety about its transformations along the death-rebirth circular movement will accompany its mystery as long as there is hope to sustain life as we know it. To be completely hopeless amounts to total annihilation. To be hopeful, but accepting of mortality as a natural part of human life, allows us to use our time in as fulfilling a way as possible.

Aronofsky has a talent for exposing flaws in human nature, with original camera moves and command of *mise-en-scène*, in *Noah* as well as in all his other movies, but he also projects the never-ending hope, exhibited in various ways. And it is always a concern how to find a conciliation after being pulled in an extreme direction, be it *obsession* ending after the realization that the true unifying pattern is the one inside you (in *π*), or the *addiction* to the American Dream giving way to American Reality (in *Requiem*), or the *reconciliation with the necessity of death* as a prerequisite for life (in *The Fountain*), or the *sacrifice of death* (in *The Wrestler*), or the *artistic sacrifice to achieve perfection* (in *Black Swan*), or finally, the *sacrifice of responsibility overturned by love* (in *Noah*). Aronofsky's filmography from 1998 to 2014, consisting of six feature films, points to a sensibility combining fierceness in its presentation of human brutality and compassion in its presentation of human weaknesses, adding a romantic strand when presenting sacrifice, death, and love. Contemporary themes lurking behind the biblical setting of *Noah* continue Aronofsky's questioning of humanity, repeating some relationships from his previous films, such as: a sense of being a chosen one (as Max in π), stubbornness to go against the views of others (as Tommy in *The Fountain*), acceptance of death (as Randy in *The Wrestler*), the challenges of parent–child relationship (as in *Black Swan*), the mentor figure (as in π and *Black Swan*). In addition to presenting a continuation of Aronofsky's own artistic preoccupations, *Noah* invites a consideration of some other directors whose filmic sensibility can be traced in its visual and narrative elements.

Noah as combination of various cinematic sensibilities

When writing about *The Fountain*, I positioned Aronofsky's sensibility in presenting the human condition between Kubrick's and Spielberg's sensibilities. While Kubrick and Spielberg did different movies, it seems that they understood each other, maybe as each other's "shadow" (to use the Jungian archetype) as evidenced by Kubrick's request that Spielberg direct his *A.I.* project. In *Noah*, Aronofsky clearly uses elements of the Spielberg filmic arsenal. For example, Noah's fighting expertise, his fascination with the task ahead, his imperfections, yet his charisma to win over the spectator, especially when compared with the bad guy, displays similarities with, say, Indiana Jones. However, Noah is no Indy—his moral turbulence, his sense of responsibility, and the unbearable weight of the decision he needs to make marks him for a sacrifice. While Spielberg's sense of adventure is present in *Noah*, the darkness and ambiguity of the character leads to the questioning of the ambiguous ending of his adventure. It is not the case that the spectator exits the theater, rejuvenated by the sense of adventure, exalted by the punishment brought upon the bad guys, and endeared to the happy ending in which the hero gets his girl. So, here comes Aronofsky's Kubrick-like sensibility in depicting elements of human nature that make us stubborn, aggressive, insensitive, and convinced of the infallibility of a carefully prepared plan. But, being a humanist does not imply providing a sugar coating to realistic flaws in human nature. Hence, Kubrick does not seem less of a humanist than Spielberg, rather just of a different sensibility.

Noah has been compared with DeMille's films, mostly his biblical epics, for example *The Ten Commandments* (Cecil B. DeMille, 1956). This is an appropriate comparison, with strong cinematography, interesting story, and a dominant leading character, and even DeMille's film received complaints about discrepancies between the film narrative and the Bible. But, *The Ten Commandments* is a different story, and Moses' character shows courage, determination, revenge—but no moral dilemmas like those facing Noah. DeMille's spectacle does not provoke questions about the environment since that was not on the agenda then. Yet, the film was politically and economically motivated. Due to the Cold War threat, social insecurities translated into increased religious sensibility, in opposition to the atheist Soviet Block. In addition, spectacles of such magnitudes were used by studios against the threat of TV.

While the biblical thematic and the presentation of a spectacle invites comparison with DeMille, Aronofsky's style has some similarity with the style of von Stroheim, a silent film auteur who was already mentioned when discussing *The Wrestler*. The work of von Stroheim shows his preoccupation with human deficiencies, be they emotional instability, arrogance, or greed. The realism of von Stroheim consists in the power of the moving image to present reality in its dual nature: the exterior of the objective world and the interior of human emotions. He achieved this by the movement of his camera, consisting of long shots without tricks of excessive montage, and by close-ups revealing details that provoke our moral sense. Without dialogue, the movement of his images increases the burden of capturing the motivations of his characters in the actions they undertake, and the emotions they develop. For many of his movies, he was also the screenwriter, moving the story forward with inter-titles often witty and ironic (e.g., referring to a prostitute as "the woman of a horizontal position"). André Bazin highly valued von Stroheim's style of the slow-moving camera emphasizing details, stating, "In his films reality lays itself bare like a suspect confessing under the relentless examination of the commissioner of police. He has one simple rule for direction. Take a close look at the world, keep on doing so, and in the end it will lay bare for you all its cruelty and its ugliness."[15]

---

[15] Bazin, *What Is Cinema?*, Vol. 1, 27.

Von Stroheim presents base human deficiencies without mercy, without DeMille's romanticism. Aronofsky's filmic sensibility has elements of DeMille's inclination for big themes, von Stroheim's fierceness in dismantling human brutality and destructive forces, Spielberg's sense of adventure and hopefulness, and Kubrick's critique of the single-mindedness and arrogance of men asking for disaster. This combination comprises auteurs from the very beginning of cinema to the current time, and provides a contemporary yet classic feel of an Aronofsky film.

In addition to the aforementioned directors, there are two older films that have some relevance with *Noah*, namely, the appeal of a biblical story to shed light on contemporary society. Fritz Lang used the biblical story of the Tower of Babel in his sci-fi silent masterpiece *Metropolis* (Fritz Lang, 1927). From the filming of *Metropolis*, the human condition has obviously changed: the machine revolution is replaced by financial and high-tech revolutions, the son creates wealth independently of his father, and resolution/mediation seems impossible. Yet, *Metropolis* presents a future story (set in 2026) that relies on the biblical story, the buildup of the Tower of Babel. The biblical story invokes Nimrod (a great-grandson of Noah, a grandson of Ham, Noah's son, who in Aronofsky's movie walks alone at the end) as the tyrant who made people dependent on him and distanced from God, which resulted in God's punishment by the creation of various languages and misunderstandings among people, instead of bringing another great flood since people did not learn from it. The biblical story of Noah is optimistic, a new beginning, and Noah's covenant with God is valid for all life on earth. The new beginning is addressed in the film *Noah* in an interesting way. Namely, the second decade of the twenty-first century seems fertile for capitalization on digital-era technology in a creative way, for example, using CGI not only as a tool to augment the visual field, but as a creative tool to augment the perception of human life. In *Noah*, CGI is used to create the "most complex animals," with each animal a bit different from the animals existing in the current animal world, suggesting a cycle of death and rebirth as a difference in repetition, evocative of the philosophy of becoming of Gilles Deleuze.[16] This seems a creative way to insinuate that there is a cyclic rhythm to life as a repetition and a difference: being born, dying, and being born again, but different. However, the remnants of the old world stayed, as a past that can never

---

[16] Gilles Deleuze, *Difference and Repetition*, trans. Paul Patton (New York: Columbia University Press, 1994).

be completely erased, in the overarching continuity of life. Human nature in all its complexity survived the flood, continuing its destiny toward other adventures.

Another film related to the story of Noah, with contemporary flavor, is *Noah's Ark* (Michael Curtiz, 1928), made during the transition of the silent film to the talkie. While Curtiz afterward gave us classics such as *Casablanca* (1943) and *Mildred Pierce* (1945), *Noah's Ark* is less known, and was afterward semi-restored. The film presents the relation of the biblical story of Noah and the contemporary story during World War I, with actors playing dual roles, biblical and contemporary, comparing the great flood with the flood of blood of World War I. The film concludes with a happy ending, but Curtiz shows his fascination with moral dilemmas, responsibility, and sacrifice. Interestingly, Curtiz's film starts with the presentation of the Tower of Babel and the worship of the golden calf symbolizing greed and the accumulation of wealth, switching to a contemporary scene of a murder due to bankruptcy, insinuating man's transformation into wickedness due to greed. In the graphic novel by Aronofsky et al., after his vision of the flood, Noah decides to warn the people and goes to Bab-ilim, a city with a central tower. His pleas for change are not accepted; he is ridiculed by Tubal-Cain, and expelled from the city.[17] This scene is not in the film, but the consideration of both stories, the story of Noah and the story of the Tower of Babylon, albeit without considering the official chronology, insinuates the circular character of human development: starting anew, then succumbing to a cataclysmic event, then repeating the pattern of behavior.

Noah's story is the perfect example of a tough moral choice. Aronofsky illustrates the psychological journey of a man with the grave responsibility of deciding who lives and who dies, and this decision is based on the verdict of who is innocent and who is not. How can complete innocence be recognized, if it exists at all? How can such a decision be made in an ethics based on moral laws proclaimed by humanity? It seems that such a decision should lead to the sense of guilt. And this is where the morality questions raised by the film *Noah* lead to Kierkegaard's writing about duty toward God and absolute faith, presented by using the story of the sacrifice of Abraham.

---

[17] Aronofsky, Handel, and Henrichon, *Noah*, 18–24, Book 1.

The sacrifice of Noah versus the sacrifice of Abraham

Kierkegaard published *Fear and Trembling* in 1843 under the pseudonym Johannes de Silencio. The book is concerned with the issue of faith and the character of Abraham in light of his sacrifice. The story about Abraham's willingness to sacrifice his son Isaak is recounted in the Bible as the ultimate story about faith and Abraham is praised as the "father of faith."

Kierkegaard is concerned with the internal ordeal that Abraham had to go through to arrive at the decision to perform the sacrifice. Viewed in terms of human ethics and morality, Abraham is a murderer. Viewed in terms of faith and belief in God, Abraham is innocent. This is a paradox of human existence, one of many paradoxes stemming from the inability to reconcile good and evil, and innocence and guilt, in finite human time. Kierkegaard is considered to be the first existentialist, prefiguring writers such as Dostoevsky and Kafka, and philosophers such as Nietzsche, Heidegger, and Sartre, among others. The credo that "existence precedes essence" implies that there are no initially given essential forms that a person inhabits, but that each person is an individual making his or her own choices, and such choices define the person. In existence, we are often required to make ethical or moral decisions, and morality is related to the preservation of the social habitat. Morality arises from the difference between good and evil, between positive and negative as understood by humanity. This duality cannot be reconciled in finite time because in finite time there is a pressure to accomplish something, to get something, to secure something, to learn something—leading to a struggle over the means of securing existence. Dualities could only be dispensed with in a timeless, absolute environment. The absolute cannot be thought because we think in concepts based on relative senses of time and space (in time something is before, something after; in space something is inside, something outside). Being stuck with mortality and finite time, the only way out is to achieve an internal spiritual enlightenment beyond thought and description in language, hence Kierkegaard's pseudonym de Silencio.

Kierkegaard argues that the religious mode of existence brings *infinity* into ethics, and we enter into the "infinite relationship with God." The impossibility of redemption due to the finality of existence, argues Kierkegaard, results with the thought that against God we are always in the wrong. With the thought of "being in the wrong," we can atone or expiate for the inability to comprehend the complexity of human nature, the mixture of good and evil residing in every human.[18] This thought produces despair and the need for repentance, which is an expression of love for God, and "the expression of the fact that evil is an essential part of me, and at the same time the expression of the fact that it is not essentially a part of me."[19] Repentance is concrete and positions an individual in the environment, the surroundings; hence, it belongs to the sphere of the ethical, producing duties. The foremost duty is to have faith in God so that the consciousness of such a duty is our "assurance of the eternal validity of his being."[20] Such a duty overrides human morality (for example, Kantian morality based on maxims and the categorical imperative).

The question of whether there is an absolute duty to God, surpassing all duties based on human morality is the basic question Kierkegaard poses in *Fear and Trembling*, and tries to answer based on the story of Abraham and Isaak. We can argue that all moral duties come from God, but such thinking results in a religion useful for social interactions, viewing God as an abstract entity supporting our own morality, and not a supreme entity that can command unconditionally. If true faith exists, it is paradoxical, outside reason and morality, unprovable and irrational. The sacrifice of Abraham is personal, different from the sacrifices by some other mythical parents of their children, because he is willing to do it for no reason other than to follow God's wish, in a "leap of faith." When Agamemnon decides to sacrifice his daughter Iphigenia, he does it for a reason, to help the Greeks win the war; hence, in his case, the reason for doing it is not personal. Because Abraham's duty to obey God is so personal, he cannot talk about it, nobody would understand it. There is nothing heroic in Abraham's story, and he goes through pain because of his duty to perform such a horrific act, but his faith in God is unshaken, absolute. Kant interprets Abraham's story completely differently: for Kant, God can only ask to perform moral duties, so if we are tempted with such a vision from God as Abraham was, it is probably a faulty vision because God would never command somebody to kill his son; it is completely contrary to the human sense of morality.

[18] The primordial existence of both good and evil in humanity and its relation to human freedom was proposed in the philosophy of F.W.J. Schelling. Schelling's philosophy characterizes human desire and yearning with the separation of *the ground* of existence from existence itself, creating the separation between darkness and light, and between good and evil, but both good and evil being *primordial*. Hence, according to Schelling, evil is natural to men as much as goodness. The evil in men did not arise because of deprivation or some lack, but because of the incompatibility of the ground with existence, that is, because evil is primary, not derived. Without being predestined, an action as actualization of the existential ground can be as much evil as it can be good, and humanity is stuck between rationality and irrationality. Schelling, *The Freedom Essay*, 36.
[19] Søren Kierkegaard, *Either/Or: A Fragment of Life*, trans. Alastair Hannay (New York: Penguin Books, 1992), 525.
[20] Ibid., 556.

In *Fear and Trembling*, in the section titled "Speech in Praise of Abraham," while writing about the greatness of men, Kierkegaard writes:

> There was one who was great in his strength, and one who was great in his wisdom, and one who was great in hope, and one who was great in love; but greater than all was Abraham, great with that power whose strength is powerlessness, great in that wisdom whose secret is folly, great in that hope whose outward form is insanity, great in that love which is hatred of self.[21]

To use the modern jargon, Abraham's task was well defined: he had to sacrifice his only son Isaak, an absolutely insane request because there was no ambiguity of whether Isaak is guilty or not since Isaak was clearly innocent. Hence, it was a pure request for the leap of faith. Noah, as presented in Aronofsky's film, faces an ambiguous and impossible task: to decide who is innocent and who is not, and to deliver a verdict who deserves to live and who does not. How could he do it? Described according to the vocabulary that Kierkegaard uses for Abraham, Noah's wisdom is based on the folly of proclaiming all humanity to be guilty, his hope to end the human race is based on the insane decision to kill his newborn grandchildren, and his strength is achieved in powerlessness to deliver the deadly blow. Finally, his heart full of love (as he confesses to Ila) results in his hatred of self, his sense of failure. But, as miraculously as Abraham's son was spared and Abraham was rewarded by his absolute faith in God, Noah's peace is restored, and Noah is rewarded by his love for humanity, seeing that innocence exists in humanity, albeit, not in its pure form, but in a mixture with guilt. Hence, Kierkegaard's quote could apply to Noah as presented in the film. Aronofsky and Handel retell the biblical story of Noah and the Great Flood by combining the notions of sacrifice, duty, love, redemption, and projecting it upon contemporary terrain.

Despite being advertised as a blockbuster, *Noah* as well as *The Fountain* need more than one viewing to fully appreciate their artistic merit. The philosophical issues about the human condition are not readily available, and *Noah* provokes by its questioning, staying clear of easy and simple answers, and in the process, delivering a strong cinematic experience. While the morality of the story plays out on the barren landscape and the worn-out faces of the protagonists, the poetry shines from many scenes, for example, from the poetical sequence of images illustrating the story of evolution; from the images of silhouettes of Noah and Naameh against the crimson sky, blurring the boundaries between interior

[21]   *Fear and Trembling*, trans. Alastair Hannay (New York: Penguin Books, 1985), 50.

Figure 6.6 Ham, Noah's son, who walks alone at the end (*Noah*, 2014)

and exterior; from the sequence presenting the original sin (snake—apple—a silhouette of Cain's hand murdering Abel) repeated three times in the film; and from the dream sequences when water consumes all and only some float toward the surface.

The film's artistic import is, to some extent, pronounced in the controversy it generated. There are scenes displaying the text from Genesis as when, in the silent movies, viewers had inter-titles to describe what was going on. It seems like a dedication to being factually correct, to read Genesis as literally as possible. And then, what is presented shows the futility of such determination, the foolishness of restricting the immensely rich text of Genesis to a set of historical facts. Just as Noah at the end cannot kill his granddaughters because all he has in his heart is love, so Aronofsky cannot stick to the predominant religious view and literal reading of Noah's story because of his artistic credo forcing him to illustrate on the big screen the human inability to separate innocence from brutality. This credo gives *Noah* a distinctly personal touch. Noah gets the inspiration, the call in his dreams and visions, to do the incredibly challenging task of preserving innocent life on earth, having detractors (Tubal-Cain) and helpers (the Watchers), and the complexity of the relations with his closest people (his family). It seems that this scenario was somewhat followed in the production of *Noah*: Aronofsky talked about his early fascination with the story of Noah, his winning essay, and the inspiration for becoming a storyteller, that is, his "call to adventure." The production of the film had detracting constraints (budget, touchy religious subject), and helpers by a whole team of creative artists. The complexity of finding the proper unifying voice, and of delivering a film of such visual imagery, allowing for criticisms and approvals from both the religious and the atheists, seems an impossible task. Aronofsky did it in his own way, creating an aesthetically strong and philosophically interesting film.

On Auteurship, Aronofsky's Themes
and Stylistic Signature

I think starting with something that is very much grounded in reality, and then trying to add to it and make it something more, helps. That often happens when an actor gets involved, especially with really talented actors. They are always thinking how to make their characters special. They don't stop at the screenplay level, they try to add to it, and bring something to it. Then your job as a director is to try to work with them and make sure those ideas don't go too far, don't contradict other ideas, so that it sort of works for the movie.

Darren Aronofsky, December 2, 2013

Considering the six Aronofsky's films from 1998 to 2014, I wish to argue that they testify to the recognizable artistic sensibility of an *auteur*. The notion of an auteur is a debatable issue, allowing for different characterizations.

The auteur theory in cinema started in postwar France with film critics' questioning of film's reliance on literature and their sensing the need to free the visual power of film from the written word of literature. In 1953, Truffaut wrote a manifesto, *A Certain Tendency of the French Cinema*, advocating for pure cinema, free from the incarceration of literature. Despite the Hollywood film factory organized and run by the studios, analysis could unearth authentic auteur-directors behind mass production and popular culture. In writing about New German Cinema, Thomas Elsaesser considers the authorship function through self-expression and self-representation.[1] The filmmaker as an artist encompasses two contradictory characteristics: as far as production is concerned, he is part of the capitalist and technological world, but ideologically he should be set apart, independent of the ideology subtending the very capitalism he acknowledges by production. The specific nature of film as art is that it is a complex and very

[1] Thomas Elsaesser, *New German Cinema: A History* (New Brunswick, NJ: Rutgers University Press, 1989).

expensive process, involving many people, so its production has to be managed and calculated economically, with a view to at least recovering the cost, if not making a profit. These constraints had to be approached in a careful way, to ensure the possibility of making another film afterward. The creativity of many auteurs can be sensed in the way they juggle the production/economic/spectator constraints with the need to offer a novel representation of an issue or a novel cinematic experience, in other words, to create a work of art.

In the third edition of *A Cinema of Loneliness*, Robert Kolker discusses some representative directors of the New Hollywood and contemporary American film (up to 2000, the book's publication date): Penn, Stone, Kubrick, Scorsese, Spielberg, and Altman.[2] Being able to exercise more individuality and more freedom in expression, these directors left personal stamps on their movies, recognizable as their style. The importance of film, argues Kolker, is unquestionable. Films sell ideologies, are deeply rooted in our culture, and have a great potential to influence spectatorship. What is presented and how it is presented can carry great weight. Hence, creative directors can leave a long-standing legacy by articulating various cultural challenges of their time through their creative prism. The notion of an *auteur* as a person leaving his/her stamp in all aspects of a movie might be outdated because a cinematic production is a very complex project involving various talents; but still, some directors exercise a strong level of control, remaining true to the same stylistic points and producing films recognizable as their work.

The poststructuralist theory has argued against the author's dominance over the text. However, despite theories of "the death of author," David Gerstner and Janet Staiger argue that during the late 1990s and early 2000s, a resurgence of the analysis of authorship justifies their anthology titled *Authorship and Film*, published in 2003.[3] The major line of investigation has been the significance of identity (of nation, ethnicity and race, class, gender, and sexual orientation). Different authors find different solutions employing elements of cinematic language to enforce their stamp of identity: trash aesthetic, aesthetic of sensuality, grassroots filmmakers, parody and satire, revisions of genres. Gerstner inquires about the placement of the author in a movie and how that resonates with the notion of authorship in other areas. The singular author of a text is easier to

---

[2]   Robert Kolker, *A Cinema of Loneliness: Penn, Stone, Kubrick, Scorsese, Spielberg, Altman* (New York: Oxford University Press, 2000).
[3]   David A. Gerstner and Janet Staiger, eds., *Authorship and Film (Afi Film Readers)* (London: Routledge, 2003).

define than the author of a film involving a complex, collaborative effort. But, since traditionally high art has been associated with authors and masterpieces, film needed to acquire the notion of an auteur, to distance itself from the connotation of mass entertainment without artistic value. Hence, regardless of a complex film production, film criticism often draws on the issue of authorship in exploring cinematic solutions. In a recent collection dedicated to Haneke's films and in arguing for Haneke's auteur status, Roy Grundmann writes:

> On the one hand, the status of auteur, particularly if freshly bestowed, signals a sense of freshness, of being new, unused, and innovative, and it also implies provocation, perhaps even rebelliousness—all of which signify a break with the status quo. On the other hand, auteurs tend to project artistic, cultural, and, in some cases, political expertise, all of which also imply a certain authority that, in turn, already invites their alignment with tradition (if only at some point in the future, when they can be assimilated into lineages and are worthy of retrospectives).[4]

Let me turn to Aronofsky's filmography. Born in 1969 in Brooklyn, New York, Aronofsky did not have issues with political turmoil and national identity like the New French Wave and the New German Wave directors. Growing up in the 1980s during the Lucas–Spielberg era, he does not fit the New American Wave (as "the cinema of loneliness") of the 1970s. Yet, with unifying (and often controversial) themes explored in his films, and with an innovative use of cinematic language, Aronofsky's films carry a recognizable signature.

Due to the complexity of a film as a composite with various artistic contributions to the narrative, visual and audio elements, crediting a single person with its artistic merit is inappropriate, and I certainly do not intend to do it. Hence, when arguing for Aronofsky's auteurship status, we should understand this status in the sense of its being a driving force behind the initial idea and the final product, and synchronizing and leading all other artistic efforts, from the involvement in the screenplay to the guidance of the actors to the visual (*mise-en-scène*, cinematography) and audio (musical score, diegetic and non-diegetic soundtrack) elements. In order to retain a recognizable sensibility over a number of films, it helps to have a more or less common group of collaborators, and many auteurs did that. For example, Fassbinder had a group of collaborators that he considered as an extended family. Aronofsky's main collaborators remain

---

[4]   Roy Grundmann, ed., *A Companion to Michael Haneke* (Oxford: Wiley-Blackwell, 2010), 7.

mostly the same in his films. The musical scores by Clint Mansell add to the poetry of Aronofsky's films, supporting the characters' travails, hopes, dreams, and harsh realities. Clint Mansell is for Aronofsky what Nino Rota was for Fellini or what Zbigniew Preisner was for Kieslowski. The cinematography of Mathew Libatique (collaborator in all films except *The Wrestler*) aids in creating the proper mood and the use of colors in framing characters' actions and states of mind. Andrew Weisblum edited the last three of Aronofsky's films. Aronofsky also occasionally uses the same lead actors (e.g., Jennifer Connelly) and often the same lead/supporting actors (e.g., Sean Gullette, Ellen Burstyn, Mark Margolis, and Stanley Herman). The repeating circle of artistic collaborators probably allows for a better understanding of diverse artistic inclinations and a greater unity in the collaborative effort of making a movie.

On Aronofsky's themes and narrative style

The themes explored in Aronofsky's filmography show individuals in extreme mental states, concentrating on the development and consequences of going overboard, that is, on the psychology of the main protagonists and the actions surrounding them. This interplay between showing the interiority of characters and showing their position in the exterior world, consisting of family, friends, mentors, and enemies, allows a wide range of visualizations: from dreams and hallucinations to scenes of pure action. Since dream and hallucination do not conform to objective space and time representations as expected in a classic movie, their inclusion allows elements of an art film (irrational cuts, convoluted sense of time and space) characteristic of European postwar auteurs. On the other hand, the action scenes (e.g., in *The Fountain* and *Noah*) testify to the influence of 1980s blockbuster movies, triggering the sense of adventure. The combination of action and psychology results in captivating narratives because we are "storytelling animals," as Jonathan Gottschall puts it and—based on research from neuroscience, biology, and psychology—argues for the importance of narratives.[5] In comparison with novels, narratives told via cinematic language offer an even greater possibility to influence our neuronal activity based on visual effects, but it takes a good story to continue reflecting on the events

---

[5] Jonathan Gottschall, *The Storytelling Animal: How Stories Make Us Human* (New York: Houghton Mifflin Harcourt, 2012).

presented on the screen. David Bordwell presents one of the first comprehensive studies on film narrative used in feature-length traditional films, relating it to the emotional impact on the viewer.[6] In a subsequent work, Ed Tan relates elements of narrative film structure to the psychological study of emotions, concluding that cinematic fiction indeed provokes viewers' genuine emotions, which could be proven experimentally by cognitive psychology.[7] While that book does not reference research on the brain's neuronal activity in triggering instantaneous bodily identification with the fictional cinematic world, resulting in affective or emotional empathy, a recent book by Elsaesser and Hagener stresses the importance of neuroscience.[8]

Hence, the emerging scientific evidence supports the claim that viewers can feel affective empathy toward fictional characters presented on the screen, regardless of whether they accept their views and/or actions or not. In addition to neuronal activity, it seems that an important factor when receiving Aronofsky's films is viewers' compliance with archetypal characters as described in Jungian analytic psychology. The collection *Jung and Film: Post-Jungian Takes on the Moving Image* (2001) edited by Hauke and Alister was the first compilation of essays connecting the narrative film experience with Jungian analytic psychology, drawing from a number of films that provoke the subjective response as well as the shared collective response by the audience.[9] In *Film after Jung: Post-Jungian Approaches to Film Theory* (2009), Greg Singh connects the experience of film (its narrative, characters, and images) with Jungian analytic psychology exploring ways in which films trigger empathy and other emotions in the spectator.[10] Singh emphasizes the relevance of embodied reaction to moving images and the generated affects, writing that "post-Jungian thought fundamentally relates to phenomenology's concerns with embodiment, appearance, and experience."[11] This statement resonates strongly with my approach toward Aronofsky's films presented in the current work. *Somatic Cinema* (2014) by Luke Hockley interprets affects in cinematic spectatorship by relating a psychoanalysis of unconscious mental processing to affective bodily engagement.[12] This provides a

---

[6] David Bordwell, *Narration in the Fiction Film* (Madison, WI: University of Wisconsin Press 1985).
[7] Tan, *Emotion and the Structure of Narrative Film: Film as an Emotion Machine.*
[8] Elsaesser and Hagener, *Film Theory: An Introduction through the Senses,* 77–79.
[9] Christopher Hauke and Ian Alister, eds., *Jung and Film: Post-Jungian Takes on the Moving Image,* (London: Routledge, 2001).
[10] Greg Singh, *Film after Jung: Post Jungian Approaches to Film Theory* (New York: Routledge, 2009).
[11] Ibid., 7.
[12] Luke Hockley, *Somatic Cinema* (New York: Routledge, 2014).

Jungian perspective on the relation between body and screen: the biology of the viewer supports the collective unconsciousness, justifying similar structures in stories that fascinate us. The bodily/mental commonality in general spectatorship provides an explanation for the shared reception of a movie. While the movie speaks to an individual, creating a subjective experience, its aesthetic quality is not individualized—it is singular. In *The Movement Image* (1986), Deleuze considers variations of movement images versus cinematic shots and relates perception images to long shots, action images to medium shots, and affection images to close-ups.[13] Deleuze argues that pure affects are not individualized, but relate to expressions on the face shown in the close-up. Let me try to interpret it. We can all experience fear, and when fear is related to an *objective* entity (my fear of spiders, your fear of snakes), it is individualized as being mine or yours. But, when a close-up of a face on the screen shows fear in the eye expression and the facial movement, there is no individuality, and yet, both you and I experience it as fear—pure fear as a singular affect.

In general, when receiving a work of art, we assume the possibility of communication, acknowledging others *implicitly*. This acknowledgement differs from an ethics based on the *explicit* consideration of and communication with others.[14] The shared experience of watching a movie generates affects that are not individualized, but singular. This might go back to our neurobiology in creating a common bodily response (e.g., increased heart rate), and to Jungian collective unconsciousness in providing a common ground for psychological responses to certain characters and actions.

Aronofsky's films are narrative, often following the line drawn by Jung–Campbell–Vogler in using archetypical characters (Jung) appearing in myths recurring over different cultures (Campbell), and adapted toward cinematic screenplays (Vogler). This was discussed in previous chapters as applicable to specific movies.

Aronofsky's characters often project their inner turbulence and psychic states onto their bodies, testifying to the psycho-physical unity and the inability to separate biology from humanity, mixing horror and melodrama elements. The

---

[13]   Gilles Deleuze, *Cinema 1: The Movement-Image*, trans. H Tomlinson and B. Habberjam (Minneapolis: University of Minnesota Press, 1986).

[14]   In *Critique of Judgment*, Kant writes that in judging aesthetically (a reflective judgment), we generate a universal from a particular. The sense of an underlying principle (purposiveness of nature) leads reflection from the particular toward the universal, that is, it views particular instances as conforming to the universal. On the other hand, it finds the universal as commonality in particular occurrences. Kant, *Critique of Judgment*.

inquisitor in *The Fountain* says that "our bodies are prisons of our souls," bringing the interplay between body and the psyche into the foreground. The question regarding the body is whether or not the body is a constraining biological relic that disables the full development of our potential (the mathematical mind in π), or our desire (the addiction in *Requiem*), or our love (in *The Fountain*), or our search for perfection (in *Black Swan*), and that leads to necessary decay (in *The Wrestler*, both the old wrestler and the old stripper). Our biology is the main reason for our environmental problems (pollution, greed for resources such as water and oil, hunger for accumulation of material wealth); however, humanity is tied up with biology and without it we can only speculate about posthumanity, androids, and the world dominated by technology and analytical intelligence devoid of obsession, addiction, madness, and quest for perfection. Our biology is also a link to our ethics and morality, and as much as we like to look into the future with hope, we have to look at it with apprehension also. Aronofsky's characters are driven by psychic needs that come into conflict with their biology and bodily functions. Since biology can be transcended only in death, it is not surprising that the way out of an existential crisis is the acceptance of death, whether as rebirth in *The Fountain*, as the gift of sacrifice in *The Wrestler*, or as the attainment of perfection in *Black Swan*. In all Aronofsky's stories, there is a bumpy road through the events of a character's adventure, driven by an unreliable vehicle called Hope, driving in predictable directions, yet ending unexpectedly. This duality of hope and apprehension is present in all of Aronofsky's films, and especially, in the latest, *Noah*. In addition, *Noah* brings to prominence a very important character: *water*.

The consideration of water as a character brings to mind the cinematic poem *H2O* (Ralph Steiner, 1929), a short film selected for preservation by the National Film Registry in 2005. Water in various forms appears in all of Aronofsky's films. From faucets dripping to toilets flushing to protagonists submerging themselves in bathtubs to the shores of Coney Island to the fountain in the title of a film and to the Big Flood—there is water. (Aronofsky is an Aquarius, and maybe astrology plays a role.) In π, *Requiem*, and *The Wrestler*, there is ocean; in *The Fountain*, there is frozen water (a snow-covered open field); and in *Black Swan*, there is an ocean on the screen on the wall of the café where the two ballerinas go to hang out. It is almost not surprising that his latest film, *Noah*, deals with the story of the most celebrated intrusion of water.

Water symbolizes the origin of life and the mystery of creation; it purifies and regenerates. For C.G. Jung, "Water in all its forms—sea, lake, river, spring—is one of the commonest typifications of the unconscious."[15] Campbell reiterates that water in mythology usually represents the unconscious. Being immersed in water and coming back represents being "born again" (e.g., in the sacrament of baptism). Sea water contains salt, whose outstanding properties—according to Jung—are bitterness and wisdom, seemingly opposing entities, but they both include feeling. Jung writes, "Tears, sorrow, and disappointment are bitter, but wisdom is the comforter in all psychic suffering. Indeed, bitterness and wisdom form a pair of alternatives: Where there is bitterness, wisdom is lacking, and where wisdom is there can be no bitterness."[16]

The ocean scenes in Aronofsky's films indeed work as regeneration moments, and as fleeting moments of consolidations between bitterness and wisdom, consciousness and unconsciousness, leading to moments of inspiration (Max in *π*), or emotional release (Harry and Marion in *Requiem for a Dream*, Randy in *The Wrestler*). However, water in Aronofsky's films comes in different forms, in the ocean as inspiration and purification, and in bathtubs as a medium to confront the unconscious. Water can attack with full force as in *Noah*, or can flow from a faucet as in *π* and *Black Swan*. It can be pure as in tears or repugnant as in vomiting. In that diversity, water can function as a metaphor for life in its ups and downs, successes and failures, a mixture of majestic and repugnant moments. Speaking of life's "downs," in Aronofsky's films, there are scenes of a character feeling repulsion or nausea, and vomiting (e.g., Marion in *Requiem* and Nina in *Black Swan*). In other scenes, those characters are also shown crying. The filth of vomit, of a dirty fluid coming out of a character's mouth is contradicted with the innocence of clear tears emanating from the eyes, pointing to contradictory bodily effects related to emotional strain. Tears are also related to life's "ups" as when Nina learns that she has got the part of the Swan Queen and cries out of joy. In *Noah*, Noah's wife Naameh has tears twice: one time out of desperation, the other time out of the joy of reconciliation. The fact that salty tears accompany our sorrow as well as our joy resonates with Jung's description of salt as a carrier of contradictory psychic states.

In all of Aronofsky's films preceding the biblical *Noah*, there are bathroom scenes, bringing into comparison the writing about Kubrick's bathrooms as in the essay by S. White in which she lucidly observes the use of bathrooms as

---

[15] C.G. Jung, *Mysterium Coniunctionis: An Inquiry into the Separation and Synthesis of Psychic Opposites in Alchemy*, trans. R.F.C. Hull (Princeton, NJ: Princeton University Press, 1970), 272.
[16] Ibid., 246.

spaces where some of most dramatic events (most obscene and most human) take place, relating the psychic and emotional states to the biological body.[17] In *π*, Max has hallucinations and collapses on his bathroom floor, and drills into his head in front of a bathroom mirror. In *Requiem for a Dream*, Marion experiences a crisis, ready to exchange sex for drugs, and calls Big Tim sitting in the bathroom. She subsequently submerges in a bathtub after the repugnant sexual encounter, either in an effort toward purification or to confront her unconscious. In *The Fountain*, Izzi and Tommy share a moment of closeness in a bathtub. In *The Wrestler*, Randy goes over bodily preparations (hair-dyeing, depilation) in the bathroom. In *Black Swan*, Nina cries out of joy, and subsequently, vomits in different bathroom scenes. Hence, the bathroom is an indispensable space when presenting humanity.

In addition to the consideration of bodily changes to externalize interior turbulence and consideration of water in various forms as a metaphor for life, the scenes of restricted places (corridors, supermarkets) appear in multiple Aronofsky films, visually supporting the sense of a character being trapped. Not only are we trapped in our body, but in our environment as well. A possible way out is in creating an illusion of multiplicity, achieved by the use of mirrors. The symbolism of mirrors suggesting decentered personality supports the visualization of the character's psychic turmoil.

On Aronofsky's cinematic style

In tracing Aronofsky's films from his first, independent, low-budget, black-and-white *π* that introduced the hip-hop montage (his debt to growing up with hip-hop music and the MTV era) to the expressive montage and color tonality in *Requiem* to the exploration of shapes in the philosophical film *The Fountain* without CGI to the use of CGI in *Black Swan* in order to externalize the interior metamorphosis of Nina to the excessive use of CGI and special effects in the epic *Noah*—it is clear that Aronofsky is set up to explore all the possibilities of emerging cinematic techniques influenced by science and technology. However, due to themes concerning extreme mental states, and the presentation

---

[17]   Susan White, "Kubrick's Obscene Shadows," in *Stanley Kubrick's 2001: A Space Odyssey: New Essays* (New York: Oxford University Press, 2006), 135–39.

of interiority spilling out via dreams and hallucinations, Aronofsky's films are maybe best characterized with fast and irrational cutting and extreme close-ups.

A two-day event titled "Movies in Your Brain: The Science of Cinematic Perception," hosted by the Academy of Motion Picture Arts and Sciences was held July 29–30, 2014.[18] A group of filmmakers and cognitive scientists discussed ways in which cinematic language has evolved and how that evolution influences both the physical (preconscious) and mental (conscious) responses of the audience. Aronofsky and Handel attended the event to discuss changes in the brain's neuronal architecture while responding to the cinematic language using various frame rates, various cutting and editing strategies, and presenting an emotional content. The club scene clip from *Black Swan* and the ten-second history of human violence sequence from the larger evolution sequence in *Noah* were used as examples of scenes capable of triggering strong, even extreme, neuronal response in the viewer, creating a gap between the emotional and the cognitive centers in the brain. In his article, "Data from a Century of Cinema Reveals How Movies Have Evolved," Greg Miller summarizes the discussion on the development of cinematic perception due to changing technologies, supported by observable data.[19] From the early days of cinema, the average shot length has decreased, complying with natural fluctuations in human attention; action scenes have increased in number, inducing stronger bodily response (heart rate) from viewers; and stronger contrasts in tonality increase the emotional impact of a scene. This discussion provides evidence for the new approach to film studies, a fertile combination of science (biology, psychology), technology, and art. A multiple Oscar winner (for sound mixing and editing), Walter Murch relates the ideal cut to the satisfaction of six criteria: emotion, story, rhythm, eye-trace, two-dimensional plane of screen, and three-dimensional space of action.[20] Namely, a good cut advances the emotional and narrative sides of the story, it has to be in sync with the intended interest of the audience, and with the geometries of the actual screen and the virtual space of action. But, why do cuts work? Murch argues that the audience is conditioned to cuts since even in real life we have cuts in perception,

[18] "Movies in Your Brain: The Science of Cinematic Perception," in *Events and Exhibitions* (2014).

[19] Greg Miller, "Data from a Century of Cinema Reveals How Movies Have Evolved," *Wired Science* (2014), http://www.wired.com/2014/09/cinema-is-evolving/?utm_content=bufferb7c99&utm_medium=social&utm_source=facebook.com&utm_campaign=buffer.

[20] Murch, *In the Blink of an Eye: A Perspective on Film Editing*, 18.

resulting from the blinking of eyes. The speed of eye-blinking is related to emerging thoughts in our brain. A concentration and fixity of thought results in less blinking, while when experiencing a turmoil of conflicting thoughts, we blink more often.[21] Moreover, we tend to blink after suddenly realizing something. Hence, both the rate of blinking and the instant of the blink should be relevant when editing the film. After all, a film needs to keep the audience fixated on the story and the images presented onscreen, using editing and cutting to provoke *simultaneous* blinking in the audience, and trying to prevent a viewer from getting detached and following his or her own thoughts. As Murch puts it:

> Your job is partly to participate, partly to control the thought process of the audience. To give them what they want and/or what they need just before they have to "ask" for it – to be surprising yet self-evident at the same time.... The paradox of the cinema is that it is most effective when it seems to fuse two contradictory elements—the general and the personal—into a kind of *mass intimacy.* The work itself is unchanging, aimed at an audience of millions, and yet—when it works—a film speaks to each member of the audience in a powerfully personal way.[22]

Aronofsky's narratives are predominantly character-based, concerned with characters' existential crises induced by extreme mental states, and with their finding a possible way out. Even the biblical story of the Great Flood serves as a fitting background for the development of a contemporary obsessive character convinced he is the chosen one, going overboard in his stubbornness, and finally, realizing the futility of such convictions. The existential feel of Aronofsky's movies justifies labeling him as an existential director, in art/philosophical parallel with an existential philosopher. In fact, my analysis of Aronofsky's films relates them to a number of existential philosophers—Kierkegaard, Jaspers, Heidegger, and Merleau-Ponty.

To draw an ordinary viewer into the character's intense interior, forcing identification and empathy, presents a challenging task. A viewer has to be initially provoked on a neuronal, prereflective level, to simulate an extreme psychic state and its bodily consequences. She or he subsequently has to be provoked into reflecting the character's choices and how they fit with the overall narrative, that is, how the plot, the sequence of scenes, supports the narrative.

---

[21]   Ibid., 61.
[22]   Ibid., 69, 142–43.

For both of these provocations (the instantaneous identification and the subsequent philosophical reflection) proper editing is crucial. Kubrick said that editing "is the only unique aspect of filmmaking which does not resemble any other art form—a point so important it cannot be overstressed.... It can make or break a film."[23] In Aronofsky's films, the fast rate of cutting provokes fast neuronal activity, disorienting thoughts, and simulating paranoia or unquenched desire, something that should happen and should happen fast as it does in obsession or addiction. Bursts of irrational cuts in hallucination scenes create surprise, freezing viewers' capacities for reflection in order to increase the gap between desire and surprise, intensifying the aesthetic and the emotional impact. The gap between desire and surprise provokes affection, a point close to Deleuze's writing about the affection-image, whose substance is "the compound affect of desire and astonishment."[24]

While camera moves in Aronofsky's films have changed appropriately with different themes, as already stated, some signature moves are employed in various films. The hip-hop montage consisting of short shots in π and *Requiem* is transformed into a sequence of fast cuts in the club scene in *Black Swan*, and into representing the story of evolution in *Noah*. The repetitive use of images underlines the repetitiveness of obsession in π and of addiction in *Requiem*, up to the repetitiveness of Noah's vision presented in the sequence depicting the original sin and the first murder. In all Aronofsky's films, the camera underlines the individuality of the characters, either by presenting their points of view or extreme close-ups of their faces, especially eyes, probing into their interiority and presenting their drives and mental states. The characters' eyes are prominent in all Aronofsky's films, and maybe the best analogy with "Kubrick's bathrooms" is "Aronofsky's eyes." And this enforces Aronofsky's thematic of human psychology and spirituality. The eyes are a two-way opening, allowing the character to observe the outside environment, and allowing the outsiders to look into their interiority, in line with the proverbial description of the eyes as windows to our soul. The eyes of Aronofsky's characters change from normal brightness toward abnormal shine and coloring, creating distorted points of view, depicting hallucinations and the descent into obsession, addiction, or madness, possibly ending with sorrow (Harry in *Requiem*), reconciliation (*Noah*), satisfaction (Nina in *Black Swan*), or acceptance (Randy in *The Wrestler*).

---

23   Walker, *Stanley Kubrick, Director: A Visual Analysis*, 42.
24   Deleuze, *Cinema 1*, 101.

The struggle of an individual with the environment is presented not only through eyes and the changing body of the individual, but also with the view of the external world. The discussions about *The Fountain* and *Black Swan* consider the difference between symmetry and asymmetry in the scenery, with symmetric scenery projecting outside indifference in contrast to the internal turbulence of a character. A self-obsessed character creates a subjective world detached from the rest of objective reality. The symmetric and orderly outside enhances the perception of brewing emotionality behind the surface. However, Aronofsky's choices depend on the narrative. In *The Fountain*, the outside environment in the sixteenth-century Spain, with all its symmetric architecture, presents a sharp contrast with a high priest shown flagellating himself in religious fervor. We see the objective side of the story, without entering the priest's psyche. The claustrophobic apartment in π conditions a viewer for identification with Max's interiority—not just his point of view, but his troubled thinking.

While Aronofsky's films employ some similar cinematic elements, the overall style changes in each film to comply with the story to be told. This change invites comparison with Kubrick, who crossed different genres, adapting his style to a story, and yet, resulting in a distinctly Kubrickian film. Thus far, Aronofsky's films contain elements of the psychological thriller, sci-fi, love story, melodrama, and historical epic genres. If he continues in dissecting human weakness, maybe one of his future films could be a satire, appropriate for depicting the irrationality of human behavior. However, a satire or a parody would change the focus from the subjectivity of his characters (who are deadly serious) to the objectivity of their actions and the corresponding consequences.

Courage to tell our own stories

Aronofsky said that he wants to tell stories that somehow relate to himself, and to tell them in his style.[25] This led to problems with the NC-17 rating for *Requiem for a Dream*, budgetary problems with *The Fountain*, political controversy for depicting the destruction of the Iranian flag in *The Wrestler*, feminist critique for the character of Nina in *Black Swan*, and a critique from religious circles for his

---

[25] In a documentary describing the production of *The Wrestler* (available on a DVD), Aronofsky explained his driving force, "If you think it's a good story, if it makes sense to you, if you work hard on it, you tell the story to a lot of friends and they think it's interesting and cool, then that's enough a reason to keep going ahead and do it."

interpretation of Genesis and his depiction of Noah in *Noah*. It takes courage to stick to our ideas.

Some directors accept invitations to do new versions of recent foreign movies. For example, Fincher did the Hollywood version of *The Girl with the Dragon Tattoo* (David Fincher, 2011), while there is a successful Swedish movie trilogy of Stieg Larsson's *Millennium* trilogy, and the three Swedish films were released in 2009, including *The Girl with the Dragon Tattoo* (Niels Arden Oplev, 2009). Nolan did *Insomnia* (Chris Nolan, 2002) as his first studio film, adapting the successful Norwegian film *Insomnia* (Erik Skjoldbjærg, 1997).

Some directors choose to direct movies about popular superheroes, working in a more or less safe environment, and hoping for a blockbuster. However, some directors are not appropriate for such work as, for example, Lee who did the superhero movie *Hulk* (Ang Lee, 2006), but he is obviously an auteur not best-suited for directing franchised superheroes. Lee's movies are diverse, always concerned with the question of what it means to be human and to achieve authenticity. His film *The Life of Pi* (Ang Lee, 2012) is a story of survival on the ocean and the name, the irrational number Pi, might symbolize humanity's incomprehension of reality, and it brings into comparison the thematic of Aronofsky's π. In that sense, Lee seems similar to Aronofsky; his movies as well as Aronofsky's project a wish to leave an authentic authorial mark.

We know that film is an illusion, but some directors project a sense of sincerity in what they depict, and how they depict it. They project frankness of expression that approaches directly, not through an indirect route of courting their spectatorship. Aronofsky's films do not present a straightforward critique of, say, a political or an economic system, or of a religious belief. They have some social connotations regarding the utilitarian nature of information (as both business and religious characters pursue Max in π), regarding the difficulty of attaining the American Dream (in *Requiem for a Dream*), or regarding the pressures of contemporary public machinery hungry for a spectacle (in *The Wrestler*). But the main theme is not the critique of the socio/political environment—environment is what it is. Rather, the main concern is about individualities caught up in a given social environment and their struggles to deal with their hopes and aspirations.

We can say that Aronofsky strongly advocates environmentalism in *Noah*. This is true, but concern for the environment and climate change surpasses ideological or religious boundaries and presents a basic problem for all of us—it boils down to the question of the value of life. In addition, *Noah*, being the least biblical presentation of a biblical story (to quote Aronofsky), is both a religious and a nonreligious film: it cannot be aligned with a straight religious belief, nor with the atheistic approach. The story of evolution poetically presented as occurring in seven days, with the evolutionary development of life, and the sudden nonevolutionary arrival of Adam and Eve stays clear of siding exclusively with either creationist or evolutionary approaches, making the point that the two approaches are not mutually exclusive and allowing spectators to make their own reading out of it.

Many spectators would agree that Kubrick is a sincere director, exposing humanity in its flaws, and many would agree that he is not misanthropic, but shows concern for humanity. Regardless of a number of blockbusters, many would agree that Spielberg projects sincerity through the wonder of an eternal child, priceless for even the most grown grownups, albeit generating some unsettling thoughts as well. Fassbinder projected sincerity and multi-dimensionality in his depiction of shaken identity in postwar Germany, and was attacked by the left and by the right, by the straight and by the gay. Haneke attacks contemporary problems without easy spectators' satisfaction, creating uncomfortable questions for the audience. Aronofsky mentioned Fellini as one of his inspirations; Fellini was attacked from the right as being leftist, and from the left as abandoning Italian neorealism. We can also include Ken Russell (viewed as a British Fellini), with his insistent and unapologetic questioning of sexuality and the Church in his films, and the list could include some other directors. We progress in technological development and the ever-stronger interaction between computers and humans: humans developing technology, and technology changing humans in turn, resulting in the disappearance of privacy. However, when privacy is lost and everything moves to the surface, is there any interiority left, something hidden that needs sincerity and courage to bring it out? Do we need any meaning outside of pure action and visual effects? Would we consider the disappearance of interiority as an existential problem facing humanity, or would interiority be just a bygone disease, such as the Black Death from the Middle Ages?

Aronofsky's filmography from 1998 to 2014 serves as a testimony to the fact that we are still concerned with the big question of what it means to be human, and that there is a rich and complex interiority within human beings. The film medium allows him to visualize, that is, externalize, human interiority. With the exception of *The Wrestler*, all Aronofsky's films include hallucinatory or dream sequences, making the spectator a kind of accomplice in whatever the characters do afterward. We get to know his characters from the inside.

Aronofsky emphasized that the visual scenery of *The Fountain* from 2006, dealing with the distant future, was all made without computer graphics, being all organic, created by putting organic matter under a microscope and finding spirals and whirls in the organic, simulating cosmic movements. In the later *Black Swan* from 2010, CGI is used quite extensively to depict the metamorphosis of Nina into Black Swan. In *Noah* from 2014, CGI is used extensively for effects, for depiction of the environment, and to create all the animals, freeing real animals from unnecessary and often painful treatment. However, the close-ups of characters' faces project human emotion. The dichotomy in the use of technology from *The Fountain* to *Noah*, separated by eight years only, serves as proof of the unstoppable march of technology—technology being immensely useful in augmenting cinematic language and extending our visual field, but also presenting the challenge of using it creatively so that human subjectivity is not buried beneath CGI-generated action scenes.

With his work in the first sixteen years (from 1998 to 2014), his six feature films, Aronofsky has established a strong artistic force in presenting the human condition as faced with existential challenges arising in the most vulnerable states, when going out of balance. Be it intellectual strain and emotional deficiency as in *π*, the seductive deadly dance with addiction as in *Requiem for a Dream*, the loss of a loved one and the impossible quest to overcome human mortality as in *The Fountain*, the inability to accept the process of aging as in *The Wrestler*, the psychical and physical strain to achieve personal liberation and artistic perfection as in *Black Swan*, and the conflict involving the heavy burden of responsibility and sacrifice as in *Noah*, Aronofsky's poetic treatment of his subjects shows a compassionate and nonjudgmental stance.

Appendix: Conversation with Aronofsky

Prior to seeing *Noah*, I had a chance to conduct an interview with Aronofsky on December 2, 2013. At that time, he was heavily involved with the postproduction of *Noah*, and it was obvious that there would be a limited time for conversation, so I decided to prepare only a few questions regarding each of his movies, and possibly, some general questions. Aronofsky has given a number of interviews, and there is a lot of material about his movies on the Internet, so I attempted to ask questions that I could not find already answered on some other occasion. A one-hour meeting was too short to cover all the questions I had in mind, but nonetheless, Aronofsky provided insightful comments regarding his work.

DA—Darren Aronofsky

JSK—Jadranka Skorin-Kapov

JSK: I will ask a few questions about each of your movies and some questions in general. First question is about π and the ants. In your movie, Max has a hypothesis that "when there is a true chaotic system, there is an order in it," but does not realize the potential in chaotic (and resilient) behavior of a low-level organic source such as ants. Combinatorial optimization includes the "Ant Colony Optimization," a class of meta-heuristic algorithms used in artificial intelligence and applied to robotic development. Did you consider the behavior of ants in relation to Max's frantic search for order inside the chaos?

DA: I think that's a good observation about the ants and there is something about the way they have their own universe, their own colony, and their own system. And sort of how that was going against Max's own system, getting in the way and disturbing him. I did write a book called the *Pi Journals* or something, I don't know if you saw it . . .

JSK: Yes

DA: Do I talk about ants there at all?

JSK: Yes, you talk about your visit to Mexico.

DA: Yeah, I talk a little bit about that, but I can't remember the real inspiration. Sometimes there are certain ideas that are circling in your head and they sort of just click, and you don't know exactly why you're putting it in, but you just go for it. I know I must have deeply believed it because I remember all we had to go through to make the ants act, it was very difficult. Also, just securing ants, getting ants, was hard, and a lot of effort went into it. It was something that I deeply believed in. It is so hard to remember motivations because it's a detail from twelve, thirteen years ago. I could remember for sure that the idea came later on in the process; it wasn't in the original script. I remember when the idea came and I kept telling to my producer: "We need ants; we need ants." He was not very receptive to it.

JSK: In a commentary to π, you mentioned ants you saw on your trip to Mexico, and suddenly, it came to me a reference I wish to ask you about: Gabriel Garcia Márquez's *One Hundred Years of Solitude*.

DA: Yeah?

JSK: His masterpiece and prophesy about the fictional Macondo where the first in line is tied to the tree and the last is carried off by the ants. The whole civilization that came to be ended up with the colony of ants.

DA: Which is similar to what I saw in Mexico.

JSK: Exactly. This is what triggered my thought.

DA: I read *One Hundred Years of Solitude*. I don't remember when I read it, sometime in college, so maybe I read it about a similar time, so maybe it was in my head when I went down to Mexico and saw it. And I loved it. I mean, it was a major book in my life. I connect, as do so many people, with Márquez.

JSK: The thing is that Márquez also wrote screenplays and was interested in film; his writing is very visual.

DA: Yeah.

JSK: In 2007, Mike Newell has put his *Love in the Time of Cholera* on film, but he never gave rights to *One Hundred Years of Solitude*.

DA: Oh, really?

JSK: So maybe he is looking...[1]

DA: It is very complicated. It is a very hard thing to do, a very, very hard thing to do.

JSK: Maybe he did not have the right director?

---

[1]   At the time of the conversation Gabriel García Márquez was alive. Sadly, "Gabo" left us on April 17, 2014.

DA: It's a complicated film to make. You have to do it in Spanish. It is very complicated.

JSK: You wrote some of your own original screenplays and the one from the book was only for the *Requiem* based on Selby's book. You mentioned Cronenberg as one of your influences. After *Videodrome*, he adapted Steven King's *The Dead Zone* and he is quoted as saying that if you want to be true to the book you have to betray the book because the two media are different and direct translation is not possible. My question is: In the future, would you continue developing original screenplays or. . .?

DA: I don't know, it depends. Certain books are really good for the screen, and certain books are not. Certain books are based on ideas that don't make great drama, and then another have great drama going on. So, I don't know. I am always looking for new material, to see what inspires me.

JSK: Since we don't have much time, let's move to your second movie, *Requiem for a Dream*. That movie reminds me of a book in late-1970s in Europe, the time when the book by Christiane F., *We Children from Bahnhof Zoo*, appeared and was very influential, and was subsequently adapted for a film.

DA: Yeah, I know *Christiane F.* film, I saw it.

JSK: Your movie is much broader, dealing with different types of addictions, but talking about those younger protagonists, you said that, in order to develop an addiction, it has to be a hole that needs to be filled. But, is it possible that one can become addicted at that age just out of sheer curiosity, even having a great family?

DA: It is just part of what we are as people. I think everyone has, to a certain extent, this ability to get addicted. It is just part of human nature. I think everyone can relate to it. I think some people are worse off than other people are. For some people, it is easier to control, for some not. I don't know if you are born with it or if it's how you are raised; I don't know, but for some reason, it ties into how we are as the animals that we are. It might be connected with the fact that we need to eat and other needs, and these are all based on things to survive.

JSK: You said that everything could be a drug, even hope.

DA: Sure, yeah. That was Selby's big idea; that in *Requiem for a Dream* the real addiction is to the American Dream. That's what he was talking about.

JSK: Well, hope is the basic addiction for gamblers.

DA: Yeah, that and the adrenaline of losing the money, the excitement of losing the money.

JSK: Is it possible to have a good addiction?

DA: You know, some people would think smoking is a good addiction, they love it. I mean, I don't know. It is the problem when it takes the course of your life, goes over the limit.

JSK: Let's go to your third one, *The Fountain*. It seems to be your most personal film. I read about production problems and all, and was thinking about a book you mentioned among your preferred books, *Hitchcock/Truffaut*. In that book, Truffaut mentions *Marnie*, Hitchcock's movie and said that this movie belongs to the class of so called "great flawed movies" that are masterpieces, but there is a gap between what one wanted to make and what came out. And he said that such movies belong only to the greatest directors, and true cinephiles would even prefer such movies over acknowledged masterpieces of those directors because they show a bigger level of sincerity. Like what your choreographer Thomas from *Black Swan* would say, they show perfection when one lets it go.

DA: Yeah, yeah.

JSK: It also reminded me of a novel by Joyce, *A Portrait of the Artist as a Young Man*, where Joyce talks about three artistic forms: lyric, epic, and dramatic. Now, I like your movie very much and it looks to me that there are lyric moments in it. In a commentary, you said that you might consider doing another version of that movie.

DA: Only slight version change. There were things we had to change for the ratings, and there were lots of ways to put the film together. There were two scenes that didn't make it, that I would probably want to put back in. But, you know, ultimately the film is what it is; it hasn't changed that much in my mind. Filmmakers are always tweaking their films and usually you don't finish a film; you abandon a film. And at a certain point, you run out of money, and it's the right time to bring it to the world. And that was the right time to bring it to the world. But there were definitely things that I knew we could play around a little bit more and see what happens. So, maybe one day, we'll get to it; we'll see what happens.

JSK: In *The Fountain* you stayed away from the CGI, it was all organic. Was that for the economic reason or in order to stay true to the theme of the film about love and death?

DA: Yes.

JSK: Both?

DA: Yes, exactly.

JSK: Which is actually great. In my family, we like to say that not to have is sometimes a blessing because you have to find creative ways to deal with it.

DA: Where did you grow up?

JSK: I grew up in Croatia.... Maybe we can move to *The Wrestler*. It was very interesting to have Mickey Rourke playing; as also in your other movie, *Black Swan*, Winona Ryder. I remember Mickey from the 1980s, from *9 1/2* weeks, and he was always a combination of contradictions, all different characteristics. He is such a great actor. I heard in the news that he was quitting acting, that he was boxing, and having him to play a role of an old wrestler, reminded me of one of my favorite directors of the silent era: Eric von Stroheim.

DA: Why?

JSK: Because of *Sunset Boulevard*.

DA: Right.

JSK: I like the work of von Stroheim; he was such a character. Seeing him in *Sunset Boulevard*, playing basically himself, was very emotional. Hearing that Mickey is in your movie, I was eager to see the film. Do you find the theme of life imitating art and art imitating life interesting?

DA: It made a lot of sense for that movie. It also made sense because of the whole theme of what is real and what is fake in wrestling. So, there is another level of playing with that, you know, because all these wrestlers, they cross the line of what's real and what's not. So, finding with Mickey of what is real and what is not added another level. It all worked together. I don't know how those things come together. They just do. You just start building ideas and then you start trying to improve them, make them more interesting, richer, keep growing and growing and growing them.

JSK: Actually, I can ask now about your characters. There is a difference between an archetype and a stereotype. Stereotypes are clichés; archetypes are templates used to build up character types. How do you build your characters as persons?

DA: Hubert Selby, Jr., always used to say to me that it is called a cliché for a reason because it is often true. So, I think it is important when you create a character to recognize what a clichés of that character might be, and then figure out how you can make it richer, more interesting. I think starting with something that is very much grounded in reality, and then trying to add to it and make it something more, helps. That often happens when an actor gets involved, especially with really talented actors. They are always thinking how to make their characters special. They don't stop at the screenplay level, they try to add to it, and bring something to it. Then your job as a director is to try to work with them and make sure those ideas don't go too far, don't contradict other ideas, so that it sort of works for the movie. But, Mickey was very tricky because he wanted to design the costumes. And for a while I resisted it, and then I realized I was making a mistake because I was not taking the advantage of what he was bringing to it, which was his taste, knowing what he looks good in. So, eventually I was able to find a good balance. You know, that's always the game. Filmmaking is so much about collaboration with other people.

JSK: You seem to be the actors' director.

DA: That's right.

JSK: There is the issue of death, of gift-giving and death in your movie. In all your movies, there is a gift-giving: Marcy Dawson gives Mecca chip to Max, Harry gives a TV to his mother, Ram gives clothes to his daughter, Izzy gives a pen to Tommy. Then, there is the issue of death. Is there a perfect gift? There are philosophical writings, Derrida, for example, that there is not possible to give a perfect gift. But then, there is a perfect gift of death, which includes responsibility as well. There is a recent movie by Haneke, *Amour*, about death as a gift, about responsibility, love, old age. What is your view on death? For example, Ram, when he jumps the final jump, is he a coward or a hero? Are there things worth dying for or do we have to live at all costs?

DA: That, you need to answer. I cannot give you an answer. But, what is your question?

JSK: What is your view on death?

DA: I cannot talk directly about that. You have to look at the movies, what the movies are about. They all talk about it in many different ways.

JSK: And what is actually great about your movies is that they talk in different ways. For example, in *The Fountain*, if I look from the perspective of a current story, it sounds optimistic; I can come to terms about my own death. If I look at it from the perspective of the future, it sounds pessimistic; I can accept my own death, but accepting the end of life on earth is difficult.

DA: Yeah, yeah, right.

JSK: This is one of the reason I connect your movies with Fassbinder because his endings are also ambiguous, either pessimistic or optimistic.

DA: Yeah.

JSK: Fassbinder said that movies should present exaggerated examples in order for a person to re-evaluate his or her values. Would you agree with that?

DA: I think that is very interesting. I've never heard that quote, but I think it's true. I think I do that. For me, Fassbinder is *Ali, Fear Eats the Soul*. That's my most special Fassbinder, the one I love the most.

JSK: It is said that Fassbinder reinvented the melodrama genre. What the French New Wave did for Hitchcock, he did for Douglas Sirk. He used the genre of melodrama, but in a new way. I think that you belong to a similar category.

DA: I've been called that before; you're not the first. And I think it's true. I looked up what *melodrama* really means and I think people have all different types of understanding what melodrama is because of the soap operas and stuff like that. I remember looking up the definition because a few people wrote about me and I was like: What does the word mean? I think it is probably pretty appropriate to describe my work.

JSK: Melodrama had a negative connotation, but actually it is not the case. I have a quote here by Sidney Lumet who said that, "In a well-written drama the story comes out of characters, the characters in a well written melodrama come out of the story."

DA: This is interesting.

JSK: As long as there is a struggle between imperfect human nature and existence, there will always be a story involving a melodrama.

DA: Yeah, interesting.

JSK: So, we will skip the *Wrestler* and move to *Black Swan*. What actually made me to have to write about your work is the quote of a choreographer from *Black Swan* who says to Nina that perfection relates to surprise, transcendence. This is basically my thesis in philosophy.

DA: Really?

JSK: I talk about your movie in a chapter about limit experiences. To me, *Black Swan* was exactly a visual analysis of what I was trying to do, so it worked perfectly.

DA: Good!

JSK: Now, when Thomas says to Nina that perfection is not just about control and relates it to surprise, how much is he speaking in your voice?

DA: Ha, ha. People made connections. I don't think I am as cruel as Thomas, but . . .

JSK: I don't think he is cruel.

DA: You don't think he is cruel? You think he is just direct?

JSK: He is very fair.

DA: Yeah, yeah. There are connections between the choreographer and the director, and it's a similar job. We try to put all this people together, try to figure out what the story is, and inspire people to do the best work they can.

I think there is some truth to that. It is a whole big question of what is perfection: Is it jazz or is it classical? Do you practice something over and over again, and make it perfect, or is it something that you practice so hard, and then you let it loose?

JSK: Probably human perfection is different than perfection of, say, Michelangelo's sculpture.

DA: Sure, yeah, yeah, exactly.

JSK: Perfection in imperfection, when you let it go, between perfect form and imperfect content.

DA: Yes.

JSK: So, I think he is a great teacher, great choreographer.

DA: So there you go. Good.

JSK: Talking about the choreographer, Vincent Cassel—he appeared in Cronenberg's movies, *Eastern Promises* and *A Dangerous Method*. He was asked to compare you and Cronenberg . . .

DA: Oh, really?

JSK: You don't know this quote?

DA: No, I don't think I heard it. What did he say?

JSK: He said that you and Cronenberg are both fascinated by body horror material and similar subjects, "And David is not actually American at all, he's Canadian. And Darren is not really American, he's from Brooklyn! And they both have a European quality to what they do. A dark European quality."

DA: Good!

JSK: So, how would you respond to that, that you are not really American because you are from Brooklyn?

DA: Well, I mean, that's not true. Brooklyn is so clearly part of America. I think the personality of Brooklyn is so distinct, although it's changed in what it is, from what it meant when I was from there and what it is now. But, more important is my view towards Europe than it is towards Hollywood. Probably because when I really started to think about filmmaking as something it might be possible to do, the movies that really excited me were movies not coming out of Hollywood. I grew up in the Lucas–Spielberg era, and those films were incredibly exciting, but I think by the time I was seventeen or eighteen, I was looking for something different. Aesthetically I wanted a very different way, I think. So, that's kind of what happened.

JSK: You also mentioned Fellini as one of your influences.

DA: Huge, huge. Everything he does, anytime I watch him; he is just amazing.

JSK: He was one of my preferred, and I recently watched some of his movies again. For example, *Amarcord*, and then watched a very good commentary, except when they talk about the family. They said, this is dysfunctional family, but I think they are not dysfunctional, this is how they are . . .

DA: Fellini did the commentary?

JSK: No, an American commentator.

DA: No, it's not at all dysfunctional. It's an Italian family, that's the point. I liked the uncle up in the tree.

JSK: He wants a woman. Also, when you translate Fellini, for example, *8 ½*, lots is lost in translation because in Italian there are lots of diminutives that add artificiality.

DA: Yeah, I am sure. You know, that's part of the problem. You don't get all that stuff if it's not your native tongue.

JSK: And Kurosawa . . .

DA: Yes, there's so much subtlety in Kurosawa. You know, I am complete outsider although I'll tell you, when I go to Japan, I feel like I understand more of what's going on because of how much Kurosawa I watched. So, I kind of get it of what's going on, a little bit.

JSK: Let me ask you something else, I am skipping some questions. In watching *Black Swan*, I recalled some other movies that I liked, say in the eighties, Saura's *Carmen*, part of his *Flamenco* trilogy.

DA: Yeah, when we were prepping the movie, we watched those movies; they are beautifully done.

JSK: Yes, and there are lots of scenes, the choreographer's scenes, the story of Carmen . . .

DA: . . . played out. We watched them all and we talked about them, and we were very impressed with them. Of course, they are more of dance movies, but they are a great work and definitely a very good homework for all of us.

JSK: Also, I think somewhat related is Haneke's *The Piano Teacher*.

DA: Sure, yeah. That was a big influence on the side of psychology of the movie, and we talked a lot about that movie and the relationship between the mother and the daughter.

JSK: Yeah, and also infliction with glass and sexual fantasies.

DA: Yeah, all that stuff. It's amazing. Haneke is so good.

JSK: Let me ask now about symmetry and asymmetry. You seem to have the visual ability to play with symmetry versus asymmetry.

DA: Yeah.

JSK: Many artists and philosophers wrote about symmetry versus asymmetry, their difference in artistic terms: If you have symmetry outside, it can actually reinforce the depiction of the chaos inside. What is your take on that?

DA: I don't know. For me, it is usually an aesthetic choice connected to what film it is. I thought *The Fountain* very much had this vision and the language that was uniform and connected. Then, when we got to *The Wrestler*, everything about Mickey is asymmetrical, from his face to his personality. So, I had to figure out how to create some sort of balance in that world. He kind of threw me for a loop, I had to change everything I was doing. But, I think that's the best thing you could do, you know. In filmmaking, you just want to keep on learning and try new things, not sticking to the same thing over and over. These people who do trilogies, like three films in a row—it would kill me. I am just not interested in it. You've got to change. Otherwise, it's like an endless nightmare because each film takes two, three years, and you talk about seven, eight years with one set of characters.

JSK: Talking about trilogies, there are good and bad trilogies. Let me explain. Maybe you were lucky, as I already said, sometimes not to have is a blessing. Maybe because of the problems with *The Fountain*, you didn't do Batman, and I think that was a blessing.

DA: Yeah.

JSK: Ang Lee did Hulk and he ... there are some directors that are not made to do franchise movies.

DA: Yeah.

JSK: There are some directors that would make an American version of a successful foreign movie. For example, Chris Nolan did a remake of *Insomnia*. Would you consider making ...

DA: I don't think so. I've never been in that situation where I wanted to do that. Usually if it is a good film, I just want to stay away.

JSK: That's okay. ... But there are trilogies that are very persuasive, like Polanski's *Apartment* trilogy, Kieslowski *Three Color Trilogy* ...

DA: Yeah, sure.

JSK: So, is there a possibility to one day have *Aronofsky's Body Trilogy*?

DA: Ha! I don't know, I haven't come up with anything that's that connected. Stylistically, I always thought that the first three films, π, *Requiem*, and *The Fountain*, were sort of connected, and then, as you probably read, I thought that *The Wrestler* and *Black Swan* were very connected thematically, body and passion, and all that stuff. *Noah* is on its own thing right now, so you know, I am not really plotting that type of thing right now, I am just following the stories that make sense. But, no, I don't have any plans for anything that big.

JSK: Maybe if you add some science fiction, body changes . . .

DA: That would be great. Would be great, but you need to get ideas, you know.

JSK: You mentioned *Noah*. As I said, I didn't see the film, only the trailer, it is great. The only thing that I read somewhere is that you used all sorts of created animals with CGI, and strange animals that do not exist. And I was thinking: what a great, creative idea.

DA: Yeah. I mean, practically it is very, very difficult to use animals. There is a political issue. It's very, very hard to work with live animals. You are also limited by the type of live animals you can get. Usually, the type of animals you can get in a zoo are classic famous animals, polar bear, the zebra, the giraffe, the elephant . . . but the animal kingdom is so much bigger, so much bigger, and I didn't want to represent the animal kingdom in a very, very simplistic way. And there would have been no way to get exotic animals outside that. And then, politically, it's a terrible thing. Even if the animals are treated incredibly well, which they are not, but even if they were, you are still asking things they need doing that they were not meant to do. You are not asking them. You are starving them and forcing them. We worked with a live monkey in *The Fountain*. I have never worked with an animal before. I worked with ants, but that was about it. And when I saw how they treated the monkey, I was stunned. I couldn't believe it. And at that point, we went through with it, but, you know, I deeply regretted doing it. I just was very ignorant on the whole way how that worked. Since then, I just had been completely uninterested in doing that again. And there is no reason for doing it any more.

JSK: Actually, I was thinking that there is something artistically important to be able to create *new* types of animals.

DA: Yeah, yeah, and that's what we did.

JSK: Using CGI not only as a technical tool, but as a creative tool.

DA; Yeah, we tried to turn it into something creative.

JSK: Now, I always have a question about your movies, if it is something pessimistic or optimistic. New animals could imply that the new cycle of life starts, as a change . . .

DA: Yeah.

JSK: And thinking about that, I went back to a very old movie, Fritz Lang's *Metropolis* from 1927, which is a future story in 2026, but based on the biblical story of the *Tower of Babel*.

DA: Yeah, yeah.

JSK: As the Bible says, Nimrod, the great grandson of Noah, created a tower, enraged God, so God made them not understand each other, because the great flood did not work. So, how do you feel about The Tower of Babel?

DA: We thought a lot about it. I mean it's very strange when you think about those stories, the creation stories, the destruction, from the first, the original sin, to the destruction of the world with Noah, and then you have the Tower of Babel. So, it seems it's the same story over and over again. Which is: arrogance of men rises up, and then they need to be destroyed and punished. You have Sodom and Gomorrah, the same story over and over again. It all goes back to the original sin, which is when we have learned the difference between right and wrong.

JSK: Noah made a covenant with God, and God said that he will never destroy life on earth again, so now you people destroy yourself.

DA: Yeah, over and over again, yeah.

JSK: Your recurring theme is water. In the movies, there is ocean; in *Black Swan* there is ocean on the screen in a cafe. What is the consideration of water in your movies?

DA: I grew up close to the ocean. I grew up two houses from the beach. And, most people don't picture Brooklyn that way, but there are beaches out there, and so I spent a lot of time on the beach as a teenager thinking about it. And, also, I am an Aquarius, so it's a water sign. So, I think, water is very important to me. The ocean and all that.

JSK: Being immersed in water is a kind of being rejuvenated ...

DA: Sure, sure.

JSK: Just one more question.

DA: Yeah.

JSK: Aronofsky's human condition between Kubrick's excess and Spielberg's narrative?

DA: Yeah, yeah, maybe.

JSK: Could your artistic sensibility be placed in the interval between Kubrick's critique of humanity's flaws and Spielberg's wonder and emotion?

DA: It's a pretty interesting observation. I guess I have a little bit more hope than Kubrick. We may be able to take control and do something about it. I am more of an optimist, probably I would say. But, I am definitely more of a pessimist than Spielberg.

JSK: I wonder how would it come out if you did *A.I.*?

DA: I have no idea. To start with, how much information was really there?

JSK: Actually, it was lot of Kubrick's ideas. There is a book from 2009 and there is a quote, one of the producers said, "Artificial Intelligence offers us the hope of the continuation of our race, albeit in a new form, following the death of biological humanity."[2] Does this sentence make any sense?

DA: You know Kurzweil, singularity?

JSK: Yeah, yeah

DA: That's what he is talking about.

JSK: But, what do you think? How is humanity connected with biology? Ethics? Morality?

DA: I think it's deep in everything that we are; it's connected to our bodies and our place on the planet. I think that separating from it is the problem.

JSK: And technology is in between. All your characters have something with body, and in *The Fountain*, the priest says that "our bodies are prisons of our souls." Would we be the same species if we get rid of biology?

DA: Not good. . . . Thank you very much.

JSK: Thank you.

---

[2]   Jane M. Struthers and Jan Harlan, eds., *A.I. Artificial Intelligence: From Stanley Kubrick to Steven Spielberg: The Vision Behind the Film* (London: Thames & Hudson, 2009).

Bibliography

Adorno, Theodor W. *Aesthetic Theory*. Translated by R. Hullot-Kentor. Minneapolis: University of Minnesota Press, 1997.

Altman, Rick. *Film/Genre*. British Film Institute, 1999.

Arendt, Hannah. *The Human Condition*. Garden City, NY: Doubleday Anchor Books, 1959.

Aristotle. *De Anima, Book II and III*. Translated by D.W. Hamlyn. Oxford: Clarendon Press, 1998.

———. *Nicomachean Ethics*. Translated by H.G. Apostle. Grinnell, Iowa: The Peripatetic Press, 1975.

———. *Poetics*. Translated by Richard Janko. Indianapolis, IN: Hackett Publishing Company, 1987.

Aronofsky, Darren. *Black Swan*. DVD, Directed by Darren Aronofsky, Twentieth Century Fox Film Corporation, Los Angeles, 2010.

———. *Π: Screenplay and the Guerilla Diaries*. London: Faber and Faber Limited, 1998.

Aronofsky, Darren, and Ari Handel. *Noah*. New York: Rizzoli, 2014.

Aronofsky, Darren, Ari Handel, and Nico Henrichon. *Noah*. Berkeley, CA: Image Comics, Inc., 2014.

Aronofsky, Darren, and Hubert Selby, Jr. *Requiem for a Dream*. London: Faber and Faber Limited, 2000.

Aronofsky, Darren, and Kent Williams. *The Fountain*. New York: Vertigo, 2005.

Balthaser, Benjamin. "Re-Staging the Great Depression: Genre as Social Memory in Darren Aronofsky's *The Wrestler*." *Cultural Logic Special Issue: Culture and the Crisis* (2010).

Bataille, Georges. *Erotism: Death and Sensuality*. Translated by Mary Dalwood. San Francisco, CA: City Lights Books, 1986.

———. "Visions of Excess." In *Theory and History of Literature*. Minneapolis: University of Minnesota Press, 1999.

Bazin, Andre. *What Is Cinema, Vol. 1*. Berkeley, CA: University of California Press, 2004.

Beames, Robert. "Interview: Vincent Cassel on *Black Swan*, Darren Aronofsky, Eastern Promises 2!" In *Whatculture.com*, 2011.

Blanchot, Maurice. *The Infinite Conversation*. Translated by Susan Hanson. *Theory and History of Literature* Vol. 82. Minneapolis: University of Minnesota Press, 1993.

———. *The Step Not Beyond*. Translated by Lycette Nelson. Albany, NY: State University of New York Press, 1992.

Bordwell, David. *Narration in the Fiction Film*. Madison, WI: University of Wisconsin Press 1985.

Boyle, Danny. *Trainspotting*. DVD, Directed by Danny Boyle, PolyGram Filmed Entertainment (Intl.) Universal City, and Miramax Films (US & Canada), New York City, 1996.

Byars, Jackie. *All That Hollywood Allows: Re-Reading Gender in 1950s Melodrama*. Chapel Hill, NC: University of North Carolina Press, 1991.

Campbell, Joseph, and Bill Moyers. *The Power of Myth*. New York: Anchor Books, Doubleday, 1988.

Carel, Havi, and Greg Tuck, eds. *New Takes in Film-Philosophy*. London: Palgrave Macmillan, 2011.

Carroll, Noel, and Jinhee Choi, eds. *Philosophy of Film and Motion Pictures: An Anthology* (Blackwell Philosophy Anthologies). Oxford: Wiley-Blackwell, 2006.

Cavell, Stanley. *Cities of Words: Pedagogical Letters on a Register of the Moral Life*. Cambridge, MA: Harvard University Press, 2004.

——. *Contesting Tears: The Hollywood Melodrama of the Unknown Woman*. Chicago: University of Chicago Press, 1996.

Cipra, Barry. "Irrationality Dominates Π." *Math Horizons* 6, no. 3 (1999): 26.

Cox, Damian, and Michael P. Levine. *Thinking through Film: Doing Philosophy, Watching Movies*. Oxford: Wiley-Blackwell, 2012.

Davis, Colin. *Critical Excess: Overreading in Derrida, Deleuze, Levinas, Žižek and Cavell*. Redwood City, CA: Stanford University Press, 2010.

Deleuze, Gilles. "The Brain Is the Screen: An Interview with Gilles Deleuze." In *The Brain Is the Screen*. Edited by Gregory Flaxman. Minneapolis: Minnesota University Press, 2000.

——. *Cinema 1: The Movement-Image*. Translated by H. Tomlinson and B. Habberjam. Minneapolis: University of Minnesota Press, 1986.

——. *Difference and Repetition*. Translated by Paul Patton. New York: Columbia University Press, 1994.

Deleuze, Gilles, and Felix Guattari. *A Thousand Plateaus: Capitalism and Schizophrenia*. Translated by Brian Massumi. Minneapolis: University of Minessota Press, 1987.

Derrida, Jacques. *The Gift of Death*. Translated by David Wills. Chicago: University of Chicago Press, 1996.

——. *Given Time: I. Counterfeit Money*. Translated by Peggy Kamuf. Chicago: University of Chicago Press, 1992.

Dewey, John. *Art as Experience*. New York: A Wideview/Perigee Book, 1980.

Duras, Marguerite. *Practicalities (Alcohol)*. New York: Grove Press, 1990.

Ebert, Robert, and Gene Siskel. *The Future of the Movies: Interviews with Martin Scorsese, Steven Spielberg, and George Lucas*. Andrews and McMeel: A Universal Press Syndicate Company, 1991.

Eggert, Brian. "Deep Focus Review: *A.I. (Artificial Intelligence*, 2001)," 2011. http://www.deepfocusreview.com/reviews/aiartificialintelligence.asp.

Eisenstein, Paul. "Devouring Holes: Darren Aronofsky's *Requiem for a Dream* and the Tectonics of Psychoanalysis." *International Journal of Žižek Studies* 1, no. 3 (2007).

——. "Visions and Numbers; Aronofsky's *Π* and the Primordial Signifier." In *Lacan and Contemporary Film*. Edited by Tod McGowan and Sheila Kunkle. New York: Other Press, 2004.

Elsaesser, Thomas. *New German Cinema: A History*. New Brunswick, NJ: Rutgers University Press, 1989.

Elsaesser, Thomas, and Malte Hagener. *Film Theory: An Introduction through the Senses*. New York: Routledge, 2010.

Failes, Ian. "Character Ark: The Visual Effects of *Noah*." *Fxguide* (2014). http://www.fxguide.com/featured/character-ark-the-visual-effects-of-noah/.

Fassbinder, Rainer Werner. *The Anarchy of the Imagination: Interviews, Essays, Notes*. Translated by Krishna Winston. Edited by Michael Totenberg and Leo A. Lensing. Baltimore, MD: Johns Hopkins University Press, 1992.

Fisher, Mark, and Amber Jacobs. "Debating *Black Swan*: Gender and Horror." *Film Quarterly* 65, no. 1 (2011): 58–62.

Flaxman, Gregory, ed. *The Brain Is the Screen*. Minneapolis: University of Minnesota Press, 2000.

Foucault, Michel. *Language, Counter-Memory, Practice*. Translated by Donald F. Bouchard and Sherry Simon. Ithaca, NY: Cornell University Press, 1977.

Frampton, Daniel. *Filmosophy*. New York: Wallflower Press, 2006.

Friedman, D. Lester. *Citizen Spielberg*. Champaign, IL: University of Illinois Press, 2006.

Gallese, Vittorio, and Michele Guerra. "Embodying Movies: Embodied Simulation and Film Studies." *Cinema: Journal of Philosophy and the Moving Image*, no. 3 (2012): 183–210.

Gerstner, David A., and Janet Staiger, eds. *Authorship and Film (Afi Film Readers)*. London: Routledge, 2003.

Gilmore, Richard A. *Doing Philosophy at the Movies*. Albany, NY: State University of New York Press, 2005.

Girard, René. *Violence and the Sacred*. London: Bloomsbury Academic, Series Continuum Impacts, 2005.

Gottschall, Jonathan. *The Storytelling Animal: How Stories Make Us Human*. New York: Houghton Mifflin Harcourt, 2012.

Grant, Barry Keith. *Film Genre: Theory and Criticism*. Metuchen, NJ: Scarecrow Press, 1977.

Grundmann, Roy, ed. *A Companion to Michael Haneke*. Oxford: Wiley-Blackwell, 2010.

Haneke, Michael. *The Piano Teacher*. DVD, directed by Michael Haneke, arte France Cinéma, Strasbourg, 2001.

Hauke, Christopher, and Ian Alister, eds. *Jung and Film: Post-Jungian Takes on the Moving Image*. London: Routledge, 2001.

Heidegger, Martin. *Being and Time*. Translated by Joan Stambaugh. Albany, NY: State University of New York Press, 1996.

Hockley, Luke. *Somatic Cinema*. New York: Routledge, 2014.

Howard, James. *Stanley Kubrick Companion*. London: B. T. Batsford Ltd., 1999.

Husserl, Edmund. *Cartesian Meditations.* Translated by Dorion Cairns. The Hague, The Netherlands: Martinus Nijhoff, 1977.

——. *On the Phenomenology of the Consciousness of Internal Time (1893–1917).* Translated by John Barnett Brough. Edited by John Barnett Brough. Dordrecht, The Netherlands: Kluwer Academic Publishers, 1991.

Jaspers, Karl. "Excerpts from Philosophy (Volume 2)." In *Existentialism.* Edited by Robert C. Solomon, 134–60. New York: The Modern Library, 1974.

——. *Reason and Anti-Reason in Our Time.* Translated by Stanley Godman. New Haven, CT: Yale University Press, 1952.

——. *Strindberg and Van Gogh: An Attempt at a Pathographical Analysis with Reference to Parallel Cases of Swedenborg and Holderlin.* Translated by Oscar Grunow and David Woloshin. Tucson, AZ: University of Arizona Press, 1977.

Joyce, James. *A Portrait of the Artist as a Young Man.* New York: Penguin Books, 1976.

Jung, C.G. *Commentary to the "Secret of the Golden Flower."* Translated by Richard Wilhelm and Cary F. Baynes. London: Kegan Paul, Trench, Trubner & Co., Ltd., 1947.

——. *Mysterium Coniunctionis: An Inquiry into the Separation and Synthesis of Psychic Opposites in Alchemy.* Translated by R.F.C. Hull. Princeton, NJ: Princeton University Press, 1970.

——. In *BBC video "Carl Jung: Face to Face."* Edited by John Freeman, 1959.

Kant, Immanuel. *Critique of Judgment.* Translated by Werner S. Pluhar. Indianapolis, IN: Hackett Publishing Company, Inc., 1987.

——. *Critique of Pure Reason.* Translated by Werner S. Pluhar. Indianapolis, IN: Hackett Publishing Company, Inc., 1996.

Kierkegaard, Søren. *Either/Or: A Fragment of Life.* Translated by Alastair Hannay. New York: Penguin Books, 1992.

——. *Fear and Trembling.* Translated by Alastair Hannay. New York: Penguin Books, 1985.

Klinger, Barbara. *Melodrama and Meaning.* Bloomington, IN: Indiana University Press, 1994.

Kolker, Robert. *A Cinema of Loneliness: Penn, Stone, Kubrick, Scorsese, Spielberg, Altman.* New York: Oxford University Press, 2000.

Kovacs, Andras Balint. *Screening Modernism: European Art Cinema, 1950–1980.* Chicago: University of Chicago Press, 2007.

Kulezic-Wilson, Danijela. "A Musical Approach to Filmmaking: Hip-Hop and Techno Composing Techniques and Models of Structuring in Darren Aronofsky's *П.*" *Music and the Moving Image* 1, no. 1 (2008): 19–24.

Lacan, Jacques. *Ecrits.* Translated by Bruce Fink. New York: W.W. Norton & Company, 2002.

Lennihan, Lydia. "The Dark Feminine in Aronofsky's *The Wrestler.*" In *Jung and Film II: The Return,* 243–52. East Sussex, UK: Routledge, Taylor & Francis Group, 2011.

Malins, Peta. "Deleuze, Guattari and an Ethico-Aesthetics of Drug Use." *Janus Head* 7, no. 1 (2004): 84–104.

Masters, Kim. "Rough Seas on 'Noah': Darren Aronofsky Opens up on the Biblical Battle to Woo Christians (and Everyone Else)." *The Hollywood Reporter* (2014). http://www.hollywoodreporter.com/news/rough-seas-noah-darren-aronofsky-679315.

Mayne, Judith. *Cinema and Spectatorship (Sightlines)*. London: Routledge, 1993.

McManus, I.C. "Symmetry and Asymmetry in Aesthetics and the Arts." *European Review* 13, no. 2 (2005): 157–80.

Miller, Greg. "Data from a Century of Cinema Reveals How Movies Have Evolved." *Wired Science* (2014). http://www.wired.com/2014/09/cinema-is-evolving/?utm_content=bufferb7c99&utm_medium=social&utm_source=facebook.com&utm_campaign=buffer.

Moreno, Christopher M. "Body Politics and Spaces of Drug Addiction in Darren Aronofsky's *Requiem for a Dream*". *GeoJournal: New directions in media geography* 74, no. 3 (2009): 219–26.

Murch, Walter. *In the Blink of an Eye: A Perspective on Film Editing*. Los Angeles: Silman-James Press, 2001.

Newport, Kyle. "The Ultimate Warrior's Final Speech to Fans on 'Monday Night Raw'." *Bleacher report* (2014). http://bleacherreport.com/articles/2022961-the-ultimate-warriors-final-speech-to-fans-on-monday-night-raw.

Oscars.org/events. "Movies in Your Brain: The Science of Cinematic Perception." In *Events and Exhibitions*, 2014.

Parker, Kathleen. "*Noah's* Arc of Triumph." *The Washington Post Opinions* (2014). http://www.washingtonpost.com/opinions/kathleen-parker-noahs-arc-of-triumph/2014/03/14/3678b092-abaa-11e3-98f6-8e3c562f9996_story.html.

Plantinga, Carl, and Greg M. Smith, eds. *Passionate Views: Film, Cognition and Emotion*. Baltimore, MD: Johns Hopkins University Press, 1999.

Powell, Anna. *Deleuze, Altered States and Film*. Edinburgh: Edinburgh University Press, 2007.

Rodowick, D.N. *Elegy for Theory*. Cambridge, MA: Harvard University Press, 2014.

Rose, Steve. "Werner Herzog on Death, Danger and the End of the World" *The Guardian* (2012). http://www.theguardian.com/film/2012/apr/14/werner-herzog-into-the-abyss.

Ryan, Tom. "Great Directors." In *Senses of Cinema*, 30, 2010.

Schelling, F.W.J. *The Ages of the World (Third Version C.1815)*. Translated by Jason M. Wirth. Albany, NY: State University of New York Press, 2000.

——. *Philosophical Investigations into the Essence of Human Freedom*. Translated by Jeff Love and Johannes Schmidt. Albany, NY: State University of New York Press, 2006.

Shaw, Daniel. *Film and Philosophy: Taking Movies Seriously*. New York: Wallflower, 2008.

Singh, Greg. *Film after Jung: Post Jungian Approaches to Film Theory*. New York: Routledge, 2009.

Skorin-Kapov, Jadranka. *The Aesthetics of Desire and Surprise: Phenomenology and Speculation*. Lanham, Maryland: Lexington Books, 2015.

Smith, Greg M. *Film Structure and the Emotion System*. Cambridge: Cambridge University Press, 2003.

Sobchack, Vivian. *The Address of the Eye: A Phenomenology of Film Experience*. Princeton, NJ: Princeton University Press, 1992.

Stoehr, Kevin L, ed. *Film and Knowledge: Essays on the Integration of Images and Ideas*. Jefferson, NC: McFarland & Company, Inc., 2002.

Struthers, Jane M., and Jan Harlan, eds. *A.I. Artificial Intelligence: From Stanley Kubrick to Steven Spielberg: The Vision Behind the Film*. London: Thames & Hudson, 2009.

Tan, Ed S. *Emotion and the Structure of Narrative Film: Film as an Emotion Machine*. Translated by Barbara Fasting. New York: Routledge (Routledge Communication Series), 2011, Reprint edition.

Thomsen, Christian Braad. *Fassbinder: The Life and Work of a Provocative Genius*. Translated by Martin Chalmers. Minneapolis: University of Minnesota Press, 1991.

Truffaut, Francois. *Hitchcock: The Definitive Study of Alfred Hitchcock, Revised Edition*. New York: Simon & Shuster Paperbacks, 1983.

Turan, Keneth. "Review: Energetic 'Noah' Goes Overboard—to Riveting Effect." *LA Times: Art and Entertainment* (2014). http://www.latimes.com/entertainment/movies/moviesnow/la-et-mn-noah-review-20140328-story.html#ixzz2xHBqitkQ&page=1.

Van Sant, Gus. *Drugstore Cowboy*. DVD, Directed by Van Sant, Artisan Entertainment, Santa Monica, CA, 1989.

Vertov, Dziga, Kevin O'Brien, and Annette Michelson. *Kino-Eye: The Writings of Dziga Vertov*. Oakland, CA: University of California Press, 1984.

Vogler, Christopher. "A Practical Guide to Joseph Campbell's the Hero with a Thousand Faces." *Raindance* (1985). http://www.thewritersjourney.com/hero%27s_journey.htm#Practical.

——. *The Writer's Journey: Mythic Structure for Writers*. Studio City, CA: Michael Wiese Productions, 2007.

Walker, Alexander. *Stanley Kubrick, Director: A Visual Analysis*. New York: W.W. Norton & Company, 1999.

Walsh, Kerry. "Why Does Mickey Rourke Give Pleasure?" *Critical Inquiry* 37, no. 1 (2010): 131–62.

Wheatley, Catherine. *Michael Haneke's Cinema: The Ethic of the Image (Film Europa)*. New York: Berghahn Books, 2009.

White, Susan. "Kubrick's Obscene Shadows." In *Stanley Kubrick's 2001: A Space Odyssey: New Essays*, 127–46: New York: Oxford University Press, 2006.

Williams, Linda. "Film Bodies: Gender, Genre, and Excess." *Film Quarterly* 44, no. 4 (1991): 2–13.

Index

Lightning Source UK Ltd.
Milton Keynes UK
UKHW02f0223200218
318162UK00005B/190/P